# Using Photographs in Social and Historical Research

# Using Photographs in Social and Historical Research

# Penny Tinkler

Los Angeles | London | New Delhi
Singapore | Washington DC

Los Angeles | London | New Delhi
Singapore | Washington DC

SAGE Publications Ltd
1 Oliver's Yard
55 City Road
London EC1Y 1SP

SAGE Publications Inc.
2455 Teller Road
Thousand Oaks, California 91320

SAGE Publications India Pvt Ltd
B 1/I 1 Mohan Cooperative Industrial Area
Mathura Road
New Delhi 110 044

SAGE Publications Asia-Pacific Pte Ltd
3 Church Street
#10-04 Samsung Hub
Singapore 049483

Editor: Jai Seaman
Assistant editor: Anna Horvai
Production editor: Vanessa Harwood
Copyeditor: David Hemsley
Proofreader: Derek Markham
Marketing manager: Ben Griffin-Sherwood
Cover design:
Typeset by: C&M Digitals (P) Ltd, Chennai, India
Printed in India at Replika Press Pvt Ltd

© Penny Tinkler 2013

First published 2013

**Library of Congress Control Number: 2012941368**

**British Library Cataloguing in Publication data**

A catalogue record for this book is available from the British Library

ISBN 978-0-85702-036-9
ISBN 978-0-85702-037-6 (pbk)

To Carolyn

# Contents

# About the Author

**Penny Tinkler** is a Senior Lecturer in Sociology at the University of Manchester. She has written several articles and chapters on photographic methods and practices. She has also written extensively on the history of girlhood, including *Constructing Girlhood: Popular Magazines for Girls Growing up in England, 1920–1950* (Taylor & Francis 1995), and on the feminization of smoking, including *Smoke Signals: Women, Smoking and Visual Culture in Britain 1880–1980* (Berg 2006).

# Acknowledgements

I am extremely grateful to all those who have generously contributed case studies and interviews and engaged in extended correspondence with me about their research: Stephen Brooke, Richard Chalfen, Kathryn Davies, Elizabeth Edwards, Patrizia Di Bello, Janet Fink, Jane Hamlett, Jennifer Mason, Darren Newbury, Annebella Pollen, James Ryan, Helene Snee and Toni Weller. I would also like to thank the many people who have responded to questions and provided photos, feedback and technical support, often at very short notice, in particular: Shirley Baker, Hannah Barker, Julia Bennett, Úna Bhroiméil, Hazel Burke, Anna Carden-Coyne, Teresa Doherty, Alexander Freund, Karen Harvey, Douglas Harper, Alice Jesmont, Annette Kuhn, Andrew Loxley, Wendy Luttrell, Phil Mizen, Lorie Novak, Alistair Thomson, Valerie Walkerdine and Sophie Woodward. I am also grateful to the archivists and librarians who have tracked down images and arranged permissions. For support and advice, thanks to my colleagues in Sociology at the University of Manchester and to the editorial and production teams at Sage. Thanks also to my friends for keeping me sane.

Special thanks go to my partner, Carolyn Jackson, to whom this book is dedicated. This book would not have been possible without her enduring support. I am immensely grateful to Carolyn for her constructive feedback and insightful comments on all my chapters, and for her valiant efforts to motivate and sustain me throughout the course of this project.

# List of Figures

# About this Book

Since the 1850s photographs have become increasingly integral to how we live our lives. They shape what we know, feel and remember about ourselves and the wider world in the present and past, and they play a part in how we work, learn, consume, relax, communicate and relate to one another. Photographs are also of growing importance in research, and they have the potential to become an important element of social inquiry; this is because there is a vast and growing stock of photographs relating to social life past and present, but also because we can generate our own photos on many topics we research.

Confronted by this exciting resource, the question is how to use photos productively in social and historical research. This book will guide researchers and students in working this out. Focusing exclusively on photographs, this book investigates how photos can be used in research and the conceptual and theoretical issues that underpin this practice. It is interdisciplinary in perspective, drawing on developments and examples from history and the social sciences. It approaches photographs as images that can be interpreted as texts and evaluated as evidence of the social and material world they depict, but it also engages with photographs as three-dimensional objects. Discussing and evaluating different research strategies the book offers new critical insights on how to think about and use photos to address questions about social and cultural life. Rather than offer readers a menu of established methods, the book is organised around what researchers do with photographs and engages with established and emergent methods as well as generic research techniques. It covers methods for working with images, for taking photos and listening to people talk about them. It also examines how to research photographic practices, that is how and why people and organisations make and use photographs and what these practices mean. There is an understandable tendency in methods literature to offer sanitised versions of how research is undertaken, even though research is often messy. This messiness is not a failing of individual researchers or research designs but an often unavoidable part of doing research on complex phenomena. Talking to researchers about their practices and experiences and integrating these 'interviews' into this book, I offer glimpses of the messy, pleasurable, challenging and productive dimensions of using photos in historical and social research.

This book foregrounds using photos to research the past, memory, biography and change; this is because these applications have so far received very little attention in methods texts. It is also because these topics are important to historians and researchers of contemporary life; the present is never static and multiple times co-exist and shape it. The book demonstrates how photos can be used to engage with these temporalities, including change and continuity, process, biography and autobiography, also the personal and collective memories[1] that shape identities, historical consciousness and perceptions of the relationship between past and present.

Focusing on the study of social and cultural life in the present and past, this book embraces two overlapping areas of scholarship. First, research within the social sciences – 'social research' – which, though often equated with the study of contemporary life, also includes historical lines of enquiry. Second, branches of history concerned with society and culture, for example, studies of rural and urban life, race and ethnicity, gender and sexuality, the family, education and material culture. Historical research can be as much about social phenomena as 'social research'.

The use of photographs has not always been acknowledged as appropriate in social science and historical research. Sociology and anthropology have long-standing but chequered relationships with photography (Chaplin 1994; Edwards 1992 and 2002; Harper 1998). Around 1900, photographs featured regularly in the *American Journal of Sociology* (Stasz 1979); similarly they had an established role in anthropology, principally as a means to document and categorise different groups of people. But by 1920 and through to the 1960s, photography almost disappeared from sociology, and with a few notable exceptions – Bateson and Mead (1942) and Collier (1967/1986) – it was sidelined in anthropology. In anthropology the decline in status is attributed to a focus on social organisation which was not perceived as a visual phenomenon (Edwards 2002), whereas in sociology it is attributed principally to the privileging of verbal over visual forms of communication and the move towards positivism (Chaplin 1994). In sociology photography re-emerged in the 1970s in the context of the sub-discipline visual sociology (Becker 1974; Wagner 1979). However, as Jon Wagner explains (2011:49), interest in visual methods was confined to disciplinary 'offshoots' until the 1990s after which these 'began coalescing around visual studies as a branch of empirical inquiry in its own right'. Today, photography has a prominent place in a growing body of visual studies and visual methods texts (e.g. Banks 2001; Harper 2012; Knowles and Sweetman 2004; Pink 2007; Prosser 1998; Rose 2007; van Leeuwen and Jewitt 2001; Wells 2000a). Photography is also gaining a heightened profile in social and cultural history; this represents a fairly recent development. Though social historians 'discovered' photography in the 1970s, in the 1990s it was still typically used only for illustration and with little critical awareness (Burke 2001; Samuel 1994). There are now a growing number of histories that utilise photos critically (e.g. Doan 2001; Edwards 1991, 2001, 2012; Freund and Thomson 2011; Hayes 2006; Kuhn and McAllister 2006; Ryan 1997), and texts that discuss ways of thinking about them (e.g. Edwards and Hart 2004a; Tagg 1988; special issue of *History and Theory*, edited by Tucker 2009). However, there are no books specifically on the range of ways of using photos in historical research, so explicit guidance on historical photo methods remains sparse, dispersed or integrated with a general discussion of images (e.g. Burke 2001).

This book consolidates and develops understanding of how photos can be used in social and historical research.

# The structure of this book

This book examines three main ways that photos are used in research: researchers work *with* photos in various ways (Chapters 2–6), they *generate* their own photos or ask research participants to take them (Chapters 7 and 8), and they *listen* to people talking about photos (Chapter 9). Throughout, I draw a distinction between two types of photographs: generated photos are those made for the research by the researcher or research participant; found photos are pre-existing photos, including personal and non-personal pictures such as documentary, survey and commercial images.

*Chapter 1 – Getting Started: Using Photos in Research* This chapter looks at five questions you need to consider before using photos in research:

- How do you conceptualise a photograph?
- Can photos constitute evidence of the social world?
- How do temporalities shape photo research?
- What can you do with photos?
- How do you combine methods in photo research?

Your answers to these questions inform how you approach and design research. How you conceptualise photos is of fundamental importance, and in this chapter I discuss the materiality of photos, debates about the characteristics of photographic images and whether they should be treated as texts. Following this I explain how your conceptualisation of photos relates to your views on the nature of social phenomena and what counts as evidence or knowledge of it; in other words your ontological and epistemological positions. The temporalities of photo research are also explored, including how we think about photos 'capturing' the present, the idea that photos have biographies, and the position and role of photos in the timings of research. To design research you need to know what you can do with photos. I explain how to use photos to generate questions and stimulate memory; how to engage with sensory and affective experiences of, and responses to, photos; and how to 'play' with photos. Photo research often involves multiple methods, so I conclude this chapter with a discussion of combining methods.

*Chapter 2 – Image Work: Five Lines of Enquiry* This chapter introduces and explains five lines of enquiry that are the foundations of productive work with photographic images:

- Identification of basic details about a photo – because you need to ground your work with images in place and time.
- Careful study of the image – attending to form and presentation.
- Consideration of material evidence – because a photo's materiality has implications for the status and meaning of the image.
- Contextual research – as this is fundamental to all work with photographs and involves researching contexts of production and audience engagements (viewing and using).
- Reflection on the slippery concept of a photograph's 'meaning'.

*Chapter 3 – Studying Found Photos* This chapter explores how researchers work with found photographs to explore questions about social and cultural life, particularly in the past. I demonstrate how the lines of enquiry discussed in Chapter 2 are the foundations of the photo-researcher's craft. I also introduce creative methods that some researchers use for inspiration when working with images. The chapter is organised around five areas of research and provides examples of how researchers use photographs and the issues they encounter in doing this:

- Using photos to learn about the people and material culture they depict.
- Mapping ideas about, and approaches to, aspects of the social world.
- Researching how and why images are made, used and reused.
- Exploring responses: popular and iconic photos.
- Seeking inspiration from photos.

*Chapter 4 – Autobiographical Methods* Autobiographical methods were developed in the 1980s and 1990s and have been used to generate intimate insights into the role of photos in family relationships, the contribution of personal photos to people's perceptions of themselves and their history, and the workings of memory. In this chapter I explain why autobiographical methods have a role to play in contemporary research and examine autobiographical methods that you can use with your own photos. I also consider the usefulness of asking research participants to employ these methods. Remembering is to the fore, also feeling and playful techniques such as imagining, juxtaposition and other creative strategies.

*Chapter 5 – Researching Photographic Practices* It is often assumed that the content of photos is what is most useful for the purposes of research, but a great deal can be learned about social and cultural life from researching photographic practices, namely how and why photographs are made, circulated, presented, used and engaged with and what these practices mean. If you are interested in photographic practices you are typically concerned to investigate: how and why photos are produced and by whom; where, how and why they are presented; who uses photos and what these practices mean; how and why photos circulate or are kept, archived and reused in particular ways and for different purposes. In this chapter I present four case studies to demonstrate different strategies that researchers use to investigate photographic practices.

*Chapter 6 – Archives and Digital Resources* This chapter considers how you can work with archives and digital photographic resources to do photo research. Understanding the practices that shape these resources is key to good research and so I explain these; in this way Chapter 6 develops the discussion of photographic practices that are the focus of the previous chapter. I start by looking at archival practices and the implications of these for photo research and then consider how researchers work in archives and the issues they confront. Digital technologies have transformed how researchers locate photographs and work with them and I consider the potential and limitations of using digital photographic databases. An important issue that I consider is the implications of digitalisation for access to the material properties of photographs.

*Chapter 7 – Generating Photos: Researchers* Moving on to photos generated specifically for the purpose of your research, Chapter 7 addresses ways that you can make your own photos in social and historical enquiry. Researchers take photos as an aide-memoire, but more importantly to generate data and to produce photos for use in photo-interviews. In this chapter I start by considering why researchers generate photos and then outline approaches to taking them. I also introduce technical considerations and what you need to think about, and do, when undertaking analysis of your photos. Focusing on the themes of process, change and continuity, I then examine principal methods involving researcher-generated photography – photo-documentation, making photos for use in interviews (see also Chapter 9), generating and sometimes collecting photos for the purposes of overtime comparisons.

*Chapter 8 – Generating Photos: Research Participants* Inviting research participants to take photos raises different issues than when researchers generate their own photos or use found pictures in research; these issues are examined in Chapter 8. I introduce projects in which research participants generate photographs and consider why researchers find it useful to ask participants to take pictures. I then outline how to set up a project in which respondents generate photos, including what guidance to give and technical matters. In the final section I discuss the analysis of respondents' photos addressing: approaches to image analysis; the importance of contextualising participants' photos; ways of incorporating participants' accounts of their pictures in to your investigation. Most projects involve talking to research participants about the photos they have taken, so this chapter is best read alongside Chapter 9.

*Chapter 9 – Photo-interviews: Listening to Talk about Photos* Listening to what people say about photos is an increasingly popular method and often integral to projects in which researchers and research participants generate photos. In this chapter I consider claims about the benefits of using photo-elicitation and evaluate why some photos are better than others at encouraging people to talk. I then explore how photo-interviews work, focusing on the relationship between looking at and talking about photos – the visual–verbal relationship. Understanding this relationship can help you make decisions about methods and inform the analysis and interpretation of photo-interview data. This discussion engages with how interviewees conceptualise photos, the temporalities of the visual–verbal relationship, and the relationship between photos, memories and verbal accounts. It concludes with suggestions about how to develop interview analysis to engage with the specificities of how interviewees engage with photos.

*Chapter 10 – Ethical Issues and Legalities* The final chapter addresses the ethics and legalities of using photos in social and historical research. I examine issues relating to three aspects of research with photos: how researchers and research participants generate photos within a project; the process of photo-elicitation; and the presentation of generated and found photos, including public and old photos and images from personal websites. I draw out key points for you to consider relating to privacy, anonymity, the dignity of participants, informed consent and copyright, but also less frequently discussed issues about the potential voyeurism of researchers and the importance of integrity in *how* photographs are represented in presentations and publications.

## Note

1 The terms 'personal' and 'collective' memory refer to interpretations of the past (within living memory) that are widely shared within a particular community (e.g. local or national) and established typically through representations in popular culture and especially the media. Collective memory provides a cultural framework within which people articulate and interpret their personal memories. It is informed and shaped by the experiences and stories of people in communities and so it is different from public history which is imposed top down, usually by governments. Popular memories of the past are modified or superseded as alternative accounts emerge and gain public exposure. For discussion see Abrams (2011).

# 1

# Getting Started: Using Photos in Research

Before you start using photos in research it is important to consider five questions:

- How do you conceptualise a photograph?
- Can photos constitute evidence of the social world?
- How do temporalities shape photo research?
- What can you do with photos?
- How do you combine methods?

These questions are at the heart of this chapter and I address each in turn. First, you need to consider how you conceptualise photos, as this is key to ascertaining how you can use them in research. Though photos are commonly thought of as images they are also objects, so you need to contemplate how the materiality of the image influences what and how you generate data using photos. There is debate about the properties of the photographic image and this also has implications for how you can use them: can an image provide evidence of what was in front of the camera? Should you treat photos as texts? Second, you need to consider how your conceptualisation of photos relates to your views on the nature of social phenomena and what counts as evidence or knowledge of it; in other words your ontological and epistemological positions. Do photos constitute evidence of what you regard as the constituents of the social world, and if so how? These deliberations provide the foundations for thinking about the methods and strategies you use to generate and analyse data. The third question concerns the temporalities of photo research. To use photos in social and historical research requires an appreciation of three temporal dimensions: the temporalities that are conjured by a photo; the life of a photo; the timings of research. Fourth, though researchers appreciate that photos can be looked at, it is helpful to think in more concrete and creative ways about what you can do with them. This includes: using photos to generate as well as answer questions and to stimulate memory; engaging with sensory and affective experiences of, and responses, to photos; and playing with images. Fifth, most research involves a combination of methods, so you need to think carefully at the design stage about how these fit together.

# How do you conceptualise a photograph?

The prevailing tendency is to think of photographs as two-dimensional images. This stems from how we apprehend them; as Batchen (1997: 2) explains, 'to see what the photo is "*of*" we ... suppress our consciousness of what the photograph "*is*" in material terms'. Some scholars dispute this way of thinking about photos and argue that they need to be conceptualised as material objects. Concentrating on photographs made from film and photographic plates, I look at both ways of thinking about photos – as objects and images – and draw out the implications for research. I then consider the impact of digitalisation on how photos are conceptualised.

## Thinking about photographs as objects

Photographs are three-dimensional objects. They are printed on paper, card, textiles and other material surfaces; in Japan in the 1990s there was a fashion for printing personal photos on stickers (Chalfen and Murui 2004). As Edwards and Hart (2004a) stress, understanding photos – what they mean, why they are or are not significant or valued, how and why they are used – involves engaging with their material properties. This is what Edwards (2002) describes as a material approach. The image is important, but its meaning and significance is inextricably connected to its materiality. This includes what the photo is printed on (e.g. the size, type and quality of paper), and how the photo is physically presented (in an album, in a frame etc.) as this shapes how people can engage with and use the photo and whether and how they can touch it. It also includes signs the photo bears of age and use which suggest the history of the photo. For example, a photo of a child placed in a locket suggests that the person in the picture is special to someone and cherished; the same photo printed on a mass-produced jigsaw puzzle has a different meaning.

Thus, a material approach is not limited to questions about the image, but directs attention to the place of the photographic image-object in personal and social life. In other words, it investigates the material contexts of production, such as: how and why photos are made in particular ways, including the implications of photographic technologies and choices at the point of taking a photo and processing it; the material form of the photograph, for example the choice of paper it is printed on and the finish used (glossy, matt, gold toning) and what these details mean to the people who make and use photos. A material approach also embraces personal and social uses of photographs, such as: how photos are circulated; where and how they are kept and presented; whether they are preserved and how; how they can be looked at and used; how photos are changed by use (damaged, worn) including deliberate acts of modification (cutting, painting over); and what people and organisations think about these practices.

## Thinking about photographs as images

The most common way to conceptualise a photo is as an image, but there is debate about the properties of images and how you should use them. There are two main issues. First, can an image provide evidence of what was in front of the camera when the photo was taken? Second, should photos be considered to be texts and treated like paintings and letters?

### Can an image provide evidence of what was in front of the camera when the photo was taken?

The answer to this question hinges on how the researcher perceives the relationship between the image and what it portrays. Approaches to the photographic image can best be understood as situated on a continuum; where they are positioned depends on how closely, if at all, the photographic image is considered to relate to the material and social world it seemingly depicts. This could be called the visual reality continuum, although I am referring to a particular understanding of reality that equates it with what is observable. Your position on the continuum will depend on how you answer the following questions, which I explore in detail. Is the photographic image a copy of the real world, or is there a more complex relationship? And if there is a more complex relationship, does the image provide some evidence of what was in front of the camera lens, or is it best conceptualised as independent of it?

At one end of the continuum are those who regard the photographic image as a transcription or copy of the real world; sometimes called a naive realist approach. The photograph is approached as transparent in the sense that it replicates the observable world. There is also an assumption that the photo tells you not only what was precisely in front of the camera lens, but that it is an accurate depiction of the 'reality' of the setting or event. The Victorians, for example, 'invested considerable faith in the power of the camera to record, classify and witness' (Wells 2000a: 55); photography was used to classify races, criminal types, 'lunatics', also to document place. This perspective still lingers; the phrase 'the camera never lies' has held, and continues to hold, considerable sway. The methodological implication of this approach is that researchers can use photos simply as a window for looking at the real world. For example, a photo of a young, slim woman with a flawless complexion would be considered evidence of what this woman looked like (Figure 1.1). Similarly, the photo in Figure 1.2 would be regarded as documenting accurately the appearance of a cottage and children in Evesham village in the 1890s.

Despite the 'temptations of realism' (Burke 2001: 21), contemporary scholars usually reject the idea that photos are mere copies of an observable reality (even if they sometimes slip into treating photos in this way). Instead, photos are approached as constructions that have a complex relationship to the world they depict; this is

**Figure 1.1**   Young woman

where a material approach to images (discussed earlier) is relevant, because a photo's construction is shaped by the material qualities and possibilities of cameras and printing processes, how people work with these materials and the choices they make about them.

One reason why images are necessarily constructions is that they are shaped by photographic technologies: 'In the mere act of transcribing world into picture, three dimensions into two, photographs necessarily manufacture the image they make' (Batchen 1997: 12). Moreover, photos never depict what the eye sees, or rather what the brain perceives (Goldstein 2007). Cameras do not register light in the same way as the human eye and they process colour differently. Additionally, a camera fixes a field of vision that is constantly changing in the human eye. Photographers can also set the depth of vision – the distance over which an image is in focus – to achieve results the naked eye cannot achieve and they can use different lenses to 'see' further or to include a wider view. For example, in his photographs of American landscapes Ansel Adams used camera settings that produce results the eye cannot replicate; the photos 'show us the American landscape as we could never view it in "reality"' (Sayer 2008: 59). Importantly, viewers often do not notice that a photo depicts the world differently from how they see it with the naked eye. This is because of historically and culturally specific 'ways of seeing' (Berger 1972) or 'scopic regimes' that are so well established within contemporary Western societies that we rarely consider them (Jenks 1995). Although some argue that in postmodern and digital societies this may be shifting (e.g. Mirzoeff 1998), these particular interpretative strategies remain commonplace. A photo's 'lure of realism' is, therefore, partly a result of how we interpret the image's visual techniques. Although a photo of a street is a two-dimensional representation of a three-dimensional reality, we rely on our interpretation of the image's visual techniques, namely use of perspective and shifts in tone, to 'see' two dimensions as three-dimensional. How people see colour is another instance of this. Before colour photography became commonplace, viewers of black and white photographs commonly interpreted shades of grey as colours (Yevonde 1940: 185–6).

Another reason why photos are always constructions is that the photographer inevitably makes choices about what to photograph and how, decisions that are often about materials or that have material affects. Although there are instances of deliberate manipulation of an image, as Brian Winston (1998: 64) insists, deliberate fraud is less common than 'fine questions of intervention' to achieve a particular effect or impression. These 'fine questions of intervention' include decisions about how to take the photo – lighting, angle and shutter speed – because these all convey meaning. Lighting, for instance, often conveys mood. As Goldstein (2007) describes, temporal and spatial editing also shapes the photographic account of a subject or scene. Temporal editing means deciding what moment to photograph and which, in a series of photos, to print. It is used to catch the moment a person smiles or the few seconds when no one is standing in front of a particular landscape. Whereas temporal editing is about which millisecond to record or print, spatial editing involves decisions about what aspect of a field of view to photograph and from what perspective. The selection process starts with taking the picture but there is often a second stage of cropping what has already been recorded, either manually or digitally. A host of other adjustments are also common once a photo has been taken, from refining colour, tone and focus to editing specific visual details. Not surprisingly, every photograph is shaped, literally, by the photographer's point of view, although there is often more to a photograph than the photographer intended.

While the construction of photos is widely acknowledged, scholars differ in their views about the relationship of the image to what was in front of the camera lens; do images provide some visual evidence of the real world that is photographed or is the image independent of it?

Occupying the middle section of the continuum are approaches that acknowledge photos as constructions, but that also regard photos as offering some evidence of what was in front of the lens. For instance, in *Camera Lucida*, Roland Barthes (2000) argues that a distinctive feature of a photograph is its 'evidential force' (p. 89). The photograph provides evidence that what is in the frame was actually in front of the camera at some point in time. This is an indexical relationship, like a footprint in sand indicating that a foot has recently been there. Importantly, Barthes does 'not take the photograph for a "copy" of reality'; instead, the photograph's significance is that 'From a real body, which was there, proceed radiations which ultimately touch me' (pp. 80, 88).

Scholars in this section of the continuum *evaluate* rather than *accept* the photo as evidence of what was once in front of the camera. This can be described as a cautious realist position, sometimes called a 'mild realist' (Winston 1998) or 'post-positivist' (Margolis and Rowe 2011) approach. Like many social scientists, Winston (1998: 66) argues that photos 'can only be considered as evidence of the real world in limited and complex ways': 'we are now too sophisticated to believe a photographic image is like a window on the world, a window unmarked by the photographer's finger-prints', but this 'is not necessarily to deny totally that you can still see something of the world.' This stance is evident also in Burke's (2001, 2010) guidance to historians on the 'pitfalls' of using photographs and other visual sources as evidence. Images, he argues, can provide evidence of social reality but they 'distort' it (Burke 2001: 30). Returning to the earlier example of a photo of a young woman (Figure 1.1), researchers point out that while the photo provides evidence that the woman was there, the photo has to be used cautiously as evidence of what this young woman really looked like and what she was doing in front of the camera. Reasons for caution include the likelihood that the picture was posed, that special lighting was used, that this was an atypical pose, and that although hundreds of photos may have been taken only one was selected, touched up and cropped before being produced as a photo of this young woman. Similarly, given there was a convention in the 1890s to depict the British countryside as a rural idyll (Thomas 1978), researchers are cautious about accepting Figure 1.2 as evidence of everyday village life: the area around the cottage may have been tidied up for the photo, or the photographer may have taken this particular stretch because it excluded background that gave a less picturesque view of the village; the children may have been dressed up and posed specially for the picture; and small details may have been edited out at the printing stage.

At the far end of the continuum scholars eschew an approach that looks at an image for evidence of the material and social world it depicts. There are variations in how strongly this position is held. Some scholars, such as Alan Trachtenberg (1990: xiii), provide fleeting acknowledgement of the 'depictive function' of photos within very narrow limits, but they regard this as unimportant for how scholars should work with photos. For Trachtenberg, photos are not simple depictions of what happened in the past, but constructions that produce a particular, visual version of history; the historian's job is to investigate how photos are used to construct particular stories about the past. Others adopt an uncompromising anti-realist position as exemplified by John Tagg (1988). Tagg takes issue with Barthes' claim that photos have 'evidential force' because of their indexical properties for two reasons. First, as discussed earlier, photographic images have a problematic relation to the material and social world because of the technologies and practices involved in producing a photo. Second, photographs are only ever made sense of by social beings, and what viewers think they see in a picture is determined by the discourses and everyday knowledge within which the image is situated. Tagg argues that the status of a photo as evidence is not a product of the photo's intrinsic – indexical – properties, but is a result of how powerful institutions at particular points in history have established some types of

**Figure 1.2**   Evesham Village.  Benjamin Stone Collection. Box 64. Print 28. Reproduced with the permission of Birmingham Libraries and Archives

photographs as accurately reproducing the observable world. Tagg makes the point that not all photographs are treated as evidence in this way, and he asks us to consider: 'under what conditions would a photograph of the Loch Ness Monster[1]... be acceptable?' (p. 5). Tagg has been very influential, but his uncompromising critique of indexicality is widely regarded as too extreme (e.g. Ryan 1997).

Many scholars are positioned somewhere between the two extremes of the continuum, neither naively realist nor anti-realist, though they vary considerably in the emphasis placed on using photos as evidence of the material and social world depicted in the image.

### Should photos be considered to be texts and treated like paintings and letters?

Some scholars argue it is productive to think of photos as texts and treat them in the same way as paintings or letters; this is often described as an interpretivist or hermeneutic approach. This approach is typically used by researchers at the far end of the reality continuum who adopt an anti-realist position on images. It also may be employed by those in the middle of the continuum as it can be used alongside a cautious realist approach. Margolis and Rowe (2011: 340; see also Burke 2001), for example, encourage cross-fertilisation: 'Our emphasis is rather on the interpenetration of postpositive [photographs have an indexical connection to what is in the real world] and hermeneutic approaches [images are texts that need interpretation] to researching historical photographs'.

If approaching a photo as a text, the scholar's job is to consider what account the image produces of the world and how this is achieved. If we take the case of a letter, the researcher does not 'confuse the words on a page with the objects or events to which they refer' (Sayer 2008: 55), instead they focus on what is being said by the combination of particular words on the page and how a particular interpretation is suggested by how the letter is presented and the discourses within which it is located. The same principle applies to working with a photograph. For example, Trachtenberg (1990: xiii) focuses on 'the point of view of the photograph itself, the interpretation it allows viewers to make of its subject', while Tagg (1988) insists that researchers consider how the meaning of a photo is made and mobilised within particular institutional contexts. For example, confronted with a photographic portrait of a man, and drawing on knowledge about prevailing discourse on masculinity and knowledge of conventions for representing various personal traits, the researcher concludes that Figure 1.3 is a representation of a serious and important thinker. The conclusion is reached by noting that the photograph focuses attention on the sitter's head and face signalling the importance of the man's identity and individuality, the heavy shadows around the figure that suggest his solemnity, and the luminous brow which represents intellectuality. Researchers might also consider how images are used. A photo in a health campaign poster of a pretty young woman, holding a cigarette and smiling to reveal tar-stained teeth, is studied for what it communicates about youthful femininity and attitudes towards the risks for women of smoking. Though there are different ways of working with photos as texts, attention to materiality is important: photos are typically approached with regard to their form and use.

**Figure 1.3**   Charles Darwin. Down House, Kent. © English Heritage

## What are the implications of digitalisation for thinking about photos?

What are the implications of digitalisation for thinking about what a photograph is? To address this question it is necessary to reflect briefly on the characteristics of film photography and digital photography (for fuller accounts see: Lister 2000; Wright 2004). Both film photography and digital photography rely on capturing light to create a photographic image, but they differ in how the light that enters the lens is registered, stored and transferred. In film photography, light enters the camera lens and reacts with the emulsion on the film; this film is then processed to produce a material photograph. The film image is analogue in nature; analogue images:

> consist of physical marks or signs of some kind (whether brush strokes ... or the silver salts of the photographic print) carried by material surfaces. The marks and signs are virtually inseparable from these surfaces. They are also continuously related to some perceivable features of the object which they represent. The light, for instance, cast across a rough wooden table top, becomes an analogous set of tonal differences in the emulsion of the photo-graph. (Lister 2000: 311)

In contrast to film/analogue photography, digital photography captures light through a lens but then a sensor *converts* the pattern of light in to a digital code; using an electric current, light is registered in binary information as a series of 1s and 0s. This digital code is decoded by a computer and displayed on a monitor as a pattern of dots – pixels – which make up a digital image; unlike film photography, there is no original print or negative.

The advent of digital photography has prompted much debate about the nature of the digital photographic image and whether it has revolutionised photography (for overviews see: Bull 2010; Lister 2000; Robins 1995). Two issues are particularly pertinent to a discussion of what is a photograph.

The first and most prominent issue is whether digitalisation undermines 'photography's apparent ability to guarantee the accuracy of what it depicts' (Bull 2010: 21). Focusing on the potential for manipulating digital images, one response has been to point out that manipulation has been a feature of film photography too (Rossler 1991). The difference with digital photography is that it is easy to change images and often impossible for viewers to detect the pro-cess, whereas in film photography alterations can usually be detected and it is sometimes possible to confirm this by studying the negative. Another response has been to point out that all photographs, whether analogue or digital, have a complex relationship to the world they depict, they are all constructions (Rossler 1991; Batchen 1997). Though the issue of the photo's veracity has par-ticular significance for researchers who look to photographs for evidence of the real world, for those who adopt an anti-realist position, digitalisation has not changed how they think about, and work with, images; they remain texts that are treated as independent of reality.

A second issue is that a digital image is a 'series of electronic pulses' (Edwards and Hart 2004a: 14) rather than an object. In many ways this does not change how we work with digital images compared to analogue ones; a material approach still has relevance for three reasons. First, digital images become objects when they are printed in various formats. Second, the material aspects of how images are presented – on a computer screen, in a digital photo frame or on a camera phone – have implications for meaning. Third, new viewing opportunities, such as passing around camera phones and touching images on screen, add material dimensions to how we engage with photographs (Edwards 2009; Rubinstein and Sluis 2008). It is also worth noting that, as Sluis (2010) points out, the storage, sorting and searching of digital imagery is also dependent on 'material structures' such as huge enterprise data centres. There is, however, one way in which digitalisation has important implications for research, this is when analogue photographs are digitalised. Though digitalisation is often conflated with copying, it does create a completely new type of photo. In the process of digitalising what was once an object, aspects of the photo's meaning, significance and biography that were embedded in its material form are lost (Sassoon 2004); the digital image is different from the material photograph it is based on.

Photographs are clearly complex and rich resources and it is necessary to be clear how you conceptualise them before you start using them in research.

# Can photos constitute evidence of the social world?

It is useful to consider how the previous discussion about the conceptualisation of photos relates to questions about ontology and epistemology, which need to be considered in any research. Ontology and epistemology are complex and are dealt with more fully in specialist texts (see, for example: Bryman 2008; Mason 2002). Here, I focus on general points to consider when using photos in research.

Ontology is your view on the nature of social entities: for example, is social reality external to the individual, imposing itself on their consciousness from without, or is it the product of individual consciousness, or a combination of the two? Your ontological position influences the kinds of research questions you deem worthwhile. Epistemology is 'your theory of knowledge, and should therefore concern the principles and rules by which you decide whether and how social phenomena can be known, and how knowledge can be demonstrated' (Mason 2002: 16). There are two main and interrelated ways in which your epistemology is important for research in general and for thinking about using photos.

First, epistemology informs your assessment of what counts as evidence or knowledge of social things: for example, is evidence that which can be observed or measured (associated with post/positivism), or is it attitudes, values and beliefs (associated with interpretivism)? If you are considering using photos, your epistemology informs your assessment of what they can, if anything, contribute to your research. Researchers use photos to generate two main types of data – visual data and interview data – and so a question is whether, given your epistemological position, these kinds of data can constitute evidence that will enable you to answer your research questions. If you are considering using photos as visual data, this question maps on to how you conceptualise photos: what can photographs reveal about the social world? Can photos provide visual evidence of what was in front of the camera and, if so, what would this provide knowledge about?

Some of the methods discussed in this book, such as systematic rephotography and the use of photos as visual records, are consistent with a broadly postpositivist stance, in the sense that they are premised on the idea that there is a social reality external to the individual and the researcher can acquire knowledge of this by looking at photographs (a cautious realist conceptualisation). But these methods can be combined with other research techniques to engage with how people understand and interpret the social world and their part in it, in other words, an interpretivist approach. For example, photos may be used as visual evidence of participants' working conditions alongside interview data in which participants talk about how they understand and experience the aspects of working life depicted in the photos. Similarly, a researcher may begin by scrutinising domestic photos to learn about how people decorated and furnished their homes in the past and use contextual information to evaluate the credibility of the visual data (a postpositivist stance premised on a cautious realist conceptualisation of photos). The contextual research might then be extended so that the researcher can explore what particular styles of furnishing and decor meant to the people who lived in these homes, or the researcher might treat the photos as texts and explore how they construct particular accounts of people and their domestic lives (an interpretivist approach).

The second aspect of your epistemological position is your view on the nature of knowledge and the relationship between the researcher and what they are researching. Do you conceive the researcher to be objective and uninfluenced by the researched, or does the researcher necessarily shape the data and findings they generate? The latter position is consistent with a reflexive approach to undertaking research using photos, and this is an approach I advocate throughout this book. Reflexivity involves 'critical self-scrutiny by the researcher' (Mason 2002: 7) throughout the research process, embracing their 'methods, values, biases, decisions and mere presence in the very situations they investigate' (Bryman 2008: 698).

In sum, having thought carefully about ontology and epistemology you need to ask yourself:

- Do photos constitute evidence (epistemological) of what you regard as constituents of the social world (ontological)?
- If so, how might they do this?

This leads to thinking about methodology, that is, the methods and strategies you can use to generate and analyse data; this is the focus of subsequent chapters in this book. In the remainder of this chapter I reflect further on the qualities of photos and general points about how you can incorporate them in to research design.

# How do temporalities shape photo research?

To use photos in historical and social research requires an appreciation of three temporal dimensions: the temporalities that are conjured by a photo; the life of a photo; and the timings of research.

## The temporalities that are conjured by a photo

With digital technology there is a moment when a person can take and view a photograph almost simultaneously, but this moment is short lived and specific to digital photography. Although photos depict what was once in the present, when we encounter these images they are always representations *of* the past that were produced in the past. The idea that a photo depicts what was once in the present, has far-reaching implications for how people think and feel about photos and how they use them. People, including researchers, try to 'capture' a present so that in the future they can revisit it; photos are made to embed memories or, as in research, to serve as a record or aide-memoire. They are also collected from different points in time to facilitate overtime comparisons. Knowing what is featured in a photo was once in the present, but is now in the past, creates an interesting and sometimes poignant tension for viewers, particularly when looking at old photos. The pastness of a photo is sometimes a reason why they move us. As Barthes (2000) argued, one of the sources of a photo's punctum – how it 'pricks' us – is the realisation that the people portrayed in a photo are now dead. Because photos are from the past and provide a representation of that time, they are one of the main ways we envisage and know the past in general and in relation to our personal lives. Photos are embedded in public histories, individual biographies and personal memories. Moreover, what Kuhn (2007: 285) describes as the peculiar capacity of photos 'to "freeze" a moment in time' means that photos, especially personal ones, are productive memory materials. Photos encourage us to remember and this can be an expected or unexpected outcome of looking at photos.

## The life of a photo

Photos exist in time; they are produced, circulated and engaged within particular historical contexts. These historical contexts are critical to interpreting photos and using them to learn about the people depicted, the photographer, users and viewers; they are also relevant to understanding how we do research with photos because our practice is shaped by the tools, approaches, concerns and discourses that are available and valid within a specific historical period. Because context is critical to working with photos, doing research with them necessitates engagement with a number of historical moments. Rather than thinking of photos as fixed in time researchers need to appreciate the life or biography of a photo over time; this includes what happens to the photo as a specific object and what happens to the image if it is reproduced and represented in different formats and settings (Edwards 2002). When found photos become research data, their biographies include their part in the research process. For instance, a loose photo propped on the mantelpiece is picked up and talked about by an interviewee; the interviewer digitally photographs the loose picture and this digital image becomes part of the data collected and analysed in a research project; later in the research the image is used in various publications and a copy is deposited in an archive; meanwhile, the original photo sits on the interviewee's mantelpiece. The photos we generate in research also have biographies; for example, a photo is made initially as an aide-memoire but is later reclassified as data and then used as an illustration in a publication.

## The timings of research

As Barbara Adam (1995) demonstrates, all research has temporalities. Research occurs *in* time and *over* time, but research with photos has particularly interesting temporal dynamics in at least three ways. First, because of the special manner in which people view and relate to photos (discussed under 'temporalities conjured by a photo'), the timing of their appearance in research has important consequences for data generated. Barthes (2000) lamented that photos block memory; but while this is not always the case they can sometimes colonise memory and imagination. In interviews, for example, the scheduling of photos – for instance, at the beginning or end – has implications for how people talk and remember. The second temporal feature is that photos can be a bridge between different stages and times in the research process, typically the collection/generation and analysis of data; this occurs when researchers revisit photos collected or generated in the course of research and where they produce photos as an aide-memoire. In some projects, photos are deliberately generated at different points in time with the aim of tracing change. The third way in which timing is important relates to the historical moment within which photo research is undertaken. This point is pertinent to all research, but it is particularly important where the technologies and related practices that are the means of research have undergone recent change or are in flux, as is the case with photography. How researchers and their research participants relate to cameras and photos will influence how photo methods work. For instance, how many researchers think about and use photographic images has changed dramatically since the 1960s and the emergence of poststructuralist perspectives (Price 2000); this has resulted in a reconsideration of photography's claim to document accurately aspects of the real world. In light of recent rapid changes in photographic technologies and at least some changes in how people use and relate to cameras and photos (Tinkler 2008; Woodward 2008), it is likely that how researchers and their participants engage with photo methods – generating and looking at photos – has also changed. Some photo methods will work differently (not always better) at different points in historical time and this is something researchers need to consider as they design research and analyse their findings, or as they compare studies undertaken at different points in time. Relatedly, the age of research participants will probably influence how they engage with photo methods; one might expect children aged five years and twelve years to use cameras in different ways. Additionally, the implications of being given a camera at twelve years of age will be different for someone who participated in research in the pre-digital 1980s compared to the present day.

So far I have considered the conceptualisation of photos and temporal issues. These discussions have implications for the fourth question that you need to consider: what can you do with photos?

# What can you do with photos?

Working with photos is often conflated with only looking at images; looking is very important though often done poorly. However, the scholarly value of photos is heightened when researchers work with them in more diverse ways: to generate questions; to stimulate memory; engaging with sensory and affective experiences of, and responses to, photos ('feeling your way'); playing with images.

## Using photos to generate questions

Research is as much about asking questions as answering them, and photos are useful in both endeavours. The potential of photos to pose questions is typically under recognised as are the skills required to do this. Howard Becker (1979) advises researchers to sidestep general questions about the truth of a photo. Instead he advocates that researchers inspect an image closely and identify what 'questions it *might* be answering' (p. 101), which is not necessarily what the photographer or the person who wrote a caption intended. Once these questions are identified researchers can evaluate the validity of the photograph's answer, drawing on other types of evidence and information about how and why the photo has been made.

Take Figure 1.4, which I found in the Imperial War Museum photo archive. It is from a collection of photographs relating to the service of Muriel de Wend in the First Aid

**Figure 1.4**   'Muriel's colleagues Sprot, Gyp and Heasy enjoying a champagne picnic in an abandoned dugout, near Ypres', November 1918. Photograph from the collection of Muriel de Wend. HU 87422 © IWM

Yeomanry (FANY) in France during the First World War. This particular photo is captioned 'Muriel's colleagues Sprot, Gyp and Heasy enjoying a champagne picnic in an abandoned dugout, near Ypres' and dated November 1918. Rather than concentrate on whether this photograph is a truthful record of what these women were doing in a dugout, I would focus instead on what questions this photo might answer, for example, about the clothes worn by FANYs or about the conditions in which FANYs worked and socialised.

Becker directs us to ask questions about the photographic image, but it is short-sighted to focus on this only. Researchers can also ask questions about the life of a photo and what it might reveal about society and social life: 'photographs have an evidential force that exceeds their surface appearances', 'they explain something of that world which made them possible in the first place' (Edwards 2006a: 256–7); they are 'the starting point for inquiry rather than its end' (Newbury 2009: 318). To ask these kinds of questions the researcher begins by looking closely at the image but then steps back from it (see Chapters 3–5). Indeed the worth of a photo in historical and social research is not restricted to what it depicts and how: a very poor quality image can be as useful for stimulating questions as an exceptionally well-preserved one; amateur photos are as useful as professional ones. Approaching photographs in this way leads to questions about why photos were made, and made in a particular way. Who were they intended for? What interests, desires and relations between people underpinned these productions? Why were people photographed in these ways and what did they think about this? How were the photos viewed and why? How were they used and reused, or kept and stored? Why were some photos circulated while others were not? What happened to these pictures over time and how did this affect their status and how people viewed, used and made sense of them? These questions embrace the materiality and mobility of photos, also their biographies. They shine a spotlight on the people involved, including those in the picture, the photographer and other facilitators of the photograph, the organisations and institutions that use and present images, and the groups of people that view and engage with them.

Returning to the photograph of the FANYs leads me to questions about why this photo was taken, specifically about the role of photography in war, friendships and the construction of identity, memory and autobiography. As I think about this photo I wonder about its transition into peacetime; how did Muriel use, and relate to, this photo after the war; who looked at it when Muriel was back home; and how might it have contributed to perceptions of Muriel, FANYs, the war? Fortunately these are questions I can begin to pursue by visiting the Documents section of the Imperial War Museum where I find the photograph affixed in an album made by Muriel after the war (all the captions are in past tense) and I am able to reflect on this picture alongside the others she took and arranged in her album, also her letters from when she served in France. The preservation of this photo also raises questions about the cultural significance of personal wartime records and the role of the Imperial War Museum.

Photos can be used to generate questions in interviews (Chapter 9). When interviewing participants about photos they have taken, questions might include: how did they decide what to photograph? Who or what is featured and why? How was it composed? What would they have liked to photograph but couldn't? Participants can also be interviewed about their personal photos (Why is it meaningful? What's happened to it over time?) or those the researcher has taken (What do you think is going on in the photo?). Discussing these kinds of questions with participants opens up a range of avenues for enquiry. Additionally, the experience of talking about photos, and in some cases of taking photos and making decisions about this, can help participants process and articulate their experiences and views (Chapter 8).

## Remembering

Photos are widely celebrated for their mnemonic potential and this can be harnessed to academic objectives; memory is a valuable resource and tool in research (see Chapters 3, 4, 7, 8, 9). This is a key reason why researchers use photos in interviews to explore the past, change, biography and the nature of personal and collective memory (shared accounts of the past). Although remembering with photos is approached typically in terms of what researchers ask interviewees to do, researchers' memories are also a resource in academic enquiry. Memories are a staple of autobiographical photowork, they can also be used creatively in studies of non-personal photos. Often researchers generate and use photos to jog their memories of working in the field, and to keep track of what and who they encounter in the process of doing research.

## Feeling your way with photos

In the same way that memories can be resources in academic enquiry, so too can sensory engagements with photos. Sometimes photos can be appreciated fully only by engaging with their haptic dimensions through touch or, when this is not feasible or is prohibited, through imagining how they could be held and looked at. The material form of a photo influences what that photo means to people and how it is used. There is an important difference between a tiny photograph of a person kept in a locket that is worn close to the skin and sometimes held in the hand, and the same image enlarged and presented in a glossy book that is cumbersome to hold. The materiality of photos is not, however, static and as they circulate they are rematerialised in various forms and acquire different properties and meanings, as in the difference between a photo in an album, on Facebook or deposited in an archive. Recognising the significance of materialisation and its haptic significance is critical for generating historically grounded and culturally specific analyses of the purpose of photos and how they have been used, viewed and valued (see Chapter 5).

Feeling your way also embraces the affective. Reflexivity is widely considered a constituent of scholarly research practice (e.g. Mason 2002; Pink 2007), and when working with photos it makes sense to note your reactions to the photos you work with. Reflexivity extends beyond how researchers think about what they see to how they are physically affected by photos as images and objects. The physical sensations produced by looking are what Rose refers to as the 'materiality of seeing' (2004); this is an important aspect of working with photos, including those generated in the research and, importantly, your own personal pictures. The emotiveness of photos is one of the reasons why they are often good at getting people to talk, though particularly in oral histories this is also why they sometimes silence people.

## Play

'Playing' with photos can be a productive research strategy though its value is not widely recognised. As many artists appreciate, quite subtle shifts in established ways of representing and presenting a subject – achieved, for example, by montage, juxtaposition, cropping and enlarging – can affect profoundly how researchers see and how they think about what they see. Playing with photos – for example, by looking at them outside of their usual contexts or alongside other images – can help researchers and research participants think and remember, it can also create new ways of seeing. For instance, different perspectives on the photograph of the FANYs can be gained by reviewing it alongside other photos of dugouts taken when they were occupied by soldiers, or photos of upper-middle-class women at leisure in Britain in civilian contexts at this time, or holiday/tourist photographs from the period. Another way researchers can engage differently with the content of photos and shift what they 'see' in a picture is by using their imagination. Imagination and juxtaposition are both vital to some 'creative' approaches to working with personal and non-personal photos (Chapters 3 and 4). Playing with photos, perhaps through the juxtaposition of recent and old, or personal and commercial, is a technique that can be used in photo-interviews to stimulate discussion and prompt reflection; researchers can also invite research participants to play with photos and reflect on these creative expressions. When you start to feel stale with your images, play can be an effective way to refresh your interest and generate new perspectives and questions.

Having discussed general ways of working with photos, I now focus on specific methods and how to combine these.

# How do you combine methods?

Using photos in research is usually a multi-method undertaking. Though it is expedient to discuss different methods in separate chapters, this fragments the process of doing research, which usually involves a combination of the photo methods discussed in this book. For instance, a project in which research participants take photos might involve preparing participants to take photos, listening to them talk about them and analysing the content of their photos. Sometimes a combination of methods is necessary to address a research question; a combination may also serve to cross-check findings – triangulation – and enhance the validity[2] of the researcher's conclusions. Because research often involves a combination of methods, researchers need to think carefully at the design stage about how these fit together; for instance, instructions given to research participants about taking photos will depend in part on what you want to do with the images and achieve in a photo-elicitation interview. Another reason why photo research is multi-method is that it usually involves contextual research, including research on aspects of photographic practices (how and why people and organisations make and use photographs and what these practices mean). Contextual research is necessary in order to work with images, to generate useful photos or to evaluate how research participants engage with a research task and approach the images they have made (Tinkler 2008). Exploring these contexts involves a host of different sources and methods.

To combine different types of photo methods, or to use photo methods alongside non-photo methods (observation, archival research, surveys etc.), involves the same deliberations as when combining non-photographic qualitative methods. There are a host of studies providing typologies and evaluations of mixed-method approaches and guidance on how best to use them (e.g. Mason 2006; Teddlie and Tashakkori 2009). The essential principle is neatly summarised by Jennifer Mason (2006: 3):

> Researchers engaging in mixed methods research need to have a clear sense of the logic and purpose of their approach and of what they are trying to achieve, because this ultimately must underpin their practical strategy not only for choosing and deploying a particular mix of methods, but crucially also for linking their data analytically.

On this last point, when combining methods or sources, you need to be clear about the kind of data each generates (for instance, a subjective verbal account of being a pupil in a classroom, compared to a photographic representation of a classroom taken by the teacher) and be careful not to slip between these data without attending to their ontological status and specificity.

## Summary

In this chapter I have introduced five questions you need to consider before using photos in research, these concern: your conceptualisation of photos; whether and how photos constitute evidence of the social world; the temporalities of research; what you can do with photos; and methods in combination. How you conceptualise photos is a fundamental consideration in social inquiry, and I have demonstrated the importance of understanding the materiality of photos and debates about the properties of the photographic image. I have also explained how your conceptualisation of photos relates to your views on the nature of social phenomena and what counts as evidence or knowledge of it. All research raises temporal issues, but I have argued that photo research raises particularly interesting ones. I have also argued that at the beginning of a project it is useful to think in diverse ways about what you can do with photos. Finally, I have explained why you need to consider photo research as a multi-method undertaking.

The issues considered in this chapter have implications for how you design research and think about photos; they should be kept in mind as you read subsequent chapters.

## Notes

1  The Loch Ness Monster is a creature reputed to live in Loch Ness in the Scottish Highlands.
2  Validity 'means you are observing, identifying, or "measuring" what you say you are' (Mason 2002: 39).

# 2

# Image Work: Five Lines of Enquiry

Image work is usually an important, and often vital, aspect of using photos in research. This applies even to studies that are concerned principally with what people *do* with photos, because how people use photos is shaped partly by who or what is depicted in them. Image work is also a feature of photo-elicitation research, though often peripheral.

In this chapter I suggest that five lines of enquiry provide the foundations for working productively with images in contemporary and historical social research. I discuss each line of enquiry separately, though in practice they overlap and inform each other, and researchers move back and forth between them. The first type of enquiry involves identification of basic details about a photo – this helps you frame what you are looking at. The second involves scrutiny of the image, because interpretation depends on noting carefully what is featured and how. Considering material evidence is the third line of enquiry; photos are often objects, or they are experienced through material forms (computer screens), and these material dimensions have implications for how images can be used and what they mean to people. Contextual research is the fourth type of enquiry and is fundamental to all work with photographs. The fifth line of enquiry involves reflecting on what kinds of meanings a photo might have, this can involve working out what *you* think a photo means, or what the photograph might mean to the photographer, viewers or the people in the photo.

These lines of enquiry inform analysis of images and their evaluation. In his influential book on using documents in social research, John Scott (1990) identifies four criteria by which documents, including photos, should be assessed: authenticity – whether the document is genuine; credibility – this corresponds with the concept of validity and involves an assessment of how and why the document was made and the selectivity, bias and prejudices that might shape it; representativeness – the degree to which the document is typical or not; and meaning. All Scott's criteria can be assessed by pursuing the following lines of enquiry. The chapter focuses on working with found photos, but these lines of enquiry – particularly contextual research and meaning – are also relevant to analysing participant-generated photographs and interrogating researcher-generated photos (see Chapters 8 and 9).

# Identifying basic details

It is helpful to start by discovering basic details about the photos you are working with. What is the photo ostensibly of? When was it taken, and by whom? In answering these questions you engage at a general level with whether the photo is authentic; for instance, is a sepia photo genuinely old or has it been digitally manipulated to look so? Identification strategies overlap with contextual research so I will consider them together, but genre and the dating of photos deserve special mention.

Genre is a term used to classify photos, films and other cultural products in terms of recognised conventions of style and subject matter. There are a host of photographic genres (e.g. portrait, landscape) and over time some have split, producing distinctive new genres (war, travel and street photography are offshoots of 'documentary' photography), though researchers should be wary that genre definitions are sometimes contested as in the case of 'documentary' (Price 2000; Wells 2000a; see also Chapter 5). Genre is not, however, simply a term of classification; as Liz Wells (2000b: 295) explains, 'genres carry with them specific sets of histories, practices, ideological assumptions and expectations, which shift over time'. Each genre has shifting conventions influencing how photos are made (for instance, whether or not it is appropriate to crop an image), what should appear and how (e.g. lighting, composition). Identification of the genre of a photo is important for assessing what an image can reveal about what is depicted and it is key to interpretation; knowledge of genre conventions can also contribute to dating pictures. General texts on photography provide a good starting point for learning about genres (e.g. Clarke 1997; Wells 2000a).

Ascertaining when a photo was taken is usually essential to deciding how to use it. Jeremy Rowe (cited in Margolis and Rowe 2011) offers tips on how to do this. Look for temporal clues in the picture such as newspapers and calendars. Consider the material form of the photo and the implications for when it was most likely made, for instance, cartes de visite (small photographic postcards, see Figure 6.5) were widespread from the late 1850s to 1870s. Note whether the photo is sepia, black and white or colour and what this suggests about age, though be mindful that ageing effects can now be produced digitally. Reflect on the content and aesthetics of the image and when these were in vogue; for instance, post-mortem photographs of children posed as if sleeping were common in Britain and North America between 1860 and 1910. Check for information about the collection or archive of which the photo was a part. Information written on the photo can be helpful, but bear in mind that details are often added some time after a photo was taken and that they may be inaccurate or contested (Kuhn 1991).

# Scrutinising images

Looking carefully at images, often repeatedly, is essential whether you approach photos as depictions of the world, texts or objects. The first step involves careful scrutiny of what is in the photo. What is the photo ostensibly of – people, place, objects etc.? If people are featured: are they posed, what is shown of them, where do they look, what are they wearing, what expressions do they have, what is the physical relationship between people, animals, objects and the environment, what props are used and how, where do they appear to be? What details of place are visible? If objects are a focus: how are these arranged, are they engaged with or used by people or animals, are the objects in situ, what is in the background? Are there details in these images that you would not expect, or details that are missing but that you think should have been included or visible? This last question is informed by what you already know about the subject matter from other sources including written sources, other pictures, oral accounts, also your own memories and experiences. If working with adverts or even postcards, words will often be a part of the image and you need to record what the words say, where they appear and what relationship they have to the photographic image. Do they, for instance, provide a description of the photo?

The second step involves noting *how* the content is conveyed. Identifying these techniques requires practice as it can be difficult to move beyond content to the visual elements that position and convey them. This involves noting: the use of lighting and shadow, colour, camera angle and geometrical perspective. All these elements create impressions and convey meaning. The spatial organisation of the photo's content, achieved in part by what is in front of the lens but also by camera angle and lens, suggests a particular relationship between image and audience and positions the viewer in a particular way. For instance, photos of children often seem to position the viewer as an adult and to diminish the child's stature and status through the use of camera angle which gives the impression that the viewer is looking down on the child; the content of the photo can also contribute to this effect, for instance the positioning of children in front of doors so that viewers can gauge the height of children. The use of light is also important. Heavy shadows typically suggest darkness, weight, gloom and solemnity. There are also historically specific meanings. In Victorian portrait photography, for instance, the illumination of the sitter's forehead typically signified intellectuality (Linkman 1993). Interpreting these details involves contextual research such as knowledge of genre and historically specific aesthetic conventions, I will discuss this shortly.

# Considering material evidence

Photographs are objects as well as images and when working with them you need to consider the photo's materiality (see Chapter 1 for explanation). The materiality of a photo has implications for the meaning and significance of the image it bears. As Elizabeth Edwards and Janice Hart (2004a: 2) explain, drawing on Roland Barthes, the material form of a photographic image 'exists in dialogue with the image itself', like a 'landscape and the window pane' through which it is viewed. As I have described elsewhere (Tinkler 2008), the importance of the material dimension becomes clear when we reflect on the meaning of our own photographic possessions. My mother gave me a 3 × 3 inch black and white photograph of herself taken when she was a child. I could scan this picture into my computer and the resulting image would be the same as that featured on the paper photograph. Whilst I might do this, I will never throw away the paper picture. For me, the computer image is not the same (in material form or meaning) as the slightly dog-eared paper picture that my mother touched and preserved and which I can now hold in my hands. To take another example, the meaning of the photograph of two girls dressed up and acting the parts of sailor and young woman (Figure 2.1) is inseparable from its material form – a commercial postcard sent in 1916 to Miss Mabel Horsfield with the cryptic message 'what about this'.

My reflections on the postcard and the photo of my mother touch on key features of what is called a material approach to photographs. Edwards (2002) identifies four main dimensions of materiality that researchers need to attend to when working with

**Figure 2.1**  Photographic postcard (author's collection)

photographs: form, presentation, physical traces of usage, biography. I introduce each before commenting on digital photographic images.

First, the researcher needs to attend to the material form of a photograph, such as the characteristics of the paper and printing finish; 'Such technical and physical choices in making photographs are seldom random even if they are not fully articulated' (Edwards 2002: 68).

Second, the researcher needs to engage with the photo's material presentation, for instance, whether framed, or placed in a locket or album. One reason for this is that meaning is produced from the interrelation of image and object. How photos are presented is often revealing about values and culturally appropriate forms of use. For example, the presentation of wedding photos in a white satin album decorated with silver bells tells us something about how wedding photos should be presented and viewed (Edwards and Hart 2004a). Material presentation is also important because it influences how we physically engage with a photo. Different embodied experiences of viewing – that is the position in which the photo has to be viewed, whether and how it can be held or touched etc. – result from different material forms.

The third aspect of a material approach is to consider signs of use as these suggest how people have engaged with a photo. Signs of use include evidence of wear and tear. Material modifications, such as the practice of adding paint or hair to a photo (Batchen 2004; Pinney 1997), can also be instructive because these illuminate how people relate to images. Edwards (2002) also points to examples in ethnography of deliberate tinkering with a photo to create new meanings, including the case of an anthropologist over-painting photos and cutting and pasting them together in different configurations and presenting the finished product as a single image.

Fourth, thinking about material alerts us to a photo-object's history. This approach dovetails neatly with the anthropological concept of the 'social biography' of things (Appadurai 1986). The point is that a photograph, or any other thing, has a history or biography; it has a trajectory through time and place as it is made, used, exchanged and reused. For example, a photo of a schoolgirl is initially propped on the mantelpiece for display by her parents and later placed in a drawer with other photos; some years later the photo is claimed by the subject who is now a young adult and placed in an album; thirty years later the subject, now in her fifties, relocates the photo to an album for her own daughter in which she narrates the history of her family. Meaning is context dependent, but aspects of the photograph's 'accumulative histories' (Edwards 2001: 13) contribute to its significance at any one point in time and are 'vital clues for understanding the historical potency of the image' (Edwards and Hart 2004a: 5).

Materiality is also relevant to working with digital images (Sassoon 2004). If images are digitalised versions of analogue photographs, the original materiality is no longer apparent. The digital format limits what you can study and it is important to take this into account when choosing to work with digitalised images (see also Chapter 6). Many photographs are now taken using digital cameras or camera-phones and these images are two-dimensional rather than three-dimensional, though our engagement with them is mediated by material objects such as computer screens. From a research perspective, the material mediation is important in the sense that it shapes how you can work with an image and, perhaps, how you think about them as you do your research.

# Doing contextual research

Contextual research is integral to making sense of photographs as images and objects, though what types of context are examined in detail will depend on your approach and the questions you address. Contextual study of photos is key to their identification; reflection on what questions they can address; assessments of authenticity, credibility and representativeness; and analysis of meaning. The aim of contextual research is not simply to provide a backdrop against which to prop and interpret photos; this would be a dry, inanimate and inadequate approach. Instead, contextual research embraces also the historically and culturally specific practices of making, presenting, circulating, viewing and using photos in public and domestic contexts (here it overlaps with research on materiality). Photos are not static and so contextual research has to be dynamic and responsive to the mobility of photographs across space and time. In this section I introduce questions that are typically addressed about

**Figure 2.2**    Class photo, 1950s (private collection)

context, starting with contexts of production and then contexts of encounter; the latter is variously called reception, viewing or audiencing.

To illustrate what constitutes contexts of production it is helpful to focus on an example, such as this official class photo taken in the mid-1950s (Figure 2.2). Contexts of production include: the skills of the photographer and their views on appropriate ways of taking school photos (informed by genre and aesthetic conventions) and of depicting these particular children in terms of their age and gender in the mid-1950s (note the girls and boys are posed differently); the camera technology and technical decisions, including the decision to use black and white photography even though colour is available; whether and how the image was edited or 'improved' at the production stage; the dictates of the particular job as prescribed by the head teacher, shaped by her/his notions of the school's identity (is it significant that the fairly new school building is in the background?) and the photo's intended audiences (parents, governors etc.); the preparations that went in to the photo (were the children asked to dress smartly for the occasion?); decisions about the size of the photograph and the paper it should be printed on; the specific conditions in which the photograph was taken – for instance, whether it had to be accommodated in the playground on a windy day and feature all the class's pupils who had to be encouraged to sit still, look in the same direction and say 'cheese' at the photographer's command. The historically-specific broader social and cultural context in which this photo was made is also relevant; this includes type of schooling and school practices (e.g. the practice of photographing pupils, policies around what pupils should wear), the likely backgrounds and prospects of the pupils, youth fashion, current ideas and debates about teenagers.

Contexts of encounter include how photos are presented; this is variable and can shift during a photo's lifetime. Individual copies of the 1950s school photo were purchased initially by parents and framed or included in albums, but following a house clearance one print is now displayed in a pub as decoration alongside other 'old' photos. Each presentational context frames a photo in a particular way – it provides a material context in which the image is seen and used (camera phone, locket, newspaper etc.), sometimes captions and co-text consisting of words and other images – and these framing mechanisms need attention. If the school photo had been published in a newspaper, contextual research would include: which paper it appeared in and the identity and status of it (for instance, whether local or national, high-brow or frivolous); how prominently the image is displayed (whereabouts it is featured and its size); how it is captioned; and what texts and images surround it.

The contexts in which photos are encountered also include the circumstances in which people view, interpret and use photos. Attending to this dimension typically involves identifying who the viewers are; when and where they encountered the photo, and how its material form (framed in a gallery, printed in a paper etc.) shaped the specific conditions of viewing and engagement. Returning to the 1950s school photo, this type of context embraces the backgrounds, views, needs and interests that shape how people view this photo and what they do with it, including: what they know and think about the particular school, the children featured (parents, teachers and pupils may see the children differently) and recent events such as public concerns about the behaviour of teenagers or debates about the advantages of different types of school (e.g. comprehensive versus grammar, single-sex versus mixed-sex); their knowledge of photographic genre and aesthetic conventions and the status they afford school photos. Of course, as with presentation this is not a static form of context. As this photo is now over 60 years old it is important to distinguish between viewers from the 1950s and present-day, including those who study it for academic purposes and those who notice it in a pub.

# Reflecting on meaning

There are several ways of approaching what an image means. Taking the example in Figure 2.3, I consider the content of the image, institutional frameworks, viewers' interpretations, the photographer's intended meaning and the subject's version of what a photo is about.

## Content of the image

It is useful to start by distinguishing between a literal meaning and an interpretation of this image. A literal meaning is a description of what is in the picture.

**Figure 2.3** 'Teds', 1956. Mary Evans Picture Library/Roger Mayne

In this instance, the photo depicts an urban street lined with a terrace of shops and residential accommodation. The shop names and the writing visible in a shop window indicate that this is an English-speaking country. The lack of cars and the boys' clothing suggests the photo was taken in the 1950s or 1960s. Twenty or more boys stand around, most in suits, and one boy is walking towards the camera with a stick in his hands.

Interpretation is more complex. A photo does not have one meaning, it is polysemic. When you interpret a photo you are necessarily doing it from a particular vantage point, therefore, you need to be aware of what you bring from your own time, place and perspective to deciphering a photo. When working with old photos you need to ensure your interpretative work is attuned to the historical period you are researching with a photo. It would be inappropriate to interpret this photo through a twenty-first century lens unless your research is using this photo to explore some aspect of the twenty-first century, such as why this type of photo is now popular. To interpret this photo within its original historical and cultural context requires some preliminary identification work; this photo is of London in the 1950s, it is seemingly a documentary type of photograph (as opposed, say, to a family photo or a photographic advert).

One way to approach interpretation is to focus on what is in the picture and how these elements work together to construct meaning. This is what semioticians do (see van Leeuwen 2001; Rose 2007). According to semioticians, an image is 'a system of signs', a sign being a 'thing-plus-meaning' (signifier + signified); the relationship between signifier and signified is culturally determined (Williamson 1978: 17). To take a simple example, the image of a white dove is a signifier and the mental concept this signifier produces in the mind of the viewer is the signified; in contemporary British culture this is probably peace. The process by which the image produces this meaning is called signification. What the analyst does when they look at a photo (and by implication this is what we all do unconsciously) is identify the signs in the image and how these are interelated in a meaningful way. In photos, according to Barthes (1977), signs work at two levels – denotation (literal or manifest meaning, a description) and connotation (cultural associations, ideas and symbolic meanings). Returning to the dove, the image denotes a particular type of bird, but it also symbolises or connotes peace. Individual visual details can be signs that connote, but so too can the ensemble of signs that constitute a photo and this produces what Barthes (1973) called 'myth'. Myths are 'very broad and diffuse concepts' such as Englishness (van Leeuwen 2001: 97); they are ideological in the sense that they naturalise dominant cultural beliefs and ideas. The power of a photograph, according to Barthes, is that 'it reproduces ideology while apparently showing what is merely obvious and natural. Photographs connote, while seeming only to denote.' (Bull 2010: 36).

Returning to the photo and adopting a Barthesian approach, a possible interpretation would be that the group of boys occupying the street, and dominating the photo, is a local gang. My interpretation is based on the fact that the boys are dressed similarly and with elements of teddy-boy style. Moreover, the composition of the photo, with a row of houses stretching off in to the distance and the boys arranged across the middle, denotes that this is where the boys have congregated and connotes that this space is their territory. Most of the boys are standing with their hands in their pockets signifying, or more specifically connoting, that they are hanging around with time on their hands. The posturing of the boys in the foreground, facing the camera, connotes confidence, possibly cockiness or hostility. The threatening connotations are consolidated by the purposeful and seemingly aggressive manner of the boy walking towards the camera with a stick held in both hands. The black and white photography connotes realism and, in conjunction with the heavy shadows in the bottom third of the photo, signifies that this is a built up urban environment. In combination these signs convey the meaning that these are local boys, many aspiring to be teddy boys, hanging around in the street and posing a potential threat to passers by including the photographer; in other words, the photo is of an urban gang. Interpretation can, however, go a stage further because this photo, that I conclude is of a local gang, becomes a sign in its own right and (keeping in mind that this photo is being viewed from a 1950s perspective) connotes troublesome urban youth; this is the myth. This way of approaching meaning identifies what Stuart Hall (1980) called a 'preferred reading', that is a culturally dominant interpretation of a text. So far I have described Barthes's model of meaning-making as moving from interpreting individual signs and their relationships, to interpreting the image as a whole. However, Barthes argues that in everyday practice the meaning-making process occurs very quickly and the viewer is usually aware of the myth before registering that they have interpreted the individual signs; the myth then confirms the interpretation of the visual details.

Interpretation of a photo can be refined using an intertextual approach and interpreting the image in relation to other contemporary texts and images. A prominent intertextual approach is derived from the work of Michel Foucault and his concept of discourse; discourse is a group of statements which structure the way a thing is thought and the way we act on the basis of that thinking (Rose 2007: 142). A Foucaudian intertextual method (Rose 2007) addresses how images construct a particular view of the world and involves studying a number of images and sometimes texts to identify elements in a discourse, attending to visible and invisible details and identifying themes. A similar intertextual method characterises iconography/iconology (Panofsky 1955/1982; see Rose 2007, van Leeuwen 2001). Intertextual methods can be combined with techniques from semiotics to articulate the specific relationships between discourses and the elements (signs) that appear in pictures. It provides a method for identifying the meaning of images and how these images contribute to, and are constituted by, the discourses in which they are enmeshed.

An intertextual approach to this photo would involve locating it in relation to contemporary discourses on male youth, teddy boys, leisure and urban living conditions in the 1950s. Within these discursive contexts, the photo seems to be about the purpose-less and wasted leisure of working-class young men and their potential threat to social order. This photo also resonates with discourses that construct teddy boys as a social 'problem', even as a menace.

Research on the social and historical context contributes other layers of interpretation. I could, for instance, draw on contextual research on local leisure and consumption practices among teenage boys to conclude that these are schoolboys with very little disposable income unlike their older counterparts in full-time work. I might also research who took the photo and for what purpose, and drawing on material lines of enquiry, consider how the photographer produced this particular photo and the implications for analysing the image.

## Institutional frameworks

Another way of approaching what this photo means shifts attention from the content of an image to how meanings are produced in specific material and social locations such as a museum, archive or newspaper. This approach characterises another discourse method derived from Foucault (Rose 2007), which explores how institutions produce meanings through forms of power/knowledge (e.g. laws, regulations) and practical techniques and practices (e.g. captions, classificatory practices). This way of approaching meaning focuses attention on the specific contexts in which a photo is seen; often it is used to produce accounts of meaning that treat contexts of viewing as static (e.g. Sekula 1986a/b; Tagg 1988), though it has the potential to engage with the multiple contexts in which photos are encountered (Edwards 2001: 12).

In relation to this photo, I would attend to the original caption – 'Teddy boy group, Princedale Road, 1956'– and what this suggests about how I should interpret the photo (earlier I commented that not all the boys looked as if they were in teddy-boy style, moreover it is debatable whether adopting elements of teddy-boy style makes someone a 'teddy boy'). Reflecting on what the photo would have meant in its original presentational context, I discover that it first appeared in an art exhibition at the Institute of Contemporary Arts and I would reflect on how this context suggested particular meanings. I would consider, for example, evidence of how the photo was displayed and captioned and think about the implications of where it was on show; the ICA was a place for artists and art that was founded in 1946 to provide an alternative to the long-established and traditionalist Royal Academy of Arts. Of course, as the photo is reused in different contexts it accrues other meanings. For instance, in the context of various archives the photo's meaning is shaped in part by how it has been catalogued and described.

Institutional meanings are not written in stone. The meaning of a photo changes with context and use, as when an anonymous, de-individualised photographic subject presented as an example of a 'type' of human (as in 'scientific' photographic surveys of colonial subjects) is named and reclaimed by kith and kin as a grandfather and respected community elder (Pinney and Peterson 2003). Photos can also be reappropriated in other ways to undermine institutional meanings. As Leigh Raiford (2009: 113) demonstrates, there is a long history of African American activists and artists reappropriating photographs of lynchings in ways that resist their dominant meanings and 'critique a dominant history that more often than not excised, degraded, and silenced them'.

## Viewers' interpretations

So far I have not engaged directly with what people from the 1950s would have made of this picture. When scholars analyse what a photo means they often, explicitly or implicitly, make assumptions about how these photos contribute to what viewers know and think, but these assumptions should be approached with caution unless they are grounded in an informed discussion of the audience. For example, in semiotic analyses of magazine covers and advertisements, both Barthes and Judith Williamson ignore who actually views an image, when and where, and the possible range of meanings generated from these encounters; they do not identify even the sources of their images because they regard this as unimportant for the purposes of demonstrating *how* meanings are produced (Ramamurthy 2000). For the purposes of social and historical research such a decontextualised approach is inadequate; image analysis needs to be grounded in historically and socially specific contextual research.

This brings us to contexts of reception. Who would have seen this picture? Where and when was it encountered? What ideas, attitudes, interests would have shaped the viewer's interpretation? The significations, discourses and institutional framings discussed above would be relevant, but these would need to be grounded in historically specific information about viewers and viewing. Drawing on this combination of research, I might identify that the principal audience for this photo in the 1950s were middle-class adults, including artists, of a liberal persuasion; given what I could discover about their backgrounds, political leanings etc., I would draw conclusions about their interpretations – what I call informed speculation. Perhaps these audiences interpreted this photo as testimony to the state's failure to provide adequately for young people, or as an example of social decay, or evidence of working-class youth culture. This photo has since been reused in different contexts, and it is possible to research meaning at these other points in time, for example, how people today interpret this photo.

It is possible to identify likely interpretations using informed speculation, but audience research reveals that people do interpret images in unpredictable ways. Hall (1980) posited that while images have a preferred reading/meaning (culturally dominant meaning) this can be negotiated or contested by viewers, but this position assumes that preferred meanings are identified and does not engage with the range of ways people respond to pictures. There are several reasons why preferred meanings are not always identified or prioritised. Meanings are shaped by the contexts in which photos are encountered, and though researchers identify the principal contexts of viewing, these are not usually the only ones. Moreover, audiences are not homogeneous and individuals may see different things in the same photo. One reason is that the photo's indexicality – its link to the real world that was in front of the lens – means there is usually more in a picture than the photographer or user intended (Pinney and Peterson 2003). It is also because people interpret the same signs differently depending on their interests and experiences. For instance, in contrast to the meanings identified so far, a teenage boy in the 1950s might interpret the picture simply as lads socialising after work. Photos can also affect people in unexpected ways. Barthes (2000) argues that while photos have a culturally coded meaning, a person's engagement with a photo cannot always be understood in terms of their decoding of these cultural signs. Alongside a culturally informed reading or 'studium', for some viewers a photo can also produce a 'punctum'. The punctum is, typically, a detail in a photo that produces an individual and subjective response from a viewer. It is not culturally coded (this has been contested, e.g. Cronin 1998; Tagg 1988) or predictable; it 'is that accident which pricks me (but also bruises me, is poignant to me)' (Barthes 2000: 27). Barthes' punctum suggests that it can be difficult to predict how people engage with and feel about a photo.

Researchers typically use interviews to identify the actual meanings that photos have for viewers (see Chapter 9). This type of research is most easily accomplished in studies of contemporary viewing because of the difficulty of asking people to recall what they thought about a photo in the past (Hagiopan 2006). Diaries and letters can provide documentary evidence of past interpretations but this is unusual. However, even in studies of contemporary life, audience research does have limitations. It is not always easy or possible for people to identify and articulate what images mean to them, moreover meanings are not static and shift over time, even in the course of an interview. Additionally, this type of research can only reveal what specific people make of an image and because it is time-consuming it typically sheds light on the actual meanings of a relatively small group of people. As researchers often want to comment on the responses of a wider group, it is necessary to integrate audience research with informed speculation on likely meanings.

## Photographer's intended meaning

A different way of approaching what this photo means is to consider what the photographer intended; this relates to contexts of production. The photographer is Roger Mayne and his speciality is urban street photography. In this instance, the context of production offers intriguing information about the photo's intended meaning:

> I was going out on a foray in North Kensington, and as always I had my camera around my neck, and I saw this group of teddy boys and even to me as a young person they were a bit sinister, so I walked down the street on the other side. I got past them, thank God I got past them, and then I heard this voice, 'take our photo Mister!'. So, of course, immediately I turned around and photographed the group, because I mean I wasn't going to miss a chance like that and I realised that they weren't sinister. They were actually being quite friendly. So I went in quite close amongst the group and got quite a lot more photographs quite close to them. (Interview with Roger Mayne, V&A Museum)[1]

Apparently the boys were not being aggressive and there is some corroboration for this interpretation in the photo: there is a woman standing in a doorway seemingly relaxed and some boys are perched against a shop front uninterested in what is going on. Importantly, Mayne initially felt threatened by the youths and the photo seems to convey this impression. An examination of the production of this photo suggests ambivalence towards the boys. It is difficult, however, to be certain of Mayne's intended meaning, though we can gain some ideas from researching his background, photographic work and the circumstances in which the photo was made.

## Subject's meaning

A different version of what was going on might emerge from talking to the boys that were photographed – the subject's meaning. In a discussion of her childhood family photos, Diane Gittens (1998) offers a very different interpretation of family relationships than is suggested by the traditional-style images her father and abuser made.

## A final word on meaning

There are many ways to approach a photo's meaning. If you are researching the meaning of images you need to be clear whose meaning you are discussing. You also need to reflect carefully on what you can claim about the viewer's interpretation of a photo. However you approach meaning, contextual research is crucial.

# Summary

In this chapter I have introduced and explained five types of enquiry that are fundamental to working productively with images: identifying basic details, scrutinising images, considering materiality, doing contextual research and reflecting on meanings. Distinguishing between these threads of enquiry is somewhat artificial, though it serves the purpose of allowing me to explain what each entails. In practice, these lines of enquiry overlap and, rather than doing each in sequence, researchers weave back and forth. Lots of questions are posed by working with images in these ways and it is rare to be able to answer them all. How researchers pursue these lines of enquiry is the focus of Chapter 3 in which I examine examples of research that use found photos to explore questions about society and social life in the past.

# Note

1  V&A Museum microsite, accessible from V&A Gallery 100 computer terminal.

# 3
## Studying Found Photos

This chapter examines how researchers work with found photos to explore social and cultural life, particularly in the past. I look at the questions researchers pose as they look at photographs (see Chapter 1) and the methods they employ to address these questions; the lines of enquiry discussed in Chapter 2 are the foundations of their craft. I also consider research that uses photos for inspiration utilising creative methods. The chapter does not provide a survey of research, but a consideration of some examples of how researchers use photographs and the issues they encounter in doing this. The examples are historical, but the approaches, methods and issues are relevant to using found photos to research the present. The chapter is organised around five areas of research, although in practice projects often combine them:

- Using photos to learn about the people and material culture they depict.
- Mapping ideas about, and approaches to, aspects of the social world.
- Researching how and why images are made, used and reused.
- Exploring responses: popular and iconic photos.
- Seeking inspiration from photos.

## Using photos to learn about the people and material culture they depict

In this section I consider whether and how the study of images can enable researchers to learn about what is depicted, starting with material culture and then the people who are the subjects of photos.

### Material culture
Photos are widely studied for evidence of material culture including details of things that contemporaries took for granted and failed to mention in texts. Seemingly

incidental and background features are often deemed particularly reliable and of interest to historians (Mifflin 2007; Samuel 1994). But even these details cannot be accepted as evidence without consideration of the photo's production.

Jane Hamlett (2006) studied photos of college rooms taken in the 1890s for what they reveal about material culture and the lives of students. Though the photos are read for detail, there is careful consideration of how the contents and impression are managed for the camera. Unfortunately, no information is available about how these photos were produced, so Hamlett studies the photos for clues. Reflecting on the meaning of things, comparing photos of different college rooms and placing the photos alongside other sources on college life, Hamlett pieces together an account of how students used material culture in self-presentation (see Box 3.1).

## BOX 3.1   MISS OWEN'S ROOM, BY JANE HAMLETT

This photograph (Figure 3.1) shows a room that belonged to Miss Owen, a student at Holloway College for women, and it was probably taken in 1898.

**Figure 3.1**   Miss Owen's Room. RHC AR/130/1 Archives, Royal Holloway, University of London

Historians often want to read photographs as social documents – and this one could be a very exciting way of finding out more about the lives of the pioneering students who were among some of the first women to experience university education in Britain. But before we go too far, we need to think about how the photograph was produced, how it might have been used, and how people at the time might have thought about the material objects that appear in it.

We know from college records that Miss Frost, who was a Mathematics lecturer at the college in the 1890s, took this photograph. This information changes how we see the photograph, and raises the possibility that Frost may have directed students to arrange their rooms. Certainly we might expect the room to be more messy in the rush of everyday life. The student may well have known that her lecturer was coming to take the photograph, and have tidied up and arranged it accordingly.

One stumbling block to successfully interpreting this image is that we don't know why it was produced and who would have looked at it at the time – and we can't tell this from other sources in the college archives. Frost may have taken the picture to show to potential students, or it may simply have been taken as a record of the daily life of the college, something which early women academics were immensely proud of.

Having said this, I believe that we can still use this photograph to reveal something about the lives of early women students. Despite the careful arrangement of the room for the photograph, we can see that it contains many individual personal goods, which tell us about what students brought to university and how they sought to personalise their rooms. Other sources, like diaries and reminiscences, confirm how much pleasure students often took in decorating them.

One particular item stands out in this room – an impressive, full-size, crocodile skin, attached to the wall above the mirror. To work out the meaning of this object, we need to think about how it would have been viewed in the late nineteenth century. One way of doing this is to look at other sources from the time. Advice manuals on how to decorate middle-class homes tell us that certain styles of decorating were associated with women, and others with men. Masculine spaces in upper-middle-class homes were often smoking rooms and billiard rooms – and here manliness was often communicated through the display of hunting trophies, like stags' heads or tiger skins. Tokens of the hunt were particularly associated with men and masculinity.

It's tempting to assume that Miss Owen's choice to display a crocodile skin was a deliberate play on the norms of gender and decorative display in the nineteenth century. By displaying a big crocodile skin in her room, anyone who came into the space could see that she felt unconstrained by expectations about how female spaces should be decorated. However, as we know very little about

*(Continued)*

Miss Owen, other than her name pencilled on the back of the photograph, it's hard to draw firm conclusions. Where did she get the crocodile skin from? Did she buy it, or was it a present from a relative in the colonies …? We can only speculate on this.

We do have another option, however, and that is to compare the photograph with 55 other photographs of student rooms at Royal Holloway that were taken by Frost at the same time. What emerges from these is a strong sense of differentiation between the rooms – as students chose to personalise relatively uniform spaces. The decision to decorate with such an impressive object must surely have been partly motivated by the need to create an individual space amidst the uniform life of the institution. It's an imperative that many students, living away from home in halls for the first time, continue to find familiar.

Hamlett demonstrates how photos can be used to explore material culture in the past, but what about over time? Photos can facilitate comparisons of material culture over time (in Chapter 7 I consider taking photos for this purpose), but for this to be convincing it needs to be based on critical visual analysis, attention to production and careful presentation of findings.

George Dowdall and Janet Golden (1989) undertook a study of 343 photographs taken between 1880 and 1980 of life in Buffalo State Hospital, an institution for the 'mentally ill'. Though the study is interesting, the tendency to lose sight of the construction of the photos is a major weakness which undermines their use of photos as evidence. For example, Dowdell and Golden point to the stark difference between a photo of a hospital corridor in 1901, soon after the hospital was opened, and one taken 'a few decades later' (p. 192). The first photo shows a wide corridor bathed in light with sofas and chairs lined intermittently along the walls and pictures on display; a nurse stands at the far end. The later photo shows the same corridor with chairs lining the walls and people sitting and standing everywhere. On first glance the contrast between the two photos is striking and seems to support Dowdell and Golden's conclusion that the hospital suffered from overcrowding in the later period. But when I looked again I was less convinced by the comparison and frustrated by the simple juxtaposition of photos. No comment is made about the likely production of the two photos and their intended audiences, and the implications for how the space is presented; this is a glaring omission for two main reasons. First, the early photo is a promotional one included in an annual report and one would expect it to present the hospital in the best possible light. There is no information about the second picture, but the blurred figure in the foreground and the poor lighting suggest it is not a professional or promotional photo. This difference in production may explain the difference in content. There are empty sofas and chairs along the corridor in the early photo suggesting space and indicating facilities for relaxation, but it is possible to imagine these seats filled with people producing a less tidy impression. Second, the way the photos are taken also creates a contrast. In the early photo the photographer looks straight down the corridor, making the most of the natural light (perhaps supplementing it with specialist lighting) and emphasising space, light and orderliness. In contrast, the second photo is taken from a height as if the intention was to look down on the people using the space and to emphasise the number. This angle, combined with poor lighting contributes to an impression of overcrowding, indeed the photo may have been intended to make this point. But could the second photo have been taken differently to introduce a different impression? The point of this example is that comparative work needs to engage with how photos are produced and to present these details to readers in order to substantiate conclusions.

## The subject's story?

Photographs can provide insights into the people depicted, but this requires thoughtful and careful research. In the following I look first at portrait photography and then types of photography that aim to provide visual evidence of aspects of social life, what can be broadly termed documentary types of photography. This includes institutional photography produced by employers, also 'documentary photography' which is 'the *practice* of photography as an engagement with and interpretation of social life' (Newbury 2006: 296), although some also stress that its purpose is to 'pave the way for social change' (Ohrn 1980 cited in Price 2000: 75; for discussion of terminology see Chapter 5).

### The people in portraits

The most fundamental point for many researchers of portraiture is that a photo records that someone was in front of the camera when the photo was taken, what Roland Barthes called 'presence' (2000). Whether the image tells us anything about how people actually looked is less easy to determine. Professional portraits are typically examples of how photographers want to present their subjects; this is particularly the case when subjects have no, or relatively little, power – children, colonial subjects and those in institutional settings. Relatedly, a person will look different depending on how a photo has been made, including conventions of genre and aesthetics: a professional portrait will differ from a police mug shot or a snapshot taken by a friend. Even the least contrived photo is still shaped by production factors leading to different visual accounts of a particular individual.

Commercial portraits can, however, sometimes reveal something of the subject's story. Though the degree of likeness can be difficult to gauge, commercial portraits often reveal how a person wanted to appear in a photo. Evaluating this is not straightforward. Even when people commissioned professional portraits you cannot assume they had control over their image. In Victorian Britain, photographers typically worked with fixed notions of how to represent women, men and children from different social classes (Linkman 1993). This relaxed in the twentieth century as commercial portrait photography increasingly became a medium through which 'individuals confirm and explore their identity' (Holland 2000: 122), but self-representation was frequently still constrained. In Britain it was commonplace for studios to offer sitters a gendered choice of looks from a catalogue.[1] Moreover, the portrait was a product of 'dynamics' and 'power relations' and shaped by a contract between sitter and photographer (Homberger 1992: 115). Unfortunately, it is rare to unravel quite how much control a sitter had over how they were depicted.

The subject could make choices at other stages in the photographic process (Williams 1986). Especially after 1900, photography studios specialised in distinctive styles of portraiture, for instance romantic photos of women or highly stylised ones, and peoples' decisions about which photographer or studio to use are therefore revealing about how they wanted to be portrayed. People also exercised their consumer rights at the proof and print stage. For example, Alice Hughes, a successful photographer around 1900, recounts how the mother of a plain girl complained about the proofs she received of her daughter and responded with a 'list of improvements' (de Ville and Haden-Guest 1981: 21). Although researchers cannot usually uncover the detailed negotiations that went into a sitting, the sitter's subsequent use of a portrait – displayed, given to family, sent to a magazine, hidden away – provides clues about whether or not they liked the image. The importance of these portraits is not principally that they recorded what people were actually like in appearance (although there could be visual verisimilitude), but that they offer insights into how people wanted to be seen; they convey social illusions, aspirations and the presentation of self (Thomas 1978). This approach can take us in interesting directions as my research on smoking demonstrates (see Box 3.2).

---

**BOX 3.2   WHY AND HOW WERE THESE WOMEN PREPARED TO APPEAR IN A PHOTO WITH A CIGARETTE?**

In my research on the feminisation of smoking in Britain (Tinkler 2006) I found some personal photos of middle and upper-working-class women smoking in the period 1910–20, at a time when few women smoked and it was widely regarded as disreputable. Did these photos prove that these women smoked? This was impossible to tell from the photos or other available evidence. But an equally interesting question is why and how were these women prepared to appear in a photo with a cigarette?

Take the example shown in Figure 3.2. In Bolton, around 1915, three women posed for a photograph. This particular copy belonged to their friend, Mrs Robinson, who donated it to the archive where it was labelled a 'joke'. The women came from fairly prosperous upper-working-class backgrounds, as indicated by the yard in which the picture was taken, the quality of the props, and information about Mrs Robinson's background. The photo, taken by an itinerant photographer, was most likely orchestrated by the women.

**Figure 3.2**   A 'joke' photograph (DPA 608/31). Reproduced by permission of the DPA, Greater Manchester County Record Office

In the photo, two of the three women, each holding a cigarette, sit either side of a table on which there are glasses of dark fluid; a soda siphon gives the impression that this is alcohol. A third woman leans on the back of her friend's chair with one hand on her hip and the other holding a cigarette. The women's poses were in clear disregard of photographic conventions, which stipulated that the pose of a 'lady' should be modest and contained. The bar/lounge setting, the alcohol and cigarettes, were essential props that worked in conjunction with the women's poses to suggest sexual licence. This photograph was a 'joke', and clearly so.

For the joke to work, the idea the photograph conveyed – that the women were 'fast' – had to be unbelievable. In this instance, the sexual propriety of the women had to be so clearly established for their intended viewers that the sexual meaning of the image could not be mistaken as real. To safeguard against misreading the photograph, its construction was also made visible. The photo was clearly contrived and no effort was made to hide this. The domestic or lounge-bar setting was achieved by using a backcloth that ended abruptly within the photographic frame, the flagstones of the yard were also visible on one side of the photo, and

*(Continued)*

there was a discarded chair in the photo which suggests that some experimenting took place before the right effect was achieved.

What does this photo reveal about the Bolton women and their relationship to smoking? The photograph testifies to the dominant idea that disreputable women smoked, but it also hints at the complex relationship for women between smoking and modernity. The significance of this photo becomes apparent when considered alongside others photos of women smoking in this period and the history of women's smoking. It is unlikely to be a coincidence that the archives reveal upper-working and middle-class women making 'joke' photographs of themselves smoking, but there is no evidence of a similar practice among women lower down the social scale; in photos the only serious female smokers were from the social elite. This difference cannot be explained simply by the cost of photos, as working-class women did purchase photos of themselves in playful poses (Linkman 1993). The answer lies in attitudes towards women who smoked. Although smoking was gradually being redefined as a signifier of feminine modernity, this applied only to the urban elite. For the upper-working-class Bolton women, posing for the camera as smokers was probably only possible, or desirable, in the context of play-acting. At this particular time, the modernity of smoking was beyond the reach of these women even if the respectability afforded by their upper-working-class status allowed them to make jokes about smoking. It would have been extremely risky for women lower down the social scale to appear in a photo with a cigarette because they could not afford to even 'joke' about their respectability. This photo reveals something about the women who posed in it, but read in its historical context and alongside similar photos it also offers insights into the relationship between smoking, class, gender and respect-ability in 1915.

If searching for evidence of what a portrait meant to the sitter, researchers need to be mindful of how photographic meanings are framed, often in ways unintended by the subject. Drawing on John Tagg (1988), Laura Doan (2001) demonstrates how the meaning of particular photos of interwar lesbians changed dramatically depending on prevailing discourses. For example, in the early 1920s the lesbian novelist and celeb-rity, Radclyffe Hall, commissioned several photos of herself that were released to the popular and elite press where they were presented as evidence that Hall was modern and chic. The same photos, following the highly publicised trial of Hall's lesbian novel, *The Well of Loneliness* (1928), were re-presented in the media (sometimes cropped and invariably recaptioned) as evidence of an aberrant mannishness and homosexuality. Meanings are slippery and so it is important to locate the photo's intended meaning within the discursive contexts of the moment of production and, where possible, evidence of what the sitter did with the photo. Of course, over time even the sitter may develop different interpretations of a photo (Seabrook 1991).

Evaluating what, if anything, a photo says about the subject involves learning as much as possible about the contexts of production, including: the photographer, their status and practices; the subject's relationship with the photographer; genres of portrait photography and aesthetic conventions; technological constraints; and the operation of the photographer's business. It is also useful to examine the portrait and compare it with others from the same period or, more specifically, by the same photographer and studio to discern whether or not the image is standardised. Where possible, it is also instructive to find out what happened to the portrait. Conclusions must always be historically and culturally specific. It is only through this type of research that researchers can begin to tease out the subject's story.

## The subjects of documentary types of photography

The subject's story is typically more evasive in documentary types of photography. Who makes these photos and for what purposes are key considerations. Focusing on institutional photographs of the coal-mining industry in the 1950s, Eric Margolis (1998) encourages a cautious approach. He points to the gaps and biases in the photographic record. Scrutinising the photos, he pinpoints what they show but also, by juxtaposing oral histories, what they do not or cannot show: 'Dangers that miners talked about all the time – falling rocks, inexperienced miners, methane gas, and so on, were elided from the images' (p. 14). He insists that only the material and techno-logical could be photographed; images cannot relay underlying social relationships and processes including exploitation and alienation. Margolis argues that meaning resides in how images are framed by captions. Without these anchors, meanings are slippery and changeable as evidenced by the recent recycling of these images as nostalgic commodities. While Margolis is right to point to the limitations of photos as evidence in and of themselves, I am not convinced that photos are always mute on social relations. Margolis makes a similar point about school photos (1999), and in this context I think he overstates his point because the physical arrangement of classrooms and the relative positioning of children and adults is suggestive, if not revealing, of social relations.

Margolis reminds us to be wary of the assumptions we make about what an image shows and why these conclusions seem obvious. This advice is useful when we consider street photographs, such as those taken of working-class inner-city districts in Britain in the 1950s and 1960s by Shirley Baker (1989, 2000). These are daytime photos of streets and not of interior spaces such as homes or public houses, and they feature children, women and elderly men. It would be easy but erroneous to con-clude that there are no men of working age in these areas, or that all women of working age are mothers, or that the young children photographed playing or wan-dering around were uncared for. This brings me to Howard Becker's (1979) point, discussed in Chapter 1, that we need to think carefully about the questions a photo can answer, and it highlights the importance of supplementary evidence. Historian Stephen Brooke argues that a contextualised analysis of Baker's photographs can offer insights into everyday life and facilitate interventions into historical debates. The key is to treat the photos as an account made by Baker to represent her observations and experiences (see Box 3.3). What the people featured in these photos thought of their lives or of being photographed in these ways is not possible to tell. Their stories are told from the photographer's perspective and interpreted through her frameworks, also those provided by publishers and exhibitors.

## BOX 3.3   THE REPRESENTATION OF WORKING-CLASS WOMEN IN THE PHOTOGRAPHY OF SHIRLEY BAKER, BY STEPHEN BROOKE

**Figure 3.3**    Street Scene, 1964. Mary Evans Picture Library/ Shirley Baker

In the 1950s and early 1960s, Shirley Baker made photographs tied to specific locations in Salford and Manchester. These photographs were, consciously, pictures chronicling an urban, working-class world on the verge of change, manifested in programmes of urban redevelopment that replaced, for example, the tenement streets of Hulme with the tower blocks of Hulme Crescents. This sense of change has been paralleled, in sociological and historical literature, by the argument that the salience of class identity in postwar Britain was on the wane. The photographs of Baker, and of other photographers of the period such as Roger Mayne, have sometimes been taken as snapshots of a vanishing world and a vanishing class. As an historian, I was interested in revisiting this interpretation of both working-class identity after 1945 and the representation of working-class life.

Baker's photographs of Manchester and Salford seem to me to present a complex picture of working-class life. As Baker explained in 1989, the 'huge "slum" clearance programme' of the sixties prompted her to 'capture some of the street life as it had been for generations before the change' (p. 15). This was, however, not attempted in a spirit of nostalgia, but as a way both of documenting those neighbourhoods and giving visual agency to those most intimately affected by rehousing: 'nobody seemed to be interested in recording the face of the people or anything about their lives'. She was particularly sensitive to the disparity of power between those who lived in these streets and those in charge of demolition and resettlement. Her photographs evince, in an unsentimental fashion, the continuing importance of working-class identity. They are illustrations to an ongoing story about the working classes, rather than portraits of a vanished world. A critical aspect of this is their representation of working-class women in both traditional and more modern roles.

It is a truism to say that using photographs as historical documents is a tricky business. Baker's photographs are evidence of the conditions of working-class life in 1950s and 1960s Manchester, not least of the complex picture they offer of the tension between poverty and affluence, whether it is seen in the deprivation of the physical environment or the clothing of the figures in that environment. But this view must be qualified by both the complexity of that picture and by the particular character of photography. Thinking about the picture's complexity means situating Baker's work within an historical understanding of how gender, generation and class worked at a particular point in time. Attending to the latter involves acknowledging the subjectivity of the perspective, researching the photographer's intentions, methods of work and conditions of production and publication. It also means reflecting upon how the photographs work as photographs: placing them in a broader framework of the history of photography (in this case late-Victorian slum photography and interwar documentary photography) and considering the photographs' interior, visual language. The last point may seem the most ephemeral and suspect to an historian, but historical meaning can be drawn from visual language or composition. In Baker's work, for example, the way that figures are framed by lines of terraced houses, by brick walls and doorways give a sense of the enclosures around working-class life (Figure 3.3). Similarly, there is an emphasis in Baker's photographs (and in those of Roger Mayne) upon physical movement, captured in the pictures by depth of field, exposure and framing. Women and children *move* through these photographs and these streets. This does have an historical meaning, an immediacy that suggests dynamism rather than stasis. It is, to borrow Geoff Dyer's (2005) phrase, the portrait of an 'ongoing moment' in the life of the working-classes rather than the 'decisive moment' (to echo Cartier-Bresson[2]) of their demise. In these ways, photographs can open up the complexities and ambiguities of historical analysis.

# Mapping ideas about, and approaches to, aspects of the social world

In this section I consider how to work with sets of photos to explore and map ideas about, and approaches to, aspects of the social world, this is sometimes conceptualised as discourse analysis. This type of research has been used to explore a host of different topics and themes including gender (e.g. Goffman 1979; McLellan 2009), male friendship (Ibson 2006) and apartheid photography (Newbury 2009). Photos are a particularly attractive source for researchers because they often reveal more than intended by the photographer or the organisations and institutions that use them in their publications and publicity. Janet Fink (2008) in a study of the yearbooks produced by the charity, National Children's Home (NCH), provides a good example of how to probe the suggestiveness of photographic representation and how to trace and explain changing approaches to children and their care (see Box 3.4).

---

**BOX 3.4   WHAT APPROACHES TO CHILDREN AND CHILDCARE ARE CONVEYED IN PHOTOGRAPHIC REPRESENTATIONS INCLUDED IN NCH YEARBOOKS 1930–60?**

Drawing on Tagg (1988) and Sekula's (1986b) work, Fink attends to the institutionally intended meanings conveyed through framing and captions. Fink is concerned, however, that in doing this she ignores individual images and what they reveal and conceal, so she also studies the photos as texts to 'tease out a variety of stories about childhood and childcare' and 'to identify, absences, contradictions and paradoxes in their narratives' (Fink 2008: 289). This textual analysis entails scrutiny of the images, and research on the social and political context in order to unpick and interpret the possible meanings of these images. Photos from the 1930s, for example, are read in relation to health discourses, child development and social training discourses, social and political anxieties, the influence of psychological and psychometric testing, new standards of welfare introduced by Children's and Young Person's Act (1933), as well as long-established discourses on the nature of children, notably nineteenth-century romantic notions of children's natural innocence. Fink also compares photos noting how similar pictures were sometimes given different meanings by their captions. For example, two photos of little boys published in 1944–5, one captioned with words from a progressive Italian-American school principal and the other from a Victorian cautionary tale, are interpreted by Fink as evidence of contestations between different sets of ideas at the time (p. 299). Fink establishes that the NCH yearbooks used photos of children in their care as evidence that the charity provided home-like situations

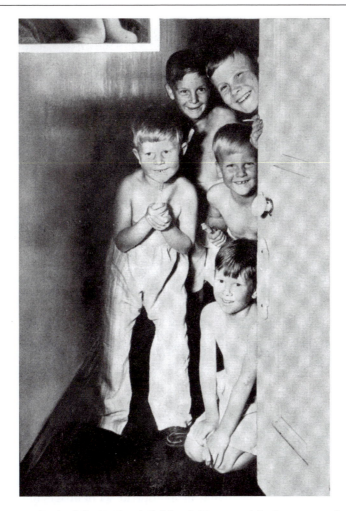

**Figure 3.4**   Year Book of the National Children's Home and Orphanage, 1936, p. 19. Image courtesy of Action for Children ©

and family-like relationships. But a closer look at the photos reveals tensions and contradictions in representations of children in this period, and negotiation of different ideas about children's needs.

Fink also traces change over time. In doing this she adopts Peter Burke's advice and approaches photos as 'special performances', using changes in the representation of children to trace 'the history of changing hopes, values and mentalities' (p. 289). Her study is organised into decades, and the use and content of images is considered within and between these periods. She traces themes in representation.

*(Continued)*

She also notes the reuse of photos of anonymous children with different captions in different yearbooks. For example, Figure 3.4 first appeared in 1936 as part of a series of photos depicting life in a Cornish branch of the NCH, and as Fink explains, it suggests spontaneity on the part of the photographer and the playfulness and wellbeing of the children in this particular home. Ten years later this photo reappeared in a feature on a Yorkshire branch; 'certain iconic images of childhood can be deployed in different periods and different contexts because meanings embedded within them – here, happiness, innocence and play – retain their resonance over time' (p. 301).

I asked Fink how she worked out a strategy to explore change. Fink explained that she was fortunate in that she owned a complete set of NCH yearbooks and so she started her research by going right through her collection several times to identify signs of change and continuity in the representation of children and to pick out themes. The decision to use a decadal structure came towards the end of this process, and it emerged from both conscious and unconscious factors. From the outset Fink was concerned to find a way to balance analysis of the images with the inclusion of sufficient political and social context. With hindsight she thinks the materiality of the collection also suggested a ten-year structure, specifically shifts in the size of the yearbooks and quality of the paper during the 1940s. In all studies, researchers have to decide their parameters. For Fink, in the context of time constraints, this was a decision not to include yearbooks from the 1960s. Additionally, what viewers made of the yearbooks would have been a very different project, though Fink points to the knowledge that likely viewers may have brought to particular images.

In order to explore and map ideas about, and approaches to, aspects of the social world you need to start by identifying an appropriate set of images in relation to your research question and resources. Before starting the analyses you need to discover, if possible, who commissioned and used the pictures, who the photographs were intended for and where the images were typically presented (a magazine, government information campaign etc.). You also need to consider whether you have access to the full range of pictures that you are interested in (from which you may take a sample), and if not, how this might influence your analysis and findings. This is followed by identification and tracking of themes, noting dominant as well as subsidiary or counter ones (content analysis techniques can be used, see Chapter 7). In tracing themes, attention is paid to patterns in content and how this is featured (composition, use of lighting and colour etc.) and also presented (status attributed to the photos – is it presented as an accurate record or an impression, its importance as indicated by size and positioning, captions, surrounding text). The analysis requires careful consideration of the detail of the images with reference to contextual information such as prevailing discourses also social conditions and historical events.

# Researching how and why images are made, used and reused

So far I have considered what photos can reveal about approaches and ideas, also about the subjects of photographs. Along the way there have been glimpses of how images are used and the individuals and groups who produce and mobilise them, it is to these aspects that I now turn. I start by examining research on how and why images are made and used, and then study the reuse of particular photos. I conclude by considering whether researchers can learn anything about photographers from studying their photographs.

Why photos are made and how they are used is important for understanding the content of images and their historical meaning and significance. Researchers should ask themselves: why represent the social and material world in particular ways? Who is making and using these images and for what purposes? These are the kinds of questions that interested historical geographer, James Ryan, when he discovered Figure 3.5: why the need for such a photograph? To address this question Ryan considered the content of the image also how and why it was made and displayed (see Box 3.5).

---

### BOX 3.5  'MRS HARRIS PHOTOGRAPHING IN THE FOREST', BY JAMES RYAN

I came across a loose print of this photograph (Figure 3.5) when researching the uses of photography in European colonialism in the late nineteenth and early twentieth century. I was particularly interested in how photographs were utilised as visual propaganda in the work of the Congo Reform Association (CRA, 1904–1914), a hugely significant international campaign against the rule of King Leopold II in the Congo.

Research on photographs involves locating them within the historical setting in which they were made and displayed. This particular photograph was made around 1904 when John and Alice Harris were working as English missionaries at the Congo Balolo Mission. Although it is unattributed it was probably made by John Harris since Mr and Mrs Harris often took photographs of each other in their daily life as missionaries.

Of course historical research into photography also needs to examine what photographs depict. This photograph shows Alice Harris, wearing a long white dress and rather splendid white hat, standing in a small clearing in a forest. Four young Congolese men sit on the ground in front of her. Their heads are turned

*(Continued)*

---

**Figure 3.5** 'Mrs Harris photographing in the forest.' Anti-Slavery International Papers (1904), J46, Bodleian Library. Rhodes House, University of Oxford

towards the white missionary so that the viewer can only see the side or back of their heads. Mrs Harris holds a camera, which she directs towards the men on the ground and the other photographer making this picture. Her gaze sits somewhere between the men and the photographer; she is clearly aware that she is being photographed. In the left foreground two large boxes of mostly photographic equipment have been placed on the ground. Their contents, including frames, boxes of film and a developing tray, seem purposefully unpacked and displayed for the viewer. If Mrs Harris actually made a photograph of this scene then it has not survived. What seems more likely is that she was simply posing with her camera and equipment for a photograph made by her husband. The photograph then becomes a photograph about photography, its human and technical operation. Why the need for such a photograph, when the operations of the photographer and camera are usually deliberately hidden from view?

To understand the content of the image requires us to place the work of John and Alice Harris in a larger historical framework. From the 1890s, reports increasingly reached Britain of the brutal coercion and forced labour being exacted on the African population by King Leopold's regime. Initial protest was fostered in

Britain by the CRA. Protestant missionary groups such as the Congo Balolo Mission, which found their operations in the Congo increasingly unstable, gradually formed strategic alliances with humanitarians for whom they supplied evidence of abuses. As English missionaries in the Congo in the early twentieth century, Mr and Mrs Harris became involved in documenting and campaigning against this oppressive regime. They were two of the most active and accomplished users of photography and made a series of 'atrocity photographs', showing men, women and children who had been subjected to colonial violence. The photographs were used widely and effectively to generate support for the CRA's campaign, which was one of the most significant popular protests over slavery and imperialism in this period. Indeed, atrocity photographs of mutilated African bodies became the visual icon of the terror of the Congo regime and of the pain and suffering of its African subjects.

In researching how photographs were used in the CRA's campaign, I have approached the photograph not merely as an image, but as a material object, made in the Congo forests for display to mass audiences in Europe and the USA. The meaning of such photographs depends on the circumstances both of their making and their subsequent exhibition and reproduction. The CRA used photographs in books, pamphlets and in lantern-slide shows where they were shown to large audiences and accompanied by spoken narrative and music. In all these instances, the question of evidence was key. How could the campaigners ensure that their evidence could be trusted? The verisimilitude of the photographic image could not, on its own, guarantee the veracity of the evidence. Reform campaigners understood that audiences had to believe in the trustworthiness of the photographer and subsequent users of the image. One way to do this was to show the missionaries themselves making photographs, to make visible the apparatus of image-making. What could be more trustworthy, audiences were being asked, than a white Christian woman like Alice Harris?

Thousands of photos were made in the past, but a few remain in circulation decades after they were taken and researchers are often interested in how and why particular images are reused. To explore the historical trajectory of a single photograph requires attending to captions, the changing 'placement' and context of an image (newspaper, art gallery etc.) and how what is visible shifts due to cropping and alteration (Shneer 2010: 32). Shneer presents a good example of this in his study of Soviet Holocaust photography, focusing on a photograph taken by Russian photographer Dmitri Baltermants in 1941 outside the town of Kerch in Southern Russia. Schneer starts with the production and initial publication of the photograph in 1942. At this time the photo was one of several presented for the purpose of documenting the mass murder in Kerch of Soviet citizens by German troops. The photograph depicts a woman – P.I. Ivanova – finding the body of her husband among those recently murdered by German troops: it was captioned 'Kerch resident P.I. Ivanova found her husband, who was tortured by the fascist executioners' (p. 37) and it was cropped to eliminate most of the background and focus on Ivanova discovering her dead husband. Shneer then traces how the photo was reused in 1965 to commemorate the Soviet experience of war. In 1965 the photo was renamed, 'Grief', and given a new caption 'We will never forget' (p. 45). What was shown of the photograph was different from 1942. The 1965 photo did not focus on Ivanova, though she is in the foreground, instead it shows a bigger picture in which people look at and search among bodies strewn across a barren and water-logged landscape. The photograph was also altered by the photographer; in the original publication the sky was a dull grey but it was darkened in 1965 producing a more dramatic effect. The 1965 photo was no longer evidence of a particular atrocity but was used to portray 'the nature of evil' and 'foster a new national memory of the war' (Shneer 2010: 43).

Reflecting on why a photo was made in a particular way and tracing its trajectory raises questions about whether researchers can use photographs to learn about a photographer's attitudes and, conscious or unconscious, viewpoint. Particularly in social history, some researchers seek insight into a society and culture by investigating how an individual photographer engages with it at a particular point in time. Take, for example, Brooke's study of the photographs produced by Bill Brandt (see also Mavor 1996). Brandt is one of the most famous documentary photographers operating in Britain in the 1930s and 1940s. During the Second World War Brandt produced photographs that contributed to dominant war discourses of stoicism, patriotism, national cohesion, but from 1944 he turned to producing 'artistic' photographs of nude women. Though seemingly different from his wartime photos, Brooke (2006: 138) argues that the nudes are in dialogue with the experiences and discourses of war; they are a 'counter-narrative of war', one that jars with nationalistic discourses emerging in the 1940s, and aligns with other counter-narratives of war including fiction by Elizabeth Bowen and Graham Green. Brooke (p. 138) insists that to understand the 'cultural meaning of the war and its aftermath' we need to explore these counter narratives and photography provides ways of doing this.

Discovering a photographer's intentions is not usually straightforward. Interviews[3] are used where feasible (see Chapters 5 and 9), also autobiographical documents, but often there are few sources to facilitate this exploration. Unsurprisingly, researchers rely heavily on careful study of the photographer's pictures and attention to contextual information – genre and aesthetic conventions, the photographer's background and previous work, the social historical context. When scrutinising the photographer's work it is important not to conflate their intentions with meaning per se. Photographs usually contain more than intended by the photographer and meanings are not reducible to the creator's intentions. It is also important to remember that most of a photographer's work is commissioned and the photographer's constructions of the world will be shaped and constrained by the demands of their employers and perceptions of potential audiences. Andrew Blaikie's (2006) account of factors shaping Bert Hardy's photo of 'Gorbals boys' produced for *Picture Post* in 1948 is a good example of this (discussed later).

Researchers also need to be mindful of the contexts in which they encounter a photographer's work. Publicly available photos represent the interests of those who present them. Sometimes it is the photographer who reuses and re-presents their own photographs, as did Russian photographer Baltermants discussed earlier; in this case the photograph is evidence of the photographer's shifting agenda. Often, however, photographers are not involved in the presentation of their work. This means that the researcher does not see the photographer's preferred version but the one that is selected, cropped, captioned and positioned to meet the needs of the user. Take, for example, a photo taken in apartheid South Africa in 1956 by Peter Magubane that appeared in *Drum* magazine with the caption 'Death in the Dark City'. The contact sheet in the archive shows that Magubane deposited at least three images of a young black man lying dead on the street. Two 'offer a graphic portrayal of murder and the indignity of death', but the image selected for publication had 'a more distanced aesthetic' with the corpse composed for the camera with arms crossed over the chest and the face covered (Newbury 2009: 30), a selection that says much about the editors.

# Exploring responses: popular and iconic photos

In this section I examine research that produces informed speculations about how people respond to particular images. I outline what is involved in informed speculation and how it is used to explain why some photos fail to resonate with viewers while others go on to achieve the status of iconic images. I start by looking at contemporary responses to photos and then at research on iconic images. In discussion of iconic images, the people who reuse images are also viewers; re-users select images because they are familiar to them and resonant, and because they think they will be recognisable and meaningful to their intended audiences. The reuse of these images contributes further to their place in shared versions of the past – collective memories.

## Informed speculation about viewers

How viewers interpret and respond to particular images is often assumed or ignored, but some researchers address these explicitly. One question that researchers explore is why some photos seem to resonate with viewers while others do not. There are two approaches to researching viewers' responses, as discussed in Chapter 2. First, there is audience research which involves discovering what individuals thought about a particular photo. Second, there is informed speculation where the researcher attempts to piece together (often because it is not possible or feasible to do audience research) how particular groups of viewers may have interpreted an image.

To produce informed speculation, the researcher starts by identifying likely viewers and establishing their relationship to particular photos. The researcher then considers: the image; information about likely viewers that may flesh out how they engaged with the picture (using evidence of viewers' choices and responses where available); the main contexts in which the image was encountered (such as a popular magazine) and how its meaning was framed (caption, co-text etc.); and pre-existing discourses, also social, economic, political and cultural events that may have shaped viewers' engagements and interpretations. Researchers may also use psychoanalytic models of how people look at images and with what effects (Burke 2001).

Informed speculations underpin historical studies of why photos were 'successful' or not in their own time, for example Gail Baylis's (2006) examination of Victorian photo postcards uses commercial success as an index of popularity (Box 3.6).

---

**BOX 3.6   WHY POSTCARDS OF WELSH 'PATCH GIRLS' WERE UNSUCCESSFUL COMPARED TO THOSE OF THE LANCASHIRE 'PIT BROW LASSES'**

**Figure 3.6**   William Clayton. Tredegar Patch Girls. © Manchester City Galleries

Gail Baylis's puzzle started when she found an album of Welsh 'patch girl' cartes de visite (photo postcards) from the 1860s compiled by commercial photographer, William Clayton. 'Patch girls' were women who worked with near-surface deposits of coal or iron ore, although the term later came to be generic for women's employment in the iron industry. What puzzled Baylis was why postcards of Welsh 'patch girls' (Figure 3.6) were unsuccessful compared to those of the Lancashire 'pit brow lasses', especially given the contemporary craze for cartes of 'exotic' others.

To resolve this puzzle Baylis starts by thinking about the purpose of commercial postcards in the 1860s: 'The issue facing William Clayton as a commercial photographer in representing the Tredegar patch girl was to signify industrial female labour but also to add a signifier of Welsh femininity' (Baylis 2006: 13). Baylis then studies the photos of the patch girls in terms of camera angles, props, stances and clothing, and drawing on semiotics she identifies what these signified. She also compares these cartes to those of Lancashire pit brow lasses. These careful readings of images are located in detailed historical context to develop a refined understanding of the signs of gender, class and ethnicity in the pictures. The contextual research includes women's labour in Wales, an examination of nineteenth-century commercial photography and the potential market for postcards and tourism in Wales, also prevailing discourses on Welshness, femininity and women's work. Baylis shows how the photographer experimented unsuccessfully with place and props (particularly the hat worn by patch girls) to find tropes that would signify ethnicity. In the context of visual tourism in the 1860s, Baylis concludes that the reason the 'patch girl' postcards were unsuccessful was that images of women's work in South Wales were not sufficiently recognisable or sufficiently distinctive to be marketable. Potential purchasers had not yet been 'taught' (p. 20) how to recognise signifiers of Welsh femininity and they could not, therefore, appreciate the cartes as photos of distinctively Welsh working women.

## Iconic images and collective memory

Some images remain in circulation long after their initial publication; they become iconic. In reflections on the Vietnam War, for instance, an image that often comes to mind for people is Nick Ut's photo of a naked Vietnamese child running down a road in pain and terror. Because iconic photos contribute to collective memory, it is important to understand how and why these particular images remain meaningful and important over time while other photos do not.

To explain iconic photos, researchers start by locating evidence of their continued use and circulation; they trace their 'social biographies' (Edwards 2002: 68). Researchers then consider the meanings ascribed to these images explicitly or implicitly through presentation and the specific contexts they are used in; this is important because photos often acquire new layers or inflections of meaning over time, what Patricia Hayes describes as 'trafficking' (2006: 11). Tracking the reuse of images is feasible if they circulate within small or defined communities, but with mass circulation images, such as Ut's Vietnam War photo, it is difficult or impossible to plot this precisely, although the main uses can be noted. Researchers then consider the historically specific cultural, social, political and economic contexts in which these photos are reused and encountered.

For example, Patrick Hagiopan (2006) explores why some Vietnam War photos have retained their influence over time and through shifting interpretations of the conflict. He starts with the origins of the photos; this entails a historically situated exploration of their production, also initial interpretations, press reactions, uses and the extent to which they seemingly influenced events during wartime. Considering the immediate impact of particular photos, he suggests that they provided evidence of atrocities, made the abstract real, and reinforced 'uncomfortable truths' thereby confirming people's suspicions (p. 208). However, Hagiopan argues it is difficult to discover effect or to claim that photos exerted independent influence because they do not appear in a vacuum and because criticisms of the war prepared the ground for them.

Hagiopan then investigates how photos were subsequently circulated and viewed and how, if at all, they retained their significance since the 1960s. He points to the mnemonic potency of photos because they enable people to look closely, repeatedly and at leisure and this leaves a stronger imprint on memory than the flash of real life or cinema. Though this may explain why some photos come to mind as appropriate illustration of a particular historical event, it is not the only reason they are repeatedly reused; these images are also relevant to shifting interpretations of historical experience (see also Moore 2006; Schwarz 2011). Reflecting on the continued resonance of particular images, he points to the difficulty of researching this except through anecdotal evidence. Audience research cannot assess impact especially with the passage of time and shifts in political discourse, but 'Material instances of the photographic act in various settings can ... provide evidence at least of the *currency* of these photographs if not of their *effect*' (Hagiopan 2006: 216).

The 'currency' of photos is often used as an index of their resonance, but contextual research is essential to make sense of this. For example, Blaikie focuses on a black and white photo entitled 'Gorbals boys' which portrays two small boys, arms linked, about to cross a road in what appears to be a deprived inner city area. The photo was taken in the Gorbals area of Glasgow, Scotland, by Bert Hardy in 1948 and has since been reproduced on the covers of autobiographies of celebrity Glaswegians, made into a poster, and 'quoted' by other professional photographers. Blaikie's analysis consists of layers of contextual research spanning from 1947 to 2005. He starts by explaining why and how this photo was made and used, investigating the production and initial publication of the photo in *Picture Post* using autobiographies, biographies, social history sources, a close reading of the photo and the issue it was published in. Blaikie explores instances of the reuse of the photo since 1948, arguing that the contexts in which this image recurs and circulates are key to understanding the image and its continued significance. Blaikie argues that for Glaswegians from working-class backgrounds, the photo fits in to collective memory of tenement life. The particular significance of the photo is heightened for many Glaswegians because the tenements portrayed in the photograph were razed in the 1950s and replaced with housing estates that were widely criticised by locals. The photo feeds nostalgia for a lost community and lost childhoods that are often associated with the myth of tenement life.

# Seeking inspiration from photos

Looking is key to working productively with photos, but researchers often cannot 'see' past their preconceived ideas, shaped by prior knowledge and experience. Art and creative methods can sometimes enable researchers to appreciate the influence of their preconceptions and to see differently. Photographic art can be good to stimulate thinking and can inspire us to engage creatively with photos in our own research (Chaplin 1994). The work of some artists can suggest new directions or questions for academic scholarship, partly because artists, in common with many academics, aim to generate fresh ways of seeing and understanding the world. Artists can also produce a visual dimension to what is otherwise invisible and through this facilitate empathic perspectives, and pose questions about the construction of dominant ways of visualising the past (see Chapters 4 and 6 for examples). Though in the past it was usually only artists and photo-therapists who worked creatively with photographs, some historians of education are now using creative methods. I first discuss the purpose and limitations of creative methods in historical and social research, then introduce key methods including juxtaposition and engagements with memory and imagination. Following this I consider creative ways of presenting found photos.

There are three main, interrelated reasons why creative methods are useful in academic work. First, these methods can help researchers engage in new ways with photographic images and can change our ways of seeing. There is much to be gained from playing with photos in order to unsettle the familiar and acquire a fresh approach to looking, thinking and questioning our sources, particularly when photos have become overly familiar because of frequent use. Second, creative methods can open up an area of research: they can be used to pose new questions, identify new avenues of enquiry, and engage with stories about a photo other than the one most obviously suggested by the image. Third, these methods can facilitate researcher reflexivity about what they bring to the act of interpreting a photo.

Creative methods are supplements to, rather than replacements for, the types of enquiry and methods discussed earlier in this chapter; they cannot be used productively on their own in academic research contexts. To use these methods constructively you need to be clear about the type and status of the knowledge produced; it is necessarily highly subjective, suggestive and impressionistic and researchers must be careful what they claim for their 'findings'. In research contexts, you need to draw also on other methods and sources to pursue your investigation and anchor your analysis (Rousmaniere 2001).

## Creative methods

Juxtaposition of photos is a prominent feature of creative methods in the history of education. It is a key component of the 'photographic montage' method developed by Ian Grosvenor, Martin Lawn and Kate Rousmaniere (1999, 2000): photos are looked at out of context and juxtaposed with one another; viewers' subjective responses and reminiscences are embraced and incorporated into the findings. Juxtaposition can involve working with a jumble of photos, also groups of related pictures. Though there are potential overlaps with comparative techniques, juxtaposition should not be conflated with these. Juxtaposition is not the systematic comparison of details of content or form with the purpose of evaluating similarities and differences, although this can be undertaken. Instead it involves a holistic assessment of groups of photos, viewed within a 'new frame of reference' (Burke and Grosvenor 2007: 158), that extends beyond what is simply observable to also embrace impressions, reactions and revelation.

The combination of juxtaposition and engagement with subjective responses is a productive strategy for 'seeing and making associations which otherwise would go unmade' (Grosvenor et al. 2000: 83) and exposing what we commonly ignore in photos. For example, when Rousmaniere (2001: 110) looked at a medley of photos of children from around the world which were categorised as 'school' photos, this prompted questions such as: how do we know a photo depicts school and what assumptions underpin this? 'When does a picture of a school not look like a picture of a school? And when we identify something as "a school", what are we ignoring?'

The literature gives few clues about how to use juxtaposition and it is easy to imagine being overwhelmed by a pile of photos. Sometimes juxtaposition occurs when you spontaneously bring together a couple of photos that are not usually viewed side by side, but here I address strategies for doing this fairly systematically. If you are going to engage creatively with photos I suggest you start by deciding what your purpose is and what photos to look at. The literature provides no guidance on how to make this decision. Should you do a random selection of photos on a topic? Do you need an inkling of what you might discover in order to select appropriate photos? There is no right answer, though what you hope to achieve from the exercise should inform your choice. In some cases it may be appropriate to do a juxtaposition exercise with a set of photos you plan to work with more systematically at a later stage. For example, Catherine Burke and Ian Grosvenor (2007) juxtaposed photos from two progressive schools to draw out their impressions of the schools' approaches to children and schooling before supplementing this with other sources and methods. You can also juxtapose photos you normally encounter and work with on a particular topic. For example, by removing photos from their usual and possibly disparate contexts (separate archives, different publications) and juxtaposing them, you might see the individual images differently but also gain a different perspective on the group. At other times, you may start with photographs relating to what you are researching and then place these alongside other photos. In this case I suggest that though you can experiment with different combinations of photos, it is helpful to have a common theme: perhaps different genres of photos on a particular theme; photos of different groups of people engaged in the same activity; or photos of a similar environment taken at different points in history. If you think that a particular juxtaposition would be productive, try it.

Once you have decided what to look at, dedicate a specific amount of time for the exercise. At this point it is worth deciding whether you want to ask other people for their impressions; group responses are often a feature of research using montage (Grosvenor et al. 2000). The exercise can be undertaken with photos laid out in front of you on a table or pinned to a noticeboard, but digital images may be more convenient if you are seeking responses from several people. Now you need to study the set. What jumps out at you? How do they make you feel? What do they make you think of or remember? What questions do they raise? What impressions do they convey? At this stage the point is not to pursue specific questions, but to identify them. It is important that you keep a record of your thoughts, reactions and impressions as details are easily forgotten. It is also essential that you are very clear about the status of these 'findings'. They are impressions and responses; they are *not* derived from careful consideration of photographs as sources that are produced in particular ways and for specific purposes.

The researcher's memories play a prominent role in the montage method and in other creative approaches to using found photos. Burke and de Castro (2007) claim this is necessary because researchers cannot resist drawing on their memories when they look at pictures of children at school, and a reflexive approach is therefore essential to understand what we bring to the act of interpretation. This point is also relevant to working with photos on other topics. In lay and academic contexts, memory and imagination are often used when we look at photos, but with little self-awareness. For example, it is because of our recourse to memories and imagination that we sometimes empathise with the people in a photo. Creative approaches can encourage reflexive engagement with these commonplace practices of looking and facilitate their development for academic purposes. Some researchers also advocate consciously using our memories to generate questions and ideas for further research (e.g. Burke and de Castro 2007). This is achieved by making a conscious effort to employ your memory when looking at photos and record what emerges from the exercise. Burke (2001) suggests identifying with someone in the photo (there are parallels with autobiographic techniques discussed in Chapter 4), a technique which draws as much on memory as imagination.

Imagination is another prominent theme in creative engagements with old photos because it can shift what we can learn from them. For example, Dónal O'Donoghue (2010: 411) asks what new interpretations might emerge if, instead of looking at a photo of a classroom as only a two-dimensional image, the researcher 'imagine[s] the three-dimensional quality of that which is captured in two dimensions' and then envisions themselves as a participant in the space depicted in the photo. O'Donoghue argues that employing this method with a photo of an empty classroom might elucidate assumptions – about children and teachers and how they interact – that are built into this environment and the arrangement of its fixtures and fittings. This imaginative exercise could also contribute to thinking about how actual pupils and teachers used and experienced this space.

## Presenting research creatively

Drawing on ideas and the practices of artists, some historians have been inspired to think creatively about how they present their research with found images (on presenting generated photos see Chapter 7). Historians Úna Bhroiméil and O'Donoghue (2009) researched gender identities and practices in teacher training colleges in Ireland 1900–38; O'Donoghue focused on masculinising practices in a male training college, and Bhroiméil on femininising practices in a female training college. Both used photographic sources and methods to make visible the historically specific ways that colleges constructed gender; they stress that this could not be achieved simply by reproducing photos from the college archives, only by re-presenting them.

**Figure 3.7**  Class. Image with text. Trainee Teachers.  Reproduced courtesy of Úna Bhroiméil

For example, Bhroiméil uses techniques of overlayering and juxtaposition to scrutinise and deconstruct photos of women trainee teachers:

> When we look at the photographs of these women we see group after group of well turned out ladies. Our impression of these women is always as an assemblage, as a unit and this can cause us to classify, categorize and bracket them together as a unified and integrated whole. This cohesion and unity of organization is petrified by the camera, fixed as a monument. (p. 177)

Using a combination of text and images, Bhroiméil transforms the photos and provides different ways of seeing them (Figure 3.7). College photos are overlaid with comments from the supervisors who observed the students' practice, and excerpts from articles in the teaching press are juxtaposed with the images. Bhroiméil also hones in on details in the group photos (Figure 3.8), a technique which disrupts their homogenising effects and exposes, to quote Walter Benjamin, 'suggestive absences and lurking presences' (p. 177). This strategy brings to light signs of intimacy and the subtle ways in which the women used dress to express their individuality.

**Figure 3.8**   Student Body 2. Photo section. Reproduced courtesy of Úna Bhroiméil

Creative presentation techniques can be used to good effect in the representation of findings. Digital technologies make it relatively easy to experiment with how pictures are presented (always ensure you keep a clearly labelled copy of the 'original' image safe), though they are not essential for this task (Frankenberger 1991). In historical and social science contexts, however, these creative representations need to be accompanied by written analysis.

# Summary

In this chapter I have considered concrete examples of how researchers use photographs to address diverse questions and how they sometimes use photos for inspiration. The examples are historical but the strategies and methods apply also to working with present-day photos and to addressing questions about contemporary life.

Some of the questions addressed in this chapter will be pursued later in this book. Strategies for researching what people do with photos will be developed further in Chapter 5, and issues relating to working in archives and with digital resources will be explored in Chapter 6. Using photos to understand more about the people depicted is taken forward in Chapter 4, but the focus is on an insider's perspective rather than an outsider's. Focusing on personal photos and the use of autobiographical methods, Chapter 4 explores research where the researcher is also the subject.

## Notes

1 Correspondence with Doug Rendall, a professional photographer working 1950s–1970s.
2 The 'decisive moment' is a term coined by photographer, Henri Cartier-Bresson; it refers to capturing on film, in a fraction of a second, the significance or essence of an event.
3 The British Library has several collections of interviews with photographers, including 'Oral History of British Photography', C459.

# 4
# Autobiographical Methods

This chapter focuses on personal photos and autobiographical methods. Remembering is to the fore, also feeling and playful techniques such as imagining, juxtaposition and other creative strategies. Autobiographical photo-work has been a fruitful area of academic enquiry, particularly in the 1980s and 1990s when researchers turned to their personal photos to explore questions about family, memory, identities and subjectivities, such as:

- How do family photographs contribute to the construction of 'family' and the production of family history?
- How do personal photographs shape contemporary self-knowledge and autobiography? As Jo Spence puts it: 'How do you know anything about your own history – most of all the history of your subjectivity and the part that images have played in its construction?' (cited in Hirsch 1997: 113).
- How does photography shape personal, familial and collective (shared popular accounts) memory?
- How can personal photographs be reworked or recreated to offer new perspectives on the past and new possibilities for the present?

In the following I look first at the 'classics' of autobiographical photo-work that emerged principally in the 1980s and 1990s, and then consider the continued relevance of autobiographical methods for social and historical enquiry. Following this I examine autobiographical methods that you can use with our own photos, and reflect on the usefulness of asking our research participants to employ these methods.

## Autobiographical photo-work of the 1980s and 1990s

In the 1980s and 1990s several studies were published that drew heavily on an analysis of the author's personal photographs (most notably J. Hirsch 1981; M. Hirsch

1997 and 1999; Kuhn, first published in 1995/2002; Spence 1986 and 1995; Spence and Holland 1991; Walkerdine 1991; Willis 1994). These, now classic, studies used autobiographical photo-work to investigate the cultural construction of gendered, classed, racialised and sexualised identities and subjectivities. The work emerged in part from a fascination with family photos and their personal and familial significance. Often underpinned by feminist agendas, the use of personal photos was justified partly by a belief in the value of focusing on the personal as a means to illuminate and explain wider social and cultural processes, an approach that dovetailed neatly with the notion that 'the personal is political'. In the following I look at the main themes in this work – constructing the self, the formation of identity and subjectivity, memory – before considering the continued relevance of this approach.

## Constructing the self

Autobiographical photo research was employed to learn about the past, but often as importantly, to understand how the past shaped the author's present self-knowledge. One reason why family photos were regarded as important in understanding present-day subjectivities is that people turn to these to trace their personal history and to make sense of their lives. This use of photos is not a passive process as personal photos are actively incorporated into the project of making a self:

> family photos may affect to show us our past, but what we do with them – how we use them – is really about today, not yesterday. These traces of our former lives are pressed into service in a never-ending process of making, remaking, and making sense of, ourselves – now. (Kuhn 1991: 22)

## The formation of identities and subjectivity

The formation of identities and subjectivity was a prominent theme in autobiographical research. Researchers reviewed personal photos, particularly of themselves as children, to stimulate memories of the past which then served as clues to the formation of their identities and subjectivities. Looking at how they had been presented to the camera, researchers sought also to understand what adults, and especially parents, had invested in them. The concept of the 'gaze' is often drawn on in the context of exploring identities and subjectivities. As Jo Spence and Rosy Martin explain, a number of theorists argue that there are 'various "gazes" which help to control, objectify, define and mirror identities to us ... Through the internalization and synthesis of these powerful gazes we learn to see and differentiate ourselves from others, in terms of our class, gender, race and sexuality' (Spence 1995: 167). Autobiographical work with personal photographs was seen to expose these overlapping discursive gazes through which we are known and come to know ourselves. In some instances, personal photos were reworked or restaged to create opportunities for the researcher to resist and challenge past constructions of themselves, and in doing so to facilitate personal and social change in the present.

Marianne Hirsch (1997) extended the analyses of how personal photos provide insights into the 'gazes' that shape familial subjectivity; she also developed a vocabulary to discuss this. Hirsch coined the term 'familial looks' to refer to how we are seen, imagined and defined by other family members, especially parents, also the expectations family have of us, and how we relate and are related to within our families. The 'familial look' is not an individual phenomenon, but inextricably connected to the prevailing dominant ideology of the family, what Hirsch calls the 'familial gaze'. The 'familial gaze' is historically and culturally variable, and in contemporary Western societies it is perpetuated principally through mainstream media representations. What people understand and experience as 'family' is shaped 'by individual responsiveness to the ideological pressures deployed by the familial gaze' (p. 10):

> photographer and viewer collaborate on the reproduction of ideology. Between the viewer and the recorded object [e.g. the little girl/daughter], the viewer encounters, and/or projects, a screen made up of dominant mythologies and perceptions that shapes the representation. Eye and screen are the very elements of ideology: our expectations circumscribe and determine what we show and what we see. (p. 7)

Hirsch argues that we have no easy access to these 'nonverbal exchanges which nevertheless shape and reshape who we are' (1997: 9–10). Photographs do, however, provide clues to these visual interactions and the power that underpins these. The camera and photography can expose the complicated and otherwise invisible network of looking that goes on within families, or what Walter Benjamin (1931/1980) called 'unconscious optics'. According to Hirsch, unconscious optics can only be uncovered by an insider because to an outsider the photo is just another family picture. The revelation of a family's unconscious optics is achieved through the production of a photo album, art installation or autobiographical writing – what she calls an 'imagetext' – which places family photos into narrative context and provides subjective commentary on them. These imagetexts allow the outsider to see, from the creator's perspective, the dynamics of family life (looks and gazes) that the creator identifies and engages with as they look at their family photos; 'Only the narratives that take shape in relation to the pictures can provide insight into the actual workings of unconscious optics' (Hirsch 1997: 119). Hirsch examines the unconscious optics exposed in the imagetexts of some of the writers considered in this chapter, namely Annette Kuhn, Jo Spence and Valerie Walkerdine.

## Memory

Through photos, families are defined and constructed, given a history and constituted in memory. While outsiders can examine a portrait to discover how a family wants to present itself to the outside world, the significance of family photos is often dependent on an insider perspective. As Patricia Holland explains (2000: 151), 'pictures do not stand alone but are enriched by memory, conversation, anecdote and whispered scandal': families and family memory are constructed in part through these layers and networks of meaning and association. What Holland calls 'the soap opera of personal life' (2000: 156) and Kuhn 'family secrets' (2002) can only be exposed by insiders, not least because the stories families tell themselves are as much about forgetting as remembering. The role of family photographs in forgetting is evident in the practice of removing photos of estranged family members or ex-partners, it is also achieved simply by decisions not to photograph particular places (e.g. an ill-kept garden), people and events (e.g. a holiday that was miserable or a bout of illness).

Memory is a dominant theme in autobiographical photo-work because family photos are expressly produced as memory material. Some scholars used personal photos explicitly to interrogate how memory works. This is a prominent theme in *Family Secrets* (Kuhn 2002: 4), which explores 'the ways memory shapes the stories we tell, in the present, about the past'. Personal memory is not approached from a physiological or psychological perspective, nor is it conceptualised as an individual store of past experiences and knowledge waiting to be dredged up. Instead, it is approached from a cultural perspective as something constructed in the present, which is shaped by social and cultural factors and entwined with collective forms of remembering.

'Memory work' is the name given to the research practice of stimulating and exploring cultural memory, it is 'a conscious and purposeful staging of memory' (Kuhn 2000: 186). Through memory work scholars aim to 'extend and deepen understanding of how personal memory operates in the cultural sphere: its distinguishing features; how, where and when it is produced; how people make use of it in their daily lives; how personal or individual memory connects with shared, public forms of memory; and ultimately, how memory figures in, and even shapes, the social body and social worlds' (2007: 283). Photos are not the only prompts to memory utilised in memory work, but they do have a special place because they appear to capture a moment in time and we almost always produce photos in order to remember. The relationship between the photographic image and memory is not, however, transparent or straightforward. As Kuhn explained, you do not learn much from looking very closely at photos:

> Photographs are produced as evidence of something, therefore, to understand what they refer to the reader must look outside the frame, to the memories the photo is intended to preserve … [Memories] do not simply spring out of the image itself, but are generated in a network, an intertext, of discourses that shift between past and present, spectator and image, and between all these and cultural contexts, historical moments. In this network, the image itself figures largely as a trace, a clue: necessary, but not sufficient, to the activity of meaning making; always pointing somewhere else. (Kuhn 2002: 12)

Family photos feature prominently in Kuhn's memory work, but memory methods can be used with all sorts of meaningful personal photos. In a recent workshop run by Kuhn, a number of participants used these methods productively to explore friendships in childhood and young adulthood.

## Are autobiographical approaches still useful today?

Autobiographical photo-work has generated important insights into the micro-politics of family life, how we use photography in the construction of self, the formation of identities and subjectivities, and the workings of memory as a cultural phenomenon. Insights from these autobiographical studies have since been drawn on in research that examines other people's personal photos. But is there any point in present-day researchers working with their personal photos? I suggest there are three main ways in which this research strategy is still important.

First, we still know little about personal photography beyond the perspectives of particular social groups in a particular historical period, mainly 1940–70. Autobiographical photo-work can be a means to explore different and contemporary families, identities and subjectivities. Additionally, autobiographical methods are useful tools for the continued exploration of memory. Recently there have been dramatic changes in cultural life and photographic technologies and we are only beginning to explore the implications of these. Researching our personal photos can facilitate exploration of cultural memory in the digital age: 'how digital technologies, by changing the material basis of our mediated memories, (re)shape the nature of our recollections and the process of remembering' (Dijck 2005: 313).

Second, one of the advantages of autobiographical work is that the researcher can interrogate and probe their responses in ways that can be difficult, unethical and time-consuming to do when working with other people. This is not surprising given the intimate level at which some of this work is conducted. Indeed, even committed researchers can shy away from interrogating their responses to some personal photos. Walkerdine (1991), for instance, admitted that in her work with personal photos she was initially reluctant to confront a 'reviled' photo of herself as a plump child. When she eventually engaged with it she generated interesting findings about herself and the micro-politics of gender and social class in the 1950s (discussed later).

Third, autobiographical work on personal photos can be a useful preliminary to researching the personal lives of *other* people. It can facilitate reflexivity about your own investments in the topics being researched and how this influences the conduct of the research and the interpretation of findings. Autobiographical photo-memory techniques have been used productively in collective memory work on the sexu-alisation of women (Haug et al. 1999) and experiences of schooling (Mitchell and Weber 1999), and in team research on modern motherhood (Thomson 2010). In the team research this strategy involved each team member writing a third-person account of the memories generated in response to a personal photo about moth-erhood. The accounts were then shared and discussed. As Rachel Thomson (2010: 9–10) explains:

> By exploring our own and each others' memories we began to engage with the emotional terrain that we would be inviting others to share with us, helping us both to gain a sense of what was possible within the research, but also to gain a perspective on the sensitivities involved.

Sharing memories can make visible the different perspectives and investments of team members in a particular topic and this, in turn, can facilitate team building and team work.

# Autobiographical methods

Having explained why I think autobiographical approaches to personal photos are still relevant to academic enquiry, I now examine how researchers can work with their personal photos. I consider two autobiographical methods: reviewing personal photos and reworking them.

## Reviewing personal photos

Studying personal photos can generate intimate insights into family, self and memory (e.g. Hirsch 1999; Kuhn 2002; Spence and Holland 1991). Researchers typically attend to what is *seen* in their photo and what is *thought* (knowledge, meanings, memories, stories, opinions) and *felt* about the photo as image and object. This method necessitates a willingness to immerse yourself in the analysis and to probe and reflect on what you think, feel and remember.

In *Family Secrets* (2002: 8) Kuhn presents a systematic approach for interpretative work on personal photographs to draw out what the researcher knows (not always consciously) and remembers about the photo and the people in it. Kuhn acknowledges her debt to Spence and Martin, their influence will be appreciated when we look at reworking personal photos.

To use Kuhn's approach, start by selecting a family photo; this may or may not feature you, but it must be personally meaningful. The aim is to elicit a wide range of associations and memories; this means engaging with the occasion depicted and using the photo as a stimulus to remembering the bigger picture – the people, relationships, places, what was going on at the time etc. To this end, Kuhn suggests approaching your chosen photo with different questions and from different perspectives. She also suggests various techniques to help you engage with, and explore, your feelings and memories such as 'visualising' yourself in the picture and taking up different vantage points in the photo, including those of objects. While the latter may seem whacky, this should be approached simply as a device to explore what you remember. The following points should guide your work:

1 Consider the human subject(s) of the photograph. Start with a simple description, and then move into an account in which you take up the position of the subject. In this part of the exercise, it is helpful to use the third person ("she", rather than "I", for instance). To bring out the feelings associated with the photograph, you may visualise yourself as the subject as she was at that moment, in the picture: this can be done in turn with all the photograph's human subjects, if there is more than one, and even with animals and inanimate objects in the picture.

2 Consider the picture's context of production. Where, when, how, by whom and why was the photograph taken?

3 Consider the context in which an image of this sort would have been made. What photographic technologies were used? What are the aesthetics of the image? Does it conform with certain photographic conventions?

4 Consider the photograph's currency in its context or contexts of reception. Who or what was the photograph made for? Who has it now, and where is it kept? Who saw it then, and who sees it now? (Kuhn 2002: 8)

Write down or audio record your memories and thoughts, then reflect on, distil and analyse these to learn about your past and the nature, characteristics and significance of memories and the role of photos in them. There are no special analytical methods, and how you do this will depend on your (discipline-specific) skills, knowledge and theoretical frameworks.

Absences and disjunctures are important features of autobiographical photo-work that Kuhn and other scholars pay particular attention to in their analyses. Reviewing her photos Kuhn exposes and interrogates both what is present and absent in them (Figure 4.1). Presences and absences are treated as evidence because photos, and especially albums, are as much about forgetting as remembering. Considering a photo of herself, aged six, apparently fascinated by the pet budgie that stands on her hand, Kuhn (2002: 14) explores what happens when absences and silences are taken as evidence. She describes the words written on the back of the photo which reveal disagreement and conflicting memories over what the photo depicts: the child amends her mother's handwritten description of the photo, 'Just back from Bournemouth (Convelescent) [sic]', by crossing out 'Bournemouth' and replacing it with 'Broadstairs' and a note, 'but I suspect the photo is earlier than this'. This evidence and the memories around it bring to the fore the mother–daughter relationship, but the silences bring her father into focus:

[The] absent presence in this little drama of remembering is my father. He is not in the picture, you cannot see him ... In another sense, however, my father is very much 'in' the picture; so much so that my mother's intervention [caption] might be read as a bid to exorcise a presence that disturbed her. The child in the photograph is absorbed with her pet bird, a gift from her father, who also took the picture. The relay of looks – father/daughter/father's gift to daughter – has a trajectory and an endpoint that miss the mother entirely. The picture has nothing to do with her. (p. 15)

Disjunctures between personal recollections and the 'evidence' of family photos are also investigated, as in Kuhn's (1991) essay, 'Remembrance'. As Holland (1991: 9) explains, 'we may feel ourselves to have been on display, shown rather than showing, the pictures concealing our "real" experience'. This can generate uncomfortable, and sometimes painful, insights into the subject's earlier experiences and the discrepancy between the needs of the subject and the family (Gittens 1998; Kuhn 1991, 2002;

**Figure 4.1**   Annette Kuhn and budgie. © Annette Kuhn

Walkerdine 1991). This emerges in Simon Watney's reflections, from the vantage point of a gay man, on photos of himself as a child:

> I have always believed that I was a grotesquely fat and unattractive child, but the little boy who stares back rather cautiously from under his sunhat is neither of these things. I thought I was fat and ugly because I thought I was *bad*.

> Many people will have memories of this order, memories that signal some kind of dysfunction between one's sense of oneself and one's parents'

expectations. These are folded in with the larger function of domestic photography, which is to impart the semblance of retrospective coherence to family life ... (Watney 1991: 29)

As Kuhn discovered, this exercise can also reveal discrepancies between the personal memories of different family members.

Juxtaposition is another technique used in autobiographical photo-work; specifically, scholars review their personal photos in relation to other found photos, namely other people's personal pictures and media images. Juxtaposing personal and other photos can produce startling and illuminating insights into one's own family photos and the relationship between personal and collective memory. Juxtaposition places personal photos in a broader context. Similarities between images should not, however, be interpreted as signs of common experience but of similar representational strategies and what Hirsch (1997) calls the 'familial gaze'.

In some instances juxtaposition occurs as an unintended consequence of researching other people's photo collections. Kirsten McAllister (2006) recalls a long-term fascination with her grandparents' photo collection, which included pictures taken during the Second World War when her Japanese-Canadian family were interned. However, her postmemory (the account she inherited) of her family's cohesion was challenged by looking at the photo collections of other Japanese-Canadian families interned during the war. Her account of this research and its impact on how she saw her own family photos points to the dialectical relationship between academic and personal viewing practices. By studying the photos of other families McAllister was able to confront signs of distress she could not initially face in her own family album.

The deliberate juxtaposition of personal and other photos is used productively in art (also phototherapy) to expose the conventions of family photography and explore the relationship between personal and collective memory. McAllister notes that alongside the illumination of archival research, her wartime postmemory was also challenged by an art installation created by Ana Chang which integrated three family portraits that were originally separated in the family's photo collection. This juxtaposition generated a stark contrast between pre-war and wartime images suggesting the stress and hardship endured by her family, it created 'synchronic shock' as 'discrete moments once separated by time and space' were collapsed 'into one visual moment' (p. 97).

Lorie Novak is another artist and academic who connects personal and other photos using various techniques, including juxtaposition and the layering of images: 'Thinking about what was and was not photographed in my family and how those choices influenced my memories and sense of self intrigues me' (1999: 15). Novak explores the relationship between personal and collective memory by juxtaposing her family snapshots with historical images drawn from books, newspapers, magazines and television (e.g. *Playback* 1992). In *Collected Visions I* (1993–4) Novak also explores the relationship between her own personal photos and those of other people focusing on representations of girls and women in families. She started by collecting snaps dating from the 1940s to 1990s from one hundred women and girls

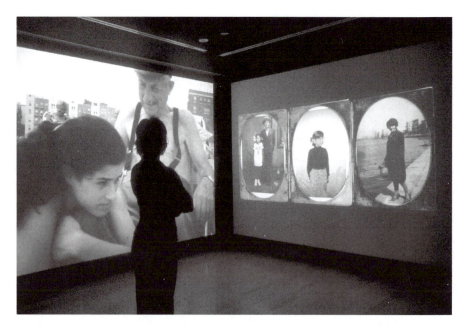

**Figure 4.2**   Photo from *Collected Visions*. Reproduced courtesy of Lorie Novak

of varied backgrounds and generations; a selection of these were then used in an image and music installation to explore representations of girlhood and the experience of coming of age. Despite the influence of feminism and changes in the roles of women, Novak was struck by the similarity in how girls and women 'present themselves' in family photos from the 1950s through to the 1990s, and how most photos 'only hinted at the female experience of coming of age' (p. 20). To stress the complexity of representations of girls and women, some photos were overlaid with open books by and about women such as Virginia Woolf's *A Room of One's Own*: 'the resulting hybrid images propose alternate narratives from the traditional ones conveyed in so many of the photographs' (p. 20).[1]

There is no specific method for utilising juxtaposition in autobiographical academic research. If you are keen to try this, you need to start by collecting examples; these may be commercial photos or other people's personal photos from the same period as your family snaps, or photographs from different social groups or different periods (see also Chapter 3). Once you have a set of photos, lay them out on a table or across the floor or wall. Now you need to look and think across the set: what do they reveal and conceal? In what ways are they similar and different (content, style, composition, posing etc.)? How do they make you feel? What questions do they raise?

In a website called *Collected Visions* (there is also an art installation around this project, see Figure 4.2), Novak has extended her work to enable visitors to relate their personal photos to other people's family pictures. *Collected Visions* consists of two archives: one of family photos submitted by visitors, the other of selected and typically brief photo stories also created by visitors (only those used in exhibitions are accessible). Interestingly, most of the contributors to the archive have opted to write about photographs that are not their own. Novak attributes this to visitors' identifications with the images of others. In looking at other people's photos, visitors often recall photos they can no longer find, or which may have never existed: 'the *Collected Visions* archive allows visitors to find images that evoke memories of their own family events that were never photographed' (p. 27). Novak also suggests that writing about the 'resonant images of others frees authors from the personal baggage surrounding their own photographs' (p. 26) and that this can liberate authors from the myths that surround their own family snaps. For the purposes of academic research, visitors' stories may be too brief and general to be useful; moreover, the opportunity to unearth and explore 'personal baggage' and 'family legends' is often what motivates researchers to work with other people's personal photos. Nevertheless, the method of using other people's personal photos to stimulate autobiographical reflections on the past and present is suggestive. The method does, however, raise interesting questions that have yet to be addressed: how does identifying with, and writing about, other people's personal photos compare to writing about one's own personal photos? How can we interpret, analyse or utilise the products of these practices in academic scholarship?[2]

## Reworking personal photos

So far I have considered ways of reviewing personal photos, but revelation can also come from taking them apart. Using creative strategies some scholars deconstruct and reconstruct personal photographs and the ways they and their families are represented in family history. Underpinning these practices is an acknowledgement of the power of photography to define us and a determination to explore how it can be 'used for its "unfixing" rather than its "fixing" qualities?' (Hirsch 1997: 12, citing Spence 1986). In this section I focus on methods for reworking personal photos. All these methods have therapeutic associations and applications: Spence's techniques for reworking the family album and restaging family photos were developed for therapeutic purposes, while Walkerdine's method of working 'below the surface' was informed by, and pursued within, a phototherapy context. While this section demonstrates the fruitful cross-fertilisation of ideas and practices across fields, the therapy applications of personal photography are beyond the scope of this book. Moreover, though phototherapy techniques can be useful for academics who decide to work on their personal photos, they are not easily dipped into and they can be emotionally demanding.

### Visual autobiography – reworking the family album

Spence is notable for her attempts to use photography in a subversive manner to bring about personal, political and social change; her work is a form of 'cultural sniping', which is the title of a posthumous collection of her work (1995). Spence has been a major influence on thinking about, and working with, personal photographs. Her work is intensely personal and political, influenced by feminism, socialism and psychoanalysis. It engages with family, identity, the body and health, and with the themes of gender, class and sexuality.

In 1979 Spence produced an exhibition about her personal photo collection which investigated her family and class background, and what it meant to be a woman. The exhibition materials were reproduced in an essay entitled 'Visual auto-biography: beyond the family album' in which Spence (1986: 82–3) explained the rationale for her work. Spence was highly critical of her collection of personal photos which provided no record of most aspects of her life including her poor health, 'the pointless years shunted around schools inside formal education (where I was downgraded for "unruly behaviour", constantly evaluated and eventually crushed into the mould of "typist")', her failed marriage, and her efforts 'to please parents and other authority figures'. Moreover, the 'passive visual moments' that did appear in her collection provided only 'surface information' about her and rendered wider social, economic and political histories invisible. Through this exhibition Spence explored the domestic photographic conventions that shaped her personal photos, a collection that was not atypical (see Chapter 5). Additionally, as she explained, she revealed 'how I had built a view of myself through other people's representations of me'. By engaging critically with her collection, and revealing alternative stories to those suggested by her snaps, Spence exposed the ideological force of family photography. In this photo-work and subsequent photography of her experiences of breast cancer and radical surgery, Spence rewrote the conventional family album, producing a very different account of her life. This 'counter memory of the "everyday"' made visible what Spence described as the 'unthinkable/unspeakable/unknowable' (Roberts 1998: 202). Through this album work and other strategies, Spence (1986: 83; 1995: 194–5) came to understand some of the ways in which her subjectivity was constructed 'as very contradictory and fragmented'; 'Out of such raw beginnings come new forms of creativity and thinking' and the potential 'to reverse the process of the way I had been constructed as a woman'.

Spence (1995: 190–5) suggests several practical exercises for reworking personal photo collections to expose, explore and revise photographic narratives of the self and family. One of these is an annotated display of 'visual autobiography' similar to that exhibited by Spence in 1979. To produce a 'self-history' display, you start by identifying one meaningful photo from each year of your life or the period you are working on. Arrange and affix this set of photos in a row, and in chronological order. Ensure there is space underneath each photo to add comments. Date each photo. Next try to remember key emotional events in your life which link to each of the years you are dealing with. Finally concentrate on recalling social and economic events for each year and on adding notes about the production of each photo – who took the photo of you, what was/is your relationship to them, and any other comments that seem relevant to you. Spence suggests doing this exercise in several sessions because it requires time and is often emotionally tiring. She also stresses the need for privacy and the importance of sharing and making public only what you feel comfortable with. The aim of this exercise is both to unpick photographic conventions and some of the roots of self-knowledge, and to generate a different narrative of the self. In light of shifts in photographic practices since Spence did her visual autobiography it will be interesting to discover how far, if at all, contemporary family photo collections tell a different story about the self.

## Staging photos – phototheatre

Phototheatre is the photographic re-enactment of scenarios and figures from one's past. In collaboration with Martin, Spence (1986, 1995) developed this technique and used it initially to stage photos from her childhood as a means to explore her memories of past experiences and feelings, including those previously repressed. But, as she explains, 'It is easy to act out being a child and be cute, but to actually go back and experience what you felt is incredibly frightening' (1986: 189). The strategy was, however, productive. Spence then extended it to explore aspects of her childhood from her mother's point of view. She did this by acting out versions of her mother and photographing these representations. As a child, Spence was evacuated and billeted with strangers on three occasions during the Second World War. These wartime events were experienced and recalled by Spence as 'abandonment' (p. 189). In phototherapy, Spence revisited herself as a child and then took up her mother's point of view by staging images of her for the camera. Through the process of constructing visual representations of her mother in different roles and remembered activities, Spence came to appreciate how difficult the wartime separation was for her mother. Spence also explored her mother's war work through which she then appreciated how liberating it was for her mother to be released from the home and to enjoy the company of other women on a daily basis.

Staging photos from the past can stimulate memories and the imagination and in these ways provide impetus and insights for academic research into uncharted aspects of past personal lives or areas of private life that are difficult to access using other methods. In research it is not undertaken solely as a means of self-discovery, not least because there is no therapeutic context to support the experience. Additionally, on its own this method is unlikely to generate data sufficient for the purposes of academic enquiry.

## Working 'below the surface'

In the context of feminist initiatives to understand the creation of gendered subjectivities, Walkerdine wrote two essays about photos of herself taken when she was a girl. Her analysis drew on insights from psychoanalysis to deconstruct and explain herself and the dynamics of working-class femininity in the 1950s. The first essay (1985) is based on reviewing a 'treasured' childhood photo of herself, but in the second (1991) she revisits this photo to explore the relationship between acceptable and unacceptable versions of herself. In the second essay she reworks images of her girlhood self to expose the conventions of photographic representation and reveal a deeply suppressed and transgressive version of herself.

The treasured photo was of Walkerdine, aged three, dressed for a fancy-dress competition as a bluebell fairy. Walkerdine suggests (1991: 35–6) that the reason she 'treasured' this image of herself was that her father played on the bluebell-fairy theme

**Figure 4.3**   Valerie. Reproduced courtesy of Valerie Walkerdine

**Figure 4.4**   From 'Behind the painted smile', New Contemporaries 1991. Reproduced courtesy of Valerie Walkerdine

when he called her Tinky, short for Tinkerbell. She explains that, as a sickly and small child, 'the fantasy of the bluebell fairy carried an enormous allure. A fairy, through her very frailty, has magic powers. My father's vision of me tied in with his own fantasies and nightmares of the disabling heart condition which finally killed him.' Walkerdine goes on to link this personal insight to the cultural significance of envisioning females as fairies, noting that in the working class the use of the fairy figure helped to 'crystallise the infantilisation' of girls and women by men and the construction of a need in women for male protection. Fairy fantasies, she continued, also promoted the notion that good girls are selfless; this fantasy was particularly important for working-class girls because it played into the 'good-girl femininity' associated with academic success and upward mobility.

In the second essay aptly titled 'Behind the painted smile', Walkerdine (1991) goes on to explore what was hidden by the bluebell-fairy photo: she did this by confronting a 'reviled' photo of herself as a 'fat' seven-year-old and by reworking other childhood representations of herself (see Figures 4.3 and 4.4). Walkerdine's method involved projecting her childhood photos onto a wall. She then placed paper on the wall and drew and coloured the projected images. Giving herself free reign to respond to the images, Walkerdine 'mutilated' (p. 37) some by, for example, sticking a piece a paper over her mouth and scribbling over her abdomen. The ways in which she reworked these images, and her reactions to these new versions of herself, were subsequently interrogated to reveal anxieties around her mouth (speaking out and saying the wrong thing) and abdomen (eating, fatness and sexuality) which she traces into adulthood. Walkerdine then made:

> more careful drawings and pastel colourings from the images. What began to happen was dramatic. I started to shade in the shadow on the photographs. I noticed that under the eyes of one sweet little image were shadows. I shaded these in heavily. I continued with other areas of the face and worked on all the images in this way, so that what emerged in the end was a series of highly disturbing portraits. I had become transformed from a sweet little girl or blank-faced fatty into a depressed, demanding and angry child … what I had done was work with what was there, as signs, as traces, in the photograph. (pp. 40–1)

In reworking girlhood photos, Walkerdine was able to explore previously suppressed memories and unravel long-standing anxieties which encouraged her to cling to debilitating gender and class specific versions of herself.

Walkerdine's methods expose the family's unconscious optics:

> If the camera gaze of the family snapshot can be said to construct the girl as a social and familial category, then resisting the image – either at the time or later in the process of rereading – becomes a way of contesting that construction, of rewriting the present by way of revising the past. Reading, rereading, and misreading thus become forms of active intervention: they enable a revision of the screens through which the familial gaze is filtered and refracted and thus a contestation of the gaze itself. In focusing on family pictures and albums, these forms of resistance not only contest but actually reveal the power of photography as a technology of personal and family memory. (Hirsch 1997: 193)

# Using autobiographical photo methods with research participants

So far I have considered how autobiographical techniques can be used by researchers to explore their own photos and memories, but can they also be used with research participants?

In my view, some reworking methods, specifically Spence's staging of photos and Walkerdine's 'working below the surface', are *not* suitable for use with research participants because their aim is to deconstruct established and often cherished versions of family and self and this is not an appropriate or ethical academic exercise. Techniques for reworking the family album, also reviewing personal photos can, however, be adapted for use in projects where research participants are asked to generate autobiographical accounts. Asking research participants to write or talk about other people's personal photos may prove a fruitful strategy for exploring how people think and feel about families without explicitly interrogating personal experiences. Kuhn's memory method can also be used to guide research participants in interrogating their own personal photos and memories, and talking and writing about them.

Kuhn (2007) has also developed collaborative versions of her memory method which are particularly suited for use in research contexts. Individuals bring along a personal photo to a workshop and first work through Kuhn's protocol on their own (method one) before revisiting the photo with a partner (method two). The advantage of the workshop is that it provides opportunities for fresh perspectives to emerge on a familiar picture. This strategy can easily be adjusted for use in a research interview. Following a preliminary meeting in which the research and Kuhn's guidelines are explained, the first memory method is undertaken privately by the research participant and then followed by the second method which takes place in discussion with the interviewer. In this kind of work research participants are actively engaged with the researcher in producing new knowledge about themselves and their past.

A third memory method (this follows methods one and two) draws on Martha Langford's oral-photographic method. This third method begins with the photograph's owner and the interviewer/analyst discussing the photo in detail using Kuhn's protocol as a guide. The dialogue prompted by the photo is then transcribed to produce a text that is then studied and interpreted. Kuhn comments that:

> an interactive performative viewing... brings to light depths and details of meaning and association that had not emerged in the group workshop, as ... it opens up readings ... that begin to unpack the intersections and continuities between the personal, the familial and the social that lie embedded in the image's many layers of meaning. (Kuhn 2007: 290)

Kuhn's analysis of Jack Yu's (Yu Chan) account of a 'treasured' family photo offers graphic illustration of the third method. Kuhn uses transcripts of her conversation with Jack to expose and then interrogate the working of memory as a cultural phenomenon. Her analysis of Jack's memories is nuanced and thoughtful. The tools of analysis are 'established procedures for analysing cultural texts, and these will be as productive and convincing as the practitioner's craft skills and insight allows' (p. 284).

Three analytical strategies are worth noting. First, Kuhn is careful to distinguish between Jack's words – 'what Jack says', 'as Jack tells it', 'Jack's comments – and her own descriptions and interpretations of them. Second, Kuhn attends to the different perspectives that Jack draws on, such as those of his mother and his adult self. Third, when reading and then writing about the transcript, Kuhn identifies and distinguishes between personal, familial and collective or popular memories. So, for example, in the following excerpt Kuhn makes clear whose memories are being referred to: 'Jack's comments on what he is wearing … are unmarked by actual memory of the occasion: he is looking back on his younger self from the standpoint of the present, or perhaps repeating a parent's memories of himself as a child' (p. 287). In the next excerpt, Kuhn identifies how Jack's account weaves references to collective memories and histories as he locates his family's story in the broader context of life in Maoist China: 'Life was still hard, says Jack, and there was still considerable uncertainty in his family, in the whole of China, about how things [the end of the Cultural Revolution] might turn out' (p. 288).

Kuhn admits that it is unclear how knowledgeable the interviewer/analyst needs to be to make a success of this third method: how important for the depth of the inquiry is the interviewer/analyst's prior knowledge of the photo's social, cultural, historical, technical contexts and antecedents? Is it necessary for the interviewer/analyst to be immersed in the culture from which the memory text emanates? Would a 'lay' cultural insider be better placed than any 'expert' outsider to interpret it?

The third memory method is a type of photo-elicitation interview because the photo's owner does not undertake the analysis and interpretation of the recorded conversation. The third method could remain an autobiographical method if the photo's owner undertook the interpretation and write-up of the interview. For the purposes of academic research this would work best if the researcher was the photo's owner and, following a recorded conversation with an interviewer, the researcher (or indeed both the interviewer and the researcher) undertook analysis of the transcript.

Though engaging research participants in autobiographical methods is an exciting idea, this should not be undertaken lightly. These methods are usually intensive in one way or another. They typically involve a high level of commitment from the research participant because they require a greater input of time and energy than conventional research methods. Moreover, though these methods can be engaging and empowering, they can also be unsettling, upsetting and challenging. Researchers who use these methods need to think carefully about whether they have the skills, time and commitment to provide adequate guidance and support for their research participants. They also need to consider whether they have the personal and academic resources to analyse what emerges from using these methods.

# Summary

Autobiographical photo methods have been tremendously important for developing insights into family, self and memory, but considerable skill is required to work with autobiographical data in ways that extend the analysis beyond the personal to address the aims of most historical and social research. This is one reason why it is not advisable for most of us to rely solely on autobiographical methods. These methods do, however, have something to offer researchers, particularly if used alongside other research strategies. Autobiographical pilot work facilitates reflexivity about our use of photo methods with research participants; 'reviewing' methods and some 'reworking' strategies can be fruitfully adjusted for use with research participants and used alongside interviews or photo-elicitation; autobiographical memory work can inform analysis of how interviewees look at and remember with their personal photos and provides insights into how photos enter collective memory; these methods also facilitate exploration of the practices and power of family photography.

Autobiographical research points to the role of photographic practices in family and personal life. These practices can also be researched in other ways and in Chapter 5 I consider how to do this.

## Notes

1  See http://cvisions.cat.nyu.edu/novak/installations.html
2  Website http://cvisions.cat.nyu.edu/ index.html

# 5

# Researching Photographic Practices

There is a tendency to assume that the value of photos lies in what they depict, but much can be learned from photographic practices, that is how and why photos are made, presented, used, circulated, stored and reused in particular social and historical contexts and what these practices mean to the people and institutions involved. Since the 1850s photos have become increasingly embedded in all aspects of daily life, and how people and institutions relate to and use them can be revealing, for example, of values, political and personal aspirations, also aspects of social and cultural practice including the intricacies of personal relationships.

Approaching photos in terms of practices often involves a shift in how you consider them; as explained in Chapter 1, you need to generate questions that engage with the life of a photo. If you are interested in photographic practices you are typically concerned to investigate: how and why photos are produced and by whom; where, how and why they are presented; who uses photos and what these practices mean; and how and why photos circulate or are kept, archived and reused in particular ways and for different purposes. This type of research embraces commercial, institutional, domestic and personal practices, also the practices of academics.

This chapter outlines different ways of researching photographic practices. There are no set methods, but if you are interested in doing this you need to consider several factors. First, what aspects of photographic practices – for instance, production, use, reuse – you are interested in. Second, the scope and scale of your research, for example, are you interested in: doing an in-depth study of a particular type of practice such as making photographic collages or memorial objects; mapping patterns of photographic practice within particular communities or institutions (families, movements etc.), perhaps with a view to undertaking cross-cultural or historical comparative work; or tracing and explaining changes in the content, form, presentation and use of particular types of photos over time? Third, the shape of your research will depend on your approach to the materiality of photos. Studies of photographic practices invariably engage with material aspects of a photo's life – its production, how it is presented and used – but some scholars adopt a micro-material approach attending to the fine details of these practices, including how people engage physically with photographic objects as they make and use them. Temporal issues are the fourth factor; are you interested in practices at a particular point in time, or in tracing changes over time?

I use four case studies to demonstrate different strategies that researchers use to investigate photographic practices. First, I look at research that seeks to identify and map patterns of photographic practices within domestic life. To do this I look at Richard Chalfen's work on domestic photography in which he investigates social conventions around producing, presenting and using photos and the role, significance and meaning of these practices in interpersonal relations. Chalfen also explores cross-cultural variations in practice and changes over time. Second, I consider research that traces and explains changes in the form, presentation and use of photos over time. To do this I focus on Darren Newbury's study of the historical development of South African apartheid photography 1948–94. The study addresses how and why particular visual accounts of apartheid were produced, circulated and reused in the public arena, and investigates the practices whereby apartheid images are re-presented and given new meanings in the context of two post-apartheid museums. The third case study, like Chalfen's, is also concerned with mapping patterns in practice, but in this instance a material approach is to the fore and attention focuses on the meaning and significance of how and why photos – as objects – are made and presented in particular ways. Here I focus on Elizabeth Edwards' study of the photographic survey movement in England 1885–1918 in which Edwards interrogates the micro-details of the material practices of a group of amateur photographers to draw out the concrete ways in which they articulated their perceptions of history. The fourth case study also hones in on material details but in the context of an in-depth study which probes the physical aspects of making and using personal photographic objects. The research, undertaken by Patrizia Di Bello, focuses on the practice among some upper-class English women in the late-Victorian period of making photocollage albums. Di Bello explores the meaning and purpose of these intricate and often humorous photographic creations by investigating the material and physical aspects of how people related to the albums, including the importance of touch.

# Mapping conventions in photographic practices

Photos play an important role in family life. In part this is because they depict family members, but it is also because of conventions around family photos. For example, the practice of taking photos of people is widely interpreted as a sign of regard and inclusion and as a means of building and maintaining personal ties; parents are expected to take photos of their children (e.g. Bourdieu 1990; Chalfen 1987; Holland 2000).

Similarly, the practice of preserving and displaying photos of family members is commonly interpreted as a demonstration of family connection and regard; it is common to remove people from family photos or displays of photos after the breakdown of a marriage (e.g. Halle 1996).

If you are interested in researching conventions in photography, such as whether and how people use mobile phone photography in personal life, or what people from different cultures do with family photos and how this might be changing, or how the practices of adults and children compare, you need to be able to identify and map people's practices. In the following I draw on Chalfen's research to suggest ways in which you might do this. I start by discussing Chalfen's model for identifying and mapping conventions around domestic photography, and the application of this model to historical and comparative research. Following this I consider issues relating to the use of online evidence of domestic photographic practices.

## Researching domestic practices

Identifying different aspects of domestic practice, and making comparisons between individuals and groups, can seem daunting. In *Snapshot Versions of Life* (1987) Chalfen outlines a method for systematically mapping the contours of what he calls 'home mode' photography which is a 'process of interpersonal and small group communication that focuses on family life mostly at home but occasionally away from home' (Chalfen 1998: 215). Chalfen aims to identify patterns in how people make and use photos and to discover the ideas, values and knowledge that underpin these practices.

Chalfen proposes a framework to guide research on domestic practices; this framework is a device to generate questions that engage with the detail and diversity of how people make and use photos in personal relationships. To build this framework of questions, Chalfen advises that researchers start by identifying five key aspects of photographic practice, what he calls 'communication events':

1  'Planning events' – 'formal or informal decisions' and actions in advance of taking a photo, for example, routines such as cleaning up in the area the photo will be taken or decisions about whether or not a type of photography (e.g. funereal) is appropriate.
2  'On camera shooting events' – action(s) that shape what 'happens' in front of the camera, such as who is regularly included or excluded, what settings are commonly used and the poses people strike.
3  'Behind camera shooting' – what people do while they are taking the photo, this might include what kinds of instructions are given to the people being photographed.
4  'Editing events' – includes processing or retouching processed film images; deleting or manipulating digital images; printing, framing, uploading images onto a website; and writing on or cutting up printed photos.
5  'Exhibition events' – ways in which photos are shown to people other than the photographer and editor.

Chalfen then identifies five 'components' that can be used to describe the operation of each aspect of 'communication events':

1  Participants – who takes, appears in and looks at these photos?
2  Settings – where and when is a photo taken?
3  Topics – what subject matter, activities, events and themes are represented in photos?
4  Message form – what is the physical form, shape or kind of picture (e.g. passport photo, framed wedding photo)?
5  Code – what social habits and conventions are responsible for how people take and edit snapshots (e.g. asking people to say 'cheese' when photographing them)?

Cross-referencing the five 'communication events' and five 'components' produces a grid of 25 cells, each of which generates questions that are useful for engaging with the detail of how we make and use photos. For example, cross-referencing shooting event (second communication event) and setting (second component) leads to questions about whether there are regularities in where pictures are taken. Cross-referencing exhibition events (fifth communication event) with message forms (fourth event) leads to questions such as: in what forms are photos exhibited? Are some forms appropriate for particular audiences and not others?

Chalfen uses the framework to guide his research on domestic practices, but his sources and methods are varied. Often his research involves: the study of family collections, supplemented by interviews to contextualise photos; photo-elicitation; sometimes a questionnaire to ascertain background details regarding the family, family photos and use of photographic technologies. Chalfen (1987) has also used his framework to analyse photographic etiquette discussed in letters to the press.

The original framework was developed for the study of photography in the 1980s, but as Chalfen explains (personal correspondence), it was 'created to be suggestive and flexible – amenable to changes in technology and to specific uses of different kinds of cameras and images'; Lehmuskallio and Sarvas (2010) have extended it to engage with ICT in non-professional photo practices. I suggest four ways the original framework can be adjusted to engage with domestic photographic practices, particularly their temporal dimensions. First, the original framework focuses only on 'exhibition events' involving at least one person other than the picture-taker or editor; this is, in part, a product of Chalfen's preoccupation with inter-personal communication. The framework can, however, be extended to embrace other meaningful social practices, such as how mums tend to look at, hold and engage with photos of their children (Rose 2004, 2010). Second, questions can be incorporated into communication events 4–5 and component 5 so that the framework engages explicitly with what people do with photos over time. Third, the focus on mapping practices does not engage explicitly with historically specific familial and social contexts, but these details can be sketched in a preliminary interview and interrogated further once patterns of photographic practices have been identified. Fourth, the original framework was not longitudinal or historical in design but Chalfen has since drawn on it productively in a comparative and longitudinal study (see Box 5.1):

> It made me check on some easily ignored relationships of the listed 'components' and 'events'. In addition to helping me talk about cross-cultural comparisons, giving specific examples, it also helped me examine issues of continuity and change through time, checking on the stability or flexibility of, for example, the choice of topics or settings for behind-the-camera shooting events, or, for instance, a change in personnel (participants) dominating different events. (Personal correspondence)

## BOX 5.1   A LONGITUDINAL AND COMPARATIVE STUDY OF THE PHOTO COLLECTIONS OF TWO JAPANESE-AMERICAN FAMILIES

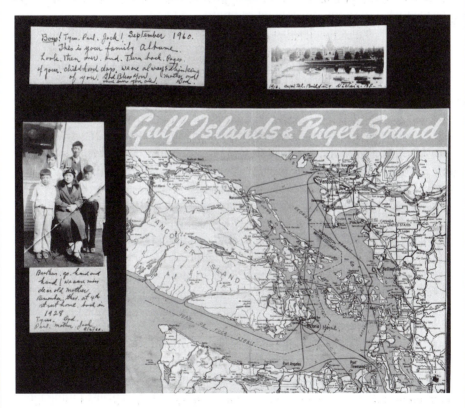

**Figure 5.1**   Inside front cover of 'Nagano's Mother 1910-1952'. Reproduced courtesy of Richard Chalfen and the George Nagano Family

*(Continued)*

*Turning Leaves* (Chalfen 1991) focuses on the photo collections of two Japanese-American families, comprising several generations each of the Nagano family and the Uyeda/Miyamura family. It is a study of photographic practices rather than of individual photos or series of them. As the study arose in part from curiosity about cultural differences in photographic practices, Chalfen wanted to explore whether Japanese-American families take the same types of photos, and for the same reasons, as their Anglo-American counterparts: is there a familial and/or cultural specificity to these pictorial records, and if so, what does it look like and how do we recognise it?

The research was done cooperatively with Lyne Horiuchi and focused on the independent study of the two collections, seeking similarities and differences between collections and comparisons over time. Drawing on Chalfen's framework, the researchers attended to the personal and social circumstances surrounding the production of photos, such as who took them and why, who decided what to shoot; the content of photos; and how they were used by family members, e.g. who decided what photos should be kept, duplicated and distributed to others.

The research entailed the examination of several thousand photos – in frames, wall displays and albums, also bundles of loose pictures. Although the content of photos was noted, the research did not concentrate on individual photos because the aim was to identify patterns of choice and what shaped these. The research also involved oral histories to ascertain personal and social histories which then served as frameworks for the analysis, and photo-elicitation interviews to identify the content of images and reconstruct the circumstances around their production. In addition, several members of each family were asked to describe how they understood what they were doing with their photos.

One challenge was how to recognise the visual representation of cultural values, this involved identifying patterns in photo content and photographic habits. The study of one of George Nagano's albums, entitled 'Nagano's Mother 1910–52', provides an example of Chalfen's approach. Nagano's album, which was about his wife, was originally produced in 1960 (eight years after Nagano's wife died) and subsequently added to and reworked until 1978. Various types of photos were included with embellishments and captions, also newspaper clippings, Christmas cards and maps. Numerous explicit forms of written communication were also featured; George 'talked' directly to his sons, his deceased wife and to himself. Chalfen analysed the patterns and content of both visual and written forms of communication in this album. These explications were contextualised using interviews to understand George's life and his relationship to photography. Chalfen also teased out and explored dominant themes in the content of photos.

One of the aims of the total Japanese-American project was to trace change over time and generations, but continuities proved more interesting. There were two aims to this strand of enquiry: to show how the Uyeda/Miyamura family recorded life over time and how Japanese traditions persisted in their photographic practices. These temporal themes were explored through an examination of how several members of the Uyeda/Miyamura family took photos, made albums and used their pictures within the extended family and over several generations (70 years in total). The researchers examined the photo collections of individual family members to explore how photos were circulated, and conducted interviews to identify what people did with the photos.

A major challenge in working with large collections is how to keep track of data. Photographic identification numbers were given to each photo in the two collections. These numbers differentiated photos by family, album and/or other type of display/storage (such as a shoebox, display, drawer). To facilitate study of these large collections, album pages were reproduced and facsimile albums with identification numbers were compiled. These facsimile albums constituted the core of the database and were the materials most used in the research and analysis stages. The researchers also produced photographic copies of each album page and item, including non-photographic material. These materials were used in photo-interviews, and later in exhibitions, presentations and displays.

It is useful to keep in mind the elements identified by Chalfen, particularly in comparative work, but rigid adherence to a systematic approach may be unproductive and time-consuming because it is difficult to answer all the questions that are generated. As Chalfen acknowledges, 'The difficulties and limitations are found in (1) the access a researcher might have to observe the entire process from "planning" to "exhibition" and (2) the ease or difficulty in reconstructing details of an "event" after the fact' (personal correspondence). Moreover, to explore some aspects of photo practices – what people do with their pictures, what these practices mean, how people feel about their pictures and the practices around them, also what is not articulated – may require in-depth interviews or ethnographies, with adequate resources you can combine approaches.

## Online photographic practices

The study of domestic photographic practices typically relies on material evidence of how photos are displayed and presented (e.g. Chalfen 1987, 1998; Halle 1996; Thomson 2011a, 2011b; Tinkler 2010), and where feasible, interviews with people about what they do with photos (see Chapter 9). Recently it has also involved studying personal websites, including personal web pages, web logs or 'blogs' – 'a website which contains a series of frequently updated, reverse chronologically ordered posts on a common web page' (Hookway 2008: 92), and social networking sites (SNS) such as Facebook and YouTube. Ways of researching personal websites are now being developed, though this area of research practice is still in its infancy. Though research on online photographic practices often uses similar research strategies to research on pre-digital practices, there are distinctive features that are worth considering: analysing the presentation and contextualisation of online photos; and the practicalities of online research.

Studying the presentation and contextualisation of photos in albums – the layout of album pages, captions etc. – is standard procedure when researching photographic practices, but online photos are often embedded in complex presentations that combine pictures, illustrations, design features, textual and sometimes audio elements. Luc Pauwels's (2008) researched photography on family websites to investigate the implications of the Internet for domestic photographic practices; this involved a survey of websites, analysis of individual sites and interviews with their creators. He argues that personal websites are a rich source of cultural information (values, aspirations etc.), and contextualise photos in a host of ways that provide insight into the personal meaning and significance of the images. Pauwels presents a guide to researching family websites that engages with their complex presentation and that is useful for approaching other types of personal websites. This 'hybrid media analysis' (Pauwels 2005: 610) involves attending to a list of website features that convey meaning:

- Analyse the photos, also other images, attending to their content, form and how they are arranged.
- List topics and issues covered in the visual and textual features, and note what is absent.
- Look at the treatment of topics and arguments, for instance the space allocated to particular topics.
- Consider whose points of view are represented and their relative status.
- Identify the intended audience.
- Investigate the structure of the website noting the 'order, flow and hierarchy of elements'.
- Identify design features – colour, the fonts used, layout, use of sound etc.
- Note available links.
- Note the overall 'look and feel'.

Doing research involving photos on personal websites poses practical challenges for researchers. Though there are no easy answers, it is useful to identify three important questions that you need to consider before starting online research (Snee, interview).[1]

### How do I keep records of the web pages I have looked at?
The problem with personal websites, especially blogs, is that they are constantly changing. This raises the question of how to keep records of the pages you have looked at. One solution is to print pages as and when you study them, but often the pages might not print as laid out on the screen. Taking notes is useful for mapping themes and general details but it is inadequate if you want to do detailed photo analysis and comparative research. Another option is to save the web page as a file,

which is possibly the best option, though you will need to be online to follow any hyperlinks (which can still change) and you will have to conduct your analysis at a computer.

## How do I sample photos on web pages?

There are two issues to consider. First, you need to identify a search facility that 'grabs' images. If you wish to use an automated 'web crawler' (specialist software for online searching) you will need to do some research to find a suitable program, as some 'grab' text only. The second and main issue for researchers is that search facilities are usually text based. You can search for images only (see Google Image search) and use web crawlers that 'grab' images. However, the way that these search facilities work is that they look for words that appear near images such as captions or links to other images. So, although your search results may be images, it is still text that is being searched, which means that you may not get the most appropriate results. So you need to decide whether to trawl through web pages to locate a sample or employ a text-based search and hope for the best (on searching see Hookway 2008; Wilkinson and Thelwall 2011).

## How do I analyse photos on personal websites?

While images can be analysed using methods and strategies discussed elsewhere in this book, the pressing issue for Internet researchers is practical. How you analyse personal websites will be dependent on the records you keep. If you have saved web pages and want to analyse them in a software package such as NVivo, you will need to convert them into a format that can be imported into the program.

# Tracing change in the form and presentation of photos

Researchers can learn a lot about a society – its values, issues, politics – by exploring and explaining what kinds of photos are made and why, and how they are presented, circulated and used. This type of research is appropriate if you are interested in tracing and explaining changes in the form and presentation of photos made for public consumption as they are used and reused at different historical moments, these might be photos commissioned and used by particular media, organisations, institutions or a state. It is also relevant to tracing how particular genres of photography change over time, such as documentary photography, although it could also be used for plotting the history of the holiday snap. This type of research is principally concerned with understanding how and why particular visual accounts of social and cultural life get made and circulate, and how they change over time; much emphasis is placed on the content of photos but always in relation to the practices that have made them possible and visible. Unlike the previous case study, emphasis is not on delineating patterns in the production of photos or in the detail of what people/viewers actually do with photos.

In the following I draw on Newbury's study of South African apartheid photography to identify and demonstrate some of the strategies you might use to trace and explain changes in images and how they are presented. Apartheid photography is sometimes described as 'documentary photography', so I will start by considering briefly what is meant by the term and why scholars, including Newbury, are cautious in using it.

## What is 'documentary' photography?

Documentary photography can be defined broadly as 'the practice of photography as an engagement with and interpretation of social life' (Newbury 2006: 296), although some also stress that its purpose is to 'pave the way for social change' (Ohrn 1980 cited in Price 2001: 75). However, 'documentary photography' is a complex term with a convoluted history. The history of this label is important because the practices of naming establish boundaries and distinctions that legitimate different responses to photos (Becker 1998; Tagg 1988). When people classify types of picture-taking Howard Becker (1998: 84–5) prompts us to ask: what have these terms been used for in the past? How does their past use constrain what can be said and done now? Who is using these terms? What are they trying to claim for the work and why?

Scholars often explain what documentary photography is by delineating its history (Price 2000; Solomon-Godeau 1991). Before 1920, almost all photography was technically documentary because of an assumption that it provided an objective and accurate record of the real world; 'the very notion of documentary photography would have seemed tautological' (Solomon-Godeau 1991: 170). However, the term 'documentary' did not enter the photographic lexicon until the late 1920s: its emergence heralded a realisation that not all photos were objective records and it conveyed a need to distinguish a particular type of photography in which accuracy and the integrity of the photographer were paramount (see Chapter 1), though some photographers saw scope for subjective expression and self-defined as artists. Though photography was used for critical social commentary in the nineteenth century, in the 1920s and 1930s documentary photography became firmly aligned with social investigation. The paradigmatical forms of documentary photography emerged in the United States and Britain. In the United States it is most notably associated with the work of the government's Farm Security Administration, while in Britain it included Mass Observation's anthropological survey of British society and photographic commissions for *Picture Post*. In these historical contexts documentary photography was heralded as capturing the facts of life and it was harnessed to various reformist political and social agendas. Western documentary photography was seriously undermined in the 1970s and 1980s by the influence of post-structuralist arguments; these arguments led to a questioning of whether realist photography could provide evidence of – document – social life.

Given the history and politics of 'documentary' photography, it is not surprising that some scholars are cautious in how they use this label. Moreover, as exemplified by this historical sketch, characterisations of documentary photography have been approached principally in terms of European and North-American practices. Newbury initially used the term 'documentary photography' to describe the photos he studied, and approached his research as offering 'an example to counter the dominance of 1930s American photography as the social documentary paradigm'. Over time, however, he became less convinced that this term adequately represented the types of photos he discusses: 'Documentary is of course a complex term and set of practices, but sometimes it has been defined rather narrowly. I don't reject the term but I consciously wanted to leave the "documentary" question open' (interview).

## Researching apartheid photography

In *Defiant Images*, Newbury (2009) researched bodies of South African photography that were explicitly or implicitly critical of apartheid. His study traced changes in the style, content and presentation of photos made during apartheid, this included a detailed examination of *Drum* magazine 1951–65, 'a monthly illustrated picture magazine, modelled on the British and American picture magazines *Life* and *Picture Post*, aimed (significantly) at an urban black African audience' (Newbury, correspondence). *Drum* was notable at the time and since for its visual reportage on life in apartheid South Africa. Newbury challenged the notion that apartheid photos are simply witnesses of history. Drawing on archival evidence and oral-history interviews with South African photographers, including contributors to *Drum,* Newbury investigated the practices through which particular visual accounts of South Africa were produced, presented and used during apartheid (see Box 5.2).

How apartheid photos are reused over time is an important question for Newbury and to address this he considers how photos that were once used in resisting apartheid are now deployed in two museums to 'commemorate the past and articulate public histories of the struggle for democracy' (p. 273). Newbury's research suggests avenues of enquiry for those interested in how museum practices shape photographic meaning and accounts of the past. He starts by detailing the location of each museum and its intended audiences, also each museum's history and controversies around their construction. He then takes the reader for a walk through each, noting the physical, aural and visual dimensions of the museum experiences and the place of photography within them. He hones in on techniques used to present photos and how these differ from the formats in which the photos were originally published or circulated: 'for example, the size at which many of the images were displayed, which has both experiential and practical consequences for the engagement with the image' (interview). Newbury also notes how photos are often unattributed, which downplays the role of the photographer and the politics and practices of photography under apartheid. The visual economy[2] is obscured 'in favour of an emphasis on the veracity and authenticity of the photograph; its ability to provide a window through which the visitor can see and experience the past' (p. 306).

## BOX 5.2   APARTHEID PHOTOGRAPHY IN SOUTH AFRICA 1948–94: AN INTERVIEW WITH DARREN NEWBURY

**Figure 5.2**   'Johannesburg Lunch-Hour', *Drum*, September 1951. © Bailey's African History Archives.  Reproduced courtesy of Bailey's African History Archives

### WHAT MOTIVATED YOU TO RESEARCH THE HISTORY OF APARTHEID PHOTOGRAPHY?

There is a large degree of serendipity in how I came to research the history of photography in South Africa. I trained as a photographer during the 1980s and was vaguely aware of *Drum* photography. At this time, as this was the height of the struggle against apartheid, I would also have seen many images of what was happening in the South African townships. I think these images seeped into my visual unconscious. Later, after doing historical research on British documentary, I travelled to South Africa and was drawn to visit the *Drum* archives. I spent no more than half an hour in the archives, but decided I wanted to come back and do research here. The coming together of social, cultural, historical and political issues in the South African photographs of this period made them ideal material for the kind of research I wanted to do. The questions I wanted to address were how and why did 'documentary' photography develop in the way that it did in apartheid South Africa (1948–94), how was this viewed and experienced by those involved, and how does the work of this period continue to shape photography in a post-apartheid era?

## HOW DID YOU APPROACH THIS RESEARCH?

Susan Sontag talks about photographs as an 'invitation to pay attention': I like to think that the research I have done is a consequence of taking that invitation seriously. The notion of an invitation also has appealing connotations, it presupposes a human other to whom one is saying 'look-see', something one might argue is inherent in the photographic act.

Taking the photograph as a starting point for enquiry means engaging in depth with what is in the photographs, at the same time as recognising that the photograph is not a transparent window onto that world. Photographs are inevitably 'of' something and it is difficult, if not impossible, to sustain an interest in photography without an interest in what those photographs document/record/depict.

While one can appreciate a 'good' or aesthetically strong image, that to my mind is not sufficient, one has to try to understand the social, historical and political context that gives rise to the image. To paraphrase something Caroline Knowles once said, I'm interested in all the other things that have to be true in order for the particular photograph to be possible. Or to borrow from Patricia Hayes (2010), there are at least three stories to be told, the story of the photograph, the story of the people in the photograph and the story of the photographer. This means asking questions about how the photographs were made, how the work of photography was organised, how the images were distributed and seen – the visual economy. This is why the archive and the interview are as important as the image itself.

## WHAT WERE THE MAIN CHALLENGES OF ARCHIVAL WORK?

Archives are seductive, yet also a source of frustration. The latter may be especially true for research on photography, where written contextual material can be as important as the images. This is for two reasons. First, photographers tend to be very poor at keeping any other sort of record than the images themselves. In many cases that is precisely why they are photographers, rather than writers. Second, contextual evidence surrounding photography is often quite fugitive. Some archives were not primarily photographic, and hence were not organised in a way that lends itself to easily locating the material I was interested in. For example, some of the most interesting archival material I found on the photographer Leon Levson was in letters written by his wife.

*(Continued)*

There were also other frustrations. Although in some cases (e.g. the *Drum* archives or the Constance Stuart Larrabee collection at the Smithsonian) archival research was relatively straightforward as there was a large body of relevant material, in other instances I had to be persistent in tracking down scattered sources. Time was another big frustration. I'm not sure I ever felt I had the time I wanted to really work through the collections, and often had to adopt a strategic approach to what could be consulted and how long I could spend reading/looking through material. Of course, the archive is also a place of silences; it is neither neutral nor transparent. During the period of apartheid having one's activities documented could be problematic, and therefore there was ambivalence around practices of documentation. Also it seems quite likely that photographer, Constance Stuart Larrabee, edited the material that went into the Smithsonian collection from the perspective of the present.

Having said all this, the archive can provide some wonderful moments of revelation, as for example, when I was able to read one of Ernest Cole's first letters home after he'd gone into exile.

## HOW DID YOU EXPLORE AND EXPLAIN DRUM'S VISUAL STYLE AND TRACK CHANGES OVER TIME?

First I sat down and looked through every issue of *Drum* from 1951 to 1965. Initially I did some of this in the British Library and the School of Oriental and African Studies Library. This is not easy given both of those libraries allow researchers to access only the issues of *Drum* they have on microfiche, which makes assessing visual style rather difficult. Despite the limitations of microfiche I vividly recall seeing the photo-essay 'Johannesburg Lunch-Hour' (Figure 5.2) and thinking this is important, this is something different.

Later, I surveyed original copies in the *Drum* archives in Johannesburg. Using a simple digital camera, I recorded picture stories and individual photographs that struck me as indicative of a particular style or interesting or unusual. I subsequently printed these images and organised them in small albums so I had an easy at-hand set of visual references that I could consult as I was writing and thinking. The access I had as a researcher at the *Drum* archives and the freedom to record material for my research, greatly facilitated my ability to analyse material when I was back in the UK. Many, if not most, photographic archives would not give this degree of freedom. Continually looking back and forth from early to later issues of the magazine, often as new questions arose, or as later information prompted me to go back and check things, allowed me to see changes in style and to be able to illustrate these.

I did most of the work looking at the published photo-essays as they appeared in *Drum*. But the ability to go back to contact sheets or negatives also allowed me to see some changes more clearly.

## WAS IT USEFUL TO INTERVIEW PHOTOGRAPHERS?

**Figure 5.3** Jürgen Schadeberg at his home in Blairgowrie, Johannesburg, April 2003. Photograph by Darren Newbury

I was not interviewing photographers solely for an account of 'what happened' and certainly they should not necessarily have the last word either in accounts of particular events or of the meaning of the images. People's

*(Continued)*

memories are faulty at the best of times and some of the events I was discussing had taken place up to fifty years earlier. Sometimes more than one photographer has claimed a particular image as theirs. These were disputes that might of themselves be interesting, and certainly say something about the lack of importance attached at the time to image credits and ownership, but they were not issues that I was concerned to resolve in favour of one photographer or another.

My approach might be described as more interpretive. Talking to photographers, and in some cases returning to the places where photographs were made, is an important part of my research approach. I am interested in photographers' accounts – their versions and perspectives on events, their experiences, how they talk about the images and construe their significance – but at the same time I recognise that they are just that, 'accounts' given in the particular context of the research interview. This doesn't mean that the events themselves don't matter, they do, and by triangulating accounts one can get nearer some sort of 'truth', but I am also interested in how photographers talk about their work and what can be understood from that. For example, some photographers are good storytellers, and one can begin to think of the photographer's story form as a genre. The fact that several photographers related stories about fooling the apartheid authorities in order to 'get the picture' says something about a specific kind of cultural resistance, regardless of whether or not every detail of every story is factually accurate.

# Identifying patterns in the materiality of photos

The material dimensions of photos are important; as Edwards and Hart (2004a: 14) explain, 'in so many ways it is the material that defines our social relations with photographs' and that shapes photographic meaning. While materiality is often considered at a general level in research on photographic practices, in this section I consider research that focuses on the detail of a photo's material form and attempts to decipher the significance of patterns in the material details of collections of photographs. This type of research is useful if you are interested in investigating how photos are manifest and what these details convey about the people or institutions that produce and present them. You might, for example, be interested in the significance of patterns in how photo albums or photographic museum exhibits are made and displayed. Often the value of this type of research will not be immediately obvious because researchers are typically unused to thinking about materiality. To demonstrate this approach I draw on Edwards' (2009; 2012) study of the English photographic survey movement, in which she explores and explains the meaning and significance of the details of how and why photographs – as objects – were made and presented in particular ways (see Box 5.3). Before I look more closely at Edwards' study I present a brief revision of what a material approach entails (for more detail, see Chapter 2).

## An eye for material: what to attend to

A material approach involves attending to four key features of a photograph (Edwards 2002). First, the material form of the photograph, this might include the size and quality of the paper and whether the finish is glossy or matt. Second, the photo's material presentation, for instance, whether it is mounted on card for archive purposes or framed for display; this is important because the meaning and significance of a photo is a product of the image and its presentation in combination. Evidence of use is the third material feature to note as it provides clues about how people have interacted with the photo. For instance, it is likely that a loose photo with crease marks across the middle and down the centre has been looked at, folded and unfolded repeatedly; these signs of use suggest the photo was highly meaningful to the owner. The fourth feature is what has happened to the photo over time and how this biography contributes to the photo's meaning, value and status.

## Researching the photographic survey movement

Edwards used a study of the English photographic survey movement 1885–1918 as 'a prism through which to consider the social practices of photography and popular historical imagination' (interview). This movement was a group of amateur photographers who used photography to record subjects of 'historical interest' for posterity, for example, ancient churches, timber cottages and also some folk customs. Edwards' research reveals that the photographers were very particular about how their photographs were produced, presented and archived and that their material practices are revealing of how they conceptualised photography, history and the future.

Central to Edwards' approach is 'the assumption that "things" are as they are for a reason – little things *matter*' (interview). Edwards' research is, therefore, attentive to the details of how the photographs were produced, presented and stored. To investigate the significance and meaning of this material evidence, Edwards looked at thousands of photographs with the aim of discerning patterns of practice within and between the local surveys that constituted the survey movement. Her research suggests ways of managing such vast amounts of material, it also highlights some of the issues involved in pursuing material interests through archival research, as Edwards recounted: '[One] institution tried to charge me three reproduction fees for publishing a card with three images on it … they saw three individual photographs and I saw one object' (interview).

## BOX 5.3    AN HISTORICAL ETHNOGRAPHY OF THE PHOTO-GRAPHIC SURVEY MOVEMENT: AN INTERVIEW WITH ELIZABETH EDWARDS

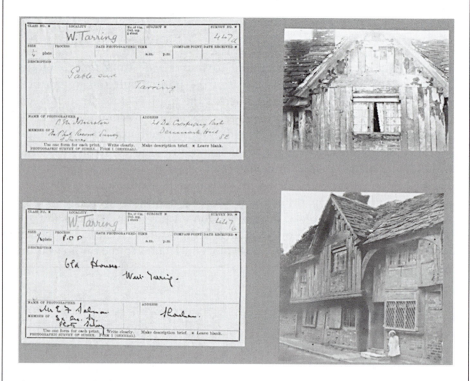

**Figure 5.4**    Buildings in West Tarring, Sussex. From the Photographic Survey of Sussex. Reproduced by kind permission of the Sussex Archaeological Society, Barbican House Museum

### WHAT MOTIVATED YOU TO RESEARCH THE PHOTOGRAPHIC SURVEY MOVEMENT?

I have a long-standing interest in the relationship between photography, identities and a sense of the past; one aspect of this is how 'self' represented 'self' to 'self', especially in terms of the visual definition of an historical past. I had known of the existence of the survey movement, but was dissatisfied with the rather predictable analyses to date. It seemed worthy of another look.

### WHAT WAS YOUR APPROACH TO RESEARCHING PHOTOS AND HOW DID IT EVOLVE?

I come from a strong anthropology and material culture background. For me photographs have never been simply images but also material objects – things made for a purpose to fulfil a certain function. Moreover, the material forms – the choices made about how and why to photograph, print, mount, label, box, rebox, remount, or remediate – had always been part of the meaning of the photograph, how it was to accomplish the work expected of it. Indeed, I saw photographic objects as 'little tools of knowledge' being made to perform information (or history if you like). It was an approach which I had used before, but not on this scale. If anything this project enabled the method to cohere and strengthen. It was forcefully underlined by the enormous emphasis and attention given to the material forms of the photographs by their originators. One could say that their desire for the photographs to record the past in the present for the benefit of the future, was expressed in terms of longevity and accuracy, both values which were materially performed. For instance it was preferable to print in platinum (which doesn't fade), mount so textual and visual information could be apprehended at one glance and so forth. Central to my method was the assumption that 'things' are as they are for a reason – little things *matter*.

## WHAT SOURCES DID YOU USE AND HOW?

It was important not to over-reify 'the archive' but instead see it as processual, spread over space and time, a 35-year period constituted through both photographic shifts and wider social changes. As such, one might describe it as a synthetic or conglomerative archive. I worked on collections scattered across local museums, archives and local studies libraries. I identified some 74 surveys, although there are certain to be others which have eluded me. I studied 17 in detail, yielding a dataset of some 55,000 photographs and over 1000 active amateur photographers. The 17 were self-selecting because they left some form of discernable archival identity. Some had good paper trails but few or no images, others had bodies of photographs but little or no paper trail. Some had both. Consequently it was essential to have a sample large enough to accommodate and balance out these unevenesses. The photographs were always at the centre of the research and I saw the paper archive and the images as a productive and equal dialogue, not simply one illustrative of the other. The other central voice in this dialogue was the photographic press. I viewed this as a primary source because its activities constituted a classic 'print community' of the survey movement and were integrally tied up with its social and material practices. Through the photographic press one could not only pick up raw data about the surveys, but also develop an understanding of survey photography in relation to other photographic practices, and how wider debates, for instance, about preservation, civic duty or rational leisure were being articulated within photography itself.

*(Continued)*

## WHAT STRATEGY DID YOU DEVISE FOR MANAGING THIS VAST AMOUNT OF DATA?

From the outset I knew that the answer to my research questions lay in the patterning of the image archive and the clustering of images around specific tropes. With so many images, detailed analysis of specific images can obscure as much as it reveals. Where I did look at specific images it was as a result of an understanding of the patterning, representative of a class of images. So it was the last act of interpretation and analysis, not the first.

I drew on the work of literature scholar Franco Moretti who has asked similar sorts of questions about genre and patterning of the whole corpus of the nineteenth-century novel (not simply the classics of 'literature'). Thinking about patterning also confirmed the importance of material approaches, because the material qualities of the photographs constituted a constant pattern.

Working with the photographs, I took detailed notes and developed a keyword and abbreviation system which could then be searched. Mostly I was guided by the photographers' own descriptions of the images – what they wanted it to say, and took that as my analytical baseline. I did not undertake formal quantitative analysis, because one is always faced with the multiple meanings of photographs, but these approaches allowed a rough quantification of the data that allowed patterning to emerge.

I also developed a database for photographers using a simple Filemaker system. This enabled me to do basic analysis of the social make-up of the survey movement and, for instance, to make well-informed qualitative statements about the number of women involved.

## DID YOU EVER FEEL OVERWHELMED BY THE DATA?

I never felt overwhelmed because I saw the body of photographs as one large 'whole' to be addressed, which in a sense contained it, rather than a mass of disparate individual images which would indeed have been overwhelming. Further, I kept very clear methodological discipline and a strong sense of my research questions: that is, without prejudging the material, I knew exactly what I needed to know from it. There were some unexpected answers.

## WHAT WERE THE MAIN CHALLENGES?

There were research difficulties. Not only was locating material difficult, often it had lost its archival integrity (the original collection was fragmented or reorganised). Institutional practices and assumptions also did not necessarily accord easily with my key approaches. For instance, some archives will let users have only a few images at a time, but if one is looking at patterning it is necessary to look through great swathes of material at once and then go through it again, and again. Others suggested I look at the photographs on micro-fiche or occasionally on-line, which is not helpful for material approaches. In effect, archival practices, focusing on image content alone, can limit the ways in which the researcher might work with and thus think about photographs.

## WHAT ADVICE WOULD YOU OFFER OTHER RESEARCHERS PLANNING TO EMPLOY A MATERIAL APPROACH TO RESEARCH A LARGE COLLECTION?

It is essential to be very clear from the outset what kind of analysis you want to undertake and why. Photographs are so ubiquitous, so analytically slippery, they promise so much but often give very little. One has to be prepared to work with them, embrace their limitations and make that the point of analytical incision. On a practical level, it is also important to find a way that works for you – keywords, coding – that enables you to retrieve not only single images but to assess the pattern of material. Working materially also requires one to really look properly and think beyond the images into the complex social and cultural spaces that photographs inhabit. This isn't simply a matter of 'looking at material in context' because that begs the question what is context? – it is the first step in interpretation, and too often rigid adherence to a limited concept of context can drain other possible approaches and meanings from photographs. In the final analysis photographs are not only 'of' things, they are things that are good to think with.

# Exploring the physical dimensions of people's relationship with photos

People act on photos in a host of ways; they arrange them in albums, draw or paint over them (Pinney 1997), combine them with lockets of hair to make photo-hair jewellery (Batchen 2004) and cut them up to produce collages (Di Bello 2007). A material approach is key to understanding the value and meaning of these photo-objects and the practices around them; why and how are they made in particular ways, what do people do with these things? This type of research typically involves in-depth study of specific photo-objects in the context of the lives of the people who create and use them; the physical dimensions of production and use are to the fore. To illustrate this way of approaching photos I consider Di Bello's study of a practice that was popular amongst elite women in late nineteenth-century England: the creation of photocollage albums. Di Bello sought to discover the meaning and significance of this practice. She stresses the importance of researching in detail the physical aspects of making and using these albums. Touch is a central consideration, so before considering Di Bello's research I will explain its importance.

## Touching photos

Touch is frequently overlooked in studies of photographs because of what Jonathan Crary calls the 'subsumption of the tactile within the optical' (cited by Schwartz 2004: 19). The haptic is an important dimension of the material presentation of a photo with implications for how photos are used and the meanings and value attached to them. For example, touch is often pivotal to *how* we view a photo. A locket containing a photo has to be held and opened before the photo can be seen, and a camera-phone photo requires close-up viewing protected from the glare of direct sunlight. Writing about the daguerreotype[3], which was popular in the 1840s and 1850s, Joan Schwartz (2004: 18) explains that it had to be held in a particular way for the image to be visible:

> Because reflections from the mirrored surface made direct examination difficult, viewing involved a haptic experience: the case must be picked up, opened carefully, cradled in the hand and tilted slowly, right to left, back and forth until, at just the right angle, the image becomes clearly visible on the surface of the plate.

Gillian Rose (2004) argues that the haptic is also involved in practices of 'seeing'. When she interviewed mothers of small children, Rose observed that the mums touched and stroked the photos of their children as they looked at them. In his research on the use of photographs in memory objects such as lockets and hair jewellery, Geoffrey Batchen (2004) similarly demonstrates that touch is central to the experience of looking. Especially in remembrance photo-objects, photos are often presented in ways that enhance their touchability and other sensory engagements. For example, a locket containing a photo and inscription has to be touched, seen and, through the act of reading out the words, experienced orally. Similarly, the incorporation of a photo into a bracelet ensures that the photograph is touched when the bracelet is picked up and worn. These features are important to the role of photos in memory.

In contemporary studies, researchers can observe how people physically engage with photos, as Rose did when she interviewed mums (2004, 2010). Historical research is more challenging. However, in both historical and contemporary research an appreciation of the haptic can be gained from handling photo-objects (see Batchen 2004: 32), but touch needs to be historically contextualised and this is tricky as Di Bello discovered.

## Researching photocollage albums

Di Bello researches how Victorian women made and used photocollage albums (see Box 5.4). Though she focuses on albums created over a century ago, the haptic dimensions of materiality are central to her work. The challenge for Di Bello is, in part, that she cannot interview or watch these women engaging with their albums. Moreover, how an upper-class Victorian woman handled her photo album is difficult to appreciate or replicate from the standpoint of today and our particular ways of standing, sitting and moving. It was only when Di Bello donned a crinoline to look at the photo albums of Victorian ladies that she gained insights into the historically specific experience of looking at an album; this embodied experience was gendered and classed, a maid or an upper-class gentlemen would have had different experiences of touching these albums.

For insights into historically specific haptic encounters, Di Bello gleaned all she could from reading accounts in letters, diaries, popular magazines and novels. Knowledge of the environment and conditions in which photos were encountered facilitated an imaginative reconstruction of holding and using a photo-object, as where Di Bello acquired an intricate knowledge of the arrangement and etiquette of the drawing rooms in which women's albums were perused. The research also entailed intensive study of the visual and material content and presentation of the photocollages.

## BOX 5.4 VICTORIAN PHOTOCOLLAGE ALBUMS: AN INTERVIEW WITH PATRIZIA DI BELLO

**Figure 5.5** 'Lady Filmer in her Drawing Room' (1860s). Collection Paul F. Walter

*(Continued)*

## WHAT DID THESE ALBUMS TYPICALLY CONTAIN?

The albums I have been working on typically combine cut-out photographs, usually cartes de visite (small photographic postcards) portraits, into drawn or painted scenarios, sometimes plausible ones – people in a drawing room – sometimes fantastic – people thrown together in a jar labelled 'Mixed Pickles', being poked at by a man holding a long pickle fork. I am not sure how 'typical' they were, but in the 1860s to 1870s it was fashionable amongst elite women to make these photocollage albums.

## WHAT QUESTIONS DID YOU SEEK TO ANSWER?

I was interested in what they meant, individually and socially. I was also interested in trying to analyse them with the close attention to details, both material and semiotic, normally used to discuss important works, those deemed to be 'of art' – I had in mind, for example, the enormous attention to detail used to discuss Picasso's collages.

## WHAT SOURCES DID YOU USE?

I initially looked for 'private' evidence – diaries or letters that would illuminate what women thought they were doing when making these albums, or explicit instruction manuals as to how to make them – I didn't find anything, and then I realised that it was the wrong thing to be looking for. These albums were not the visual equivalent of private journals or secret diaries, but items for display, not just to family and friends but the wide range of acquaintances that would frequent an elite woman's drawing room. They were not family albums but 'Society' albums. At the same time, while related to the many decorative crafts elite women were supposed to excel at, photocollage was not a mainstream socially prescribed activity – it already had the subversive connotations of later, twentieth-century collage and photomontage.

## HOW DID YOU WORK WITH THE ALBUMS?

I did not have a strategy at the outset, it evolved as I went on. I decided that since these were meant to be seen by people who did not know the ladies who had created them, I would immerse myself in the popular culture of the time. I read women's magazines, trying to get plausible narratives of upper-class women's lives, especially the social aspects since many of the album pages seemed to represent or hint at social situations. I read 'silver fork' novels and almost all of Trollope's, also etiquette manuals, 'drawing room' books, and periodical pieces that mentioned albums or women and photography. At one point, I eagerly wore a crinoline and corset at a V&A hands-on exhibition, to understand how easy or not certain poses would be.

I was surprised by how passing remarks on photographs and albums, gathered from different sources, became fruitful when gathered together and analysed. It was, however, initially frustrating as I felt sure that a lot of album pages hinted at double entendre or implied gossip, but I could not quite work out the details. Of course, this is one of the ways in which these albums worked – outsiders would just see the craft, and perhaps find the arrangements beautiful or amusing. Insiders, however, would know the people and the gossip about them to 'get' the joke.

Take, for example, Lady Filmer's drawing room scene (Figure 5.5) – I knew from other album pages (which incidentally are scattered across collections as the album was split by the dealer) that the small man was her husband, and I was taking a leap of faith in the image by reading the central female figure by the table covered with albums, pot of glue and a paper knife as Lady Filmer. Well, her attention is not towards her husband, but towards the man on the other side of the table, who has been cut out from a larger-scaled photograph. This might have been an accident – she did not have a photograph in the same scale. But it seemed also a pointed choice – that, as in a medieval painting, size was used intentionally as an indication of importance.

It was only after research into celebrity carte-de-visite culture and its embrace by the Royal family that I realised the big man in the picture is actually the Prince of Wales. This was a great clue – as a Royal and man, much research has been done on the various gossip and scandals around him. Indeed, rumours of his 'flirtation' with Lady Filmer went all the way to Queen Victoria when the two were seen 'spooning at Ascot'. Flirtation went on to become not just the gossip-story told or suggested by the album pages, but the key to how women used photocollage not to create an explicit alternative or resistant language, but to flirt with meaning.

## HOW DID YOU EXPLORE TOUCH?

Making these albums was a tactile experience – obsessive touching was involved in the painstakingly painted or rendered details, careful cutting around people's bodies and faces – actually quite hard to do. But also looking at albums involves touching and the body – cradling them on one's lap, fingering the pages. Imagine doing it with someone else, this implies a certain physical intimacy that would not be required by looking at paintings together. This was understood at the time – looking at albums, even before photography, often featured in narratives as a way to flirt with someone. I realised it was important to imagine the actual gestures associated with making and viewing the albums. Cutting up heads of

*(Continued)*

people – even if it is to reposition them in painted bodies – creates a frisson of violence. Equally, 'arranging' people at dinner was one of the skills a hostess was supposed to have mastered until it looked effortless. Arranging them as photographs meant you could have exactly the right guests, doing the right things, with the right people, so arranging them on a page implied a degree of control one could only aspire to in real social life.

But also, touch itself was highly meaningful – that's why servants wore gloves or handed things over on a tray, to show that they had not touched them. A 'lady's touch was supposed to be particularly powerful, and to have the power to make things harmonious, tasteful and cleansed from the taint of the workplace and the money used to buy them. Imagine then the connotations of photographs of people as heads on stamps – this was not just a way of saying 'you are my queen/my king' (only the monarch appeared on stamps in the nineteenth century), but also turning people into cheap, casually handled, perhaps even licked, pieces of paper.

## HOW ARE YOUR RESEARCH STRATEGIES RELEVANT TO CONTEMPORARY STUDIES?

The insistence in the 1970s and 1980s on the importance of semiotics has made us focus on meaning, in opposition to modernist ideas about aesthetic values. It has also at times made writers on photography fail to notice the material and sensual properties of photographs as objects. In other words, photographs are not just images carrying meaning like a truck carries a container. The 'how', not just of their making but of their use, is also involved in making meaning. And a photograph's relationship with meaning is intrinsically flirtatious – we are never sure whether it means or does not mean what it seems to be saying or implying.

# Summary

Through an examination of four case studies, this chapter has introduced key strategies that researchers use to investigate what people and institutions do with photos, including strategies for: mapping conventions in domestic photography across cultures and time; tracing and explaining changes in the form and presentation of photos made for public consumption as they are used and reused at different historical moments; attending to, and deciphering the significance of, patterns in the materiality of photographs; probing the physical dimensions of the production and use of personal photographic objects, attending to the importance of touch. These types of research explain the role and significance of photographs in personal and social life and how people and institutions mobilise them for a range of purposes. They also provide valuable context to inform how we make sense of individual photos, as discussed in Chapters 2 and 3, and how we can work with the private collections, archives and online databases through which we locate these sources. The practices that underpin archives and digital databases are explored further in the next chapter.

## Notes

1  I am indebted to sociologist, Helene Snee, who has worked extensively on personal websites, especially blogs (2011), for insights into practical issues.
2  The term 'visual economy' refers to the historically specific political, social, economic and cultural conditions in which images are made, circulated, used, and 'appraised, interpreted, and assigned historical, scientific and aesthetic worth' (Poole 1997: 10). The term 'visual economy' is often preferred over 'visual culture' because the former engages with the unequal power relations within which images exist.
3  Photographic image made by a process invented by Louise-Jacques-Mandé Daguerre in 1839: 'It is a positive image on a metal plate with a mirror-like silver surface ... Each one is unique and fragile and needs to be protected by a padded case' (Wells 2000a: 47).

# 6

# Archives and Digital Resources

Photo research often involves archival work and, increasingly, the use of digital photographic databases. This chapter focuses on the opportunities and issues that researchers encounter when using these resources. It extends the discussion of photographic practices started in Chapter 5 by attending to the practices that shape archives and digital resources. Although the term 'archive' can refer to a coherent body of documents that may be physically dispersed, here I am concerned principally with the archive as a particular place – physical or virtual – where documents are kept. An important aspect of working with any collection of photographs is thinking about its biography and the implications of photographic practices for interpretation. Particularly when working with photographs that are pre-digital in origin, this exploration builds up in layers. You start by thinking about the original collection, for example a survey or a family photo collection: when was it started, by whom and for what purposes? What principles, policies and practices have shaped it? How did it evolve? If collections are archived, or digitalised, additional layers of practice need to be considered; these layers of practice are central to this chapter.

The chapter begins with a consideration of non-digital photographic archives and the practices that shape these. I then look at archival research and review specific issues that researchers encounter when working in archives and with large photo collections. Digital resources are the focus of the next part of this chapter, where I outline the contribution of digitalisation to photographic research and consider issues relating to the use of digital resources, and especially digital photographic archives.

## Archival research

Understanding archives is important for how researchers work with them. Alan Sekula (1986a: 156; see also 1986b) refers to the 'illusory neutrality of the archive'

**Figure 6.1**   050210 Archive Boxes 002. Mass Observation Archive, University of Sussex. Photograph by Annebella Pollen

because they seem merely to store materials and the politics of this process is often 'fudged or denied because ordering seems to be already there in the photos, i.e. the photos depict/interpret reality and the archive merely catalogues this'. The impression of neutrality is erroneous. Archives are not neutral depositories, they are necessarily selective and there are absences; a point conveyed graphically by Warren Neidich's artistic recreations of archival images (see Box 6.1). Reflecting on the politics of archiving is an important aspect of working with archival materials. For example, in his search of two United States federal government archives for images of race, gender and physical ability in American public schools, Eric Margolis (1999) notes that while photos of Native Indian children in federally funded boarding schools are over-represented, there are few photos of African-American, Latino and Asian pupils, or children with disabilities. Assimilation, order and harmony are made visible while cultural diversity, disorder and conflict are eliminated. As Margolis concludes: 'Collections made under conditions of racial segregation are themselves segregated and continue to reproduce images of hierarchy and dominance' (p. 7).

This point is echoed by Darren Newbury (2009: 306) as he reflects on apartheid photographs deposited in South African archives: 'it is not enough to see these as "images of" apartheid, they are literally images within apartheid' in that their existence, content and circulation has been shaped by the politics of apartheid. Newbury notes the explicit or implicit forms of censorship that have shaped the photographic archives including how, in the context of post-apartheid agendas, some photographers have chosen to archive only selected images that show their work in a positive light. He also notes the politics of what was deemed worthy of careful preservation. For instance, *Drum* magazine (see Chapter 5) was notable in the 1950s and 1960s and since for its visual reportage on life in apartheid South Africa, but until the mid-1980s photographs relating to the magazine were stashed, almost forgotten, in a barn. The difficulty is that it is not always possible to know what is absent from an archive, and even if you identify that certain types of photos are missing, it is not easy to ascertain why: were photos taken but not preserved or archived, or were they not taken? Margolis is optimistic that the web may make a wider selection of images available as people upload photos that were not previously deemed of sufficient worth to be archived, but there would still be the 'deficiencies of photography itself' in that 'many things were not photographed' (1999: 34).

The 'illusory neutrality of the archive' also arises at the level of photographic meaning. Archives, Sekula explains, are 'contradictory in character' (1986a: 156). On the one hand, the original photographic meanings are lost as photos are relocated to an archive from their original contexts and uses, such as when photos embedded in the life and history of a particular family are relocated to an archive and catalogued as 'domestic photographs'. On the other hand, meaning is reconfigured *within* the archive as photos are given captions and text and are classified, catalogued and, quite often, combined under a particular themed umbrella. New meanings are also generated by material practices in the archive as demonstrated by Elizabeth Edwards' (2002: 71) account of the biography of a set of ethnographic photos. Since 1884 Cambridge University Museum of Archaeology and Anthropology had collected images from travellers, scientists, explorers and missionaries, but in 1935–40 this archive changed the format within which these images were made available. Instead of a collection of photos of different sizes and shapes, printed on different types of paper and presented in diverse forms, a new set of standardised prints were made either by rephotographing the original photos or by making prints from the original negatives; all these 'prints were mounted on 20.5 cm × 25.5 cm grey cards and numbered, with area divisions, on the top left-hand corner in black ink ... the captions are filed separately typed on 7.5 cm × 12.5 cm cards.' These new photo-objects bear little relation to the original ones beyond the content of the image. Part of their history has been lost and this changes how the photos are viewed and understood. 'The standardized surfaces of the photographs and the unifying tonal range of the black and white glossy silver prints suggest uniformity, comparability' which reinforces the museum's classification of these photos as a cohesive set of images rather than a series of pictures produced for different purposes, by different groups and with different histories and meanings. Other material practices are also meaningful. For instance, photos encountered together in an archival box accrue meanings in part from their juxtaposition with one another (Edwards and Hart 2004b).

---

**BOX 6.1 RECONSTRUCTING THE 'VISUAL ARCHIVE'**

In *American History Reinvented*[1] (Neidich and Day 1989), artist Warren Neidich recreates a series of photographs of white American families to expose racism in the 'visual archive' (archive refers here to a coherent body of documents rather than a particular location). Though there were middle-class African-Americans and many black photographers in America between 1840 and 1900 (Willis 1994), the dominant visual memory of America is of white European-American people. There are few photographs of African-Americans in circulation and these typically portray black people in supporting roles as the servants and staff of white Americans. As Lynda Day (Neidich and Day 1989: 26) suggests, 'the shape of the visual archive must make a powerful and lasting impression on our view of a particular time, or of the participation of a particular group of people in that moment'. Neidich's photographs challenge this view of history and make visible the constructedness of the photographic images that contribute to collective memory (shared popular accounts). Neidich achieves these two objectives through a set of paired photographs. On the left-hand side of each diptych, he reconstructs a mid-nineteenth century photograph of some aspect of American cultural life, substituting black subjects for white and showing African-Americans as comfortably middle class: though this is consistent with written records it is inconsistent with shared visualisations of the past. The right-hand side of each diptych features a photo that is almost a mirror image of the left-hand side. Here Neidich produces photographs that, viewed in relation to the left-hand side, reveal how edits – cropping, retouching, mirror imaging – can alter an image to convey a different impression from the original. Neidich demonstrates how images he has made of middle-class African-Americans taking a prominent role in public life alongside white Americans can be altered to remove or marginalise African-Americans and suggest they are of lowly status. In doing this, Neidich raises questions about the construction of the photographs that dominate in the visual archive.

---

It is important that you factor the archive in to your analysis; you need to be wary of the archive's impression of innocence and reflect on what kinds of histories are preserved, reworked or obscured in it. Doing this requires consideration of what is and is not in the archive and why. Identifying and explaining the absences and presences involves attending to the history, purpose, philosophy and practices of the archive, and pinpointing gaps in the archive by drawing on non-photographic sources on social life. Factoring the archive into your analysis also requires attention to how meanings are suggested by being part of an archive, by the organisation of the archive and the specific practices through which photos are made available. Recently, some researchers have developed 'participatory archives' in which research participants are involved in coding and archiving the photographic data generated from research in their communities (Mitchell 2011). If using these archives, or even family collections, you still need to reflect on the politics and practices of archiving.

Although you need to be mindful of the politics of archiving it is important to avoid a simplistic and determinist model of the archive and its effects. Attending to how institutions mobilise meanings should alert researchers to the ways meanings are suggested, often quite powerfully, but this should not blind us to the possibility of resisting, rejecting or seeing beyond these meanings to other interpretations. Additionally, researchers need to be wary of homogenising archives; they cannot be understood simply as the product of a universal and unchanging set of policies and practices. Archives are built over time and shaped by shifting agendas, resources and practices that create uneven results; as Edwards (2001: 7) puts it, it is useful to recognise the 'micro-intentions, as much as a universalizing desire' in the creation of archives.

I now consider some aspects of doing archival research and of factoring the archive in to your analysis.

## Doing archival research

Doing archival research requires reflection on archival practices. In some instances, how photos are archived is also a focus of research. This is the case in Annebella Pollen's study of amateur photographs produced initially for submission to a UK charity event 'One Day for Life' (ODfL) in 1987 and subsequently deposited in the Mass Observation Archive (see Box 6.2). Pollen was interested in how 'amateur photography might be described, historicised and evaluated, both in the past and in the present'. But rather than approach the ODfL photographs as fixed in one point of time, and try to grasp what they might mean by interpreting the images, Pollen approached the photos as objects that are made and circulated and which accrue different meanings as they are used and reused. Drawing on Ariella Azoulay (2008), Pollen describes her approach as 'watching' photos as they are used and reused rather than simply fixating on the images and 'looking' at them.

---

**BOX 6.2   RESEARCHING THE ONE DAY FOR LIFE PROJECT: AN INTERVIEW WITH ANNEBELLA POLLEN**

**WHAT IS THE ODfL PROJECT?**

One Day for Life (ODfL) was an ambitious fundraising endeavour organised in the 1980s by The Search 88 Cancer Trust. 'Ordinary people everywhere' were

---

**Figure 6.2** Open Box. Photograph by Annebella Pollen

asked to take a photograph of everyday life in Britain on 14 August 1987, accompanied by a pound donation per print, in order to raise money for charity and to compete to be published. Selection panels – first regional camera clubs, and later professional and 'celebrity' photographers – chose 'winners' from the c.55,000 submissions and these 350 were published as a bestselling book, *One Day for Life: Photographs by the People of Britain, Taken on a Single Day* (Search 88: 1987). All the photographs were subsequently deposited in the Mass Observation Archive (MOA) at the University of Sussex.

*(Continued)*

## HOW DID YOU START?

I was concerned to trace the patterns and tropes that might emerge from engagement with the material as a whole, rather than focusing on exceptional, singular images. This meant looking at every photograph in the archive and taking detailed notes about their physical, material and visual properties. In this way, I plotted the boundaries of the archive's 'image repertoire' (Frosh 2003). Although participants were able to take a photograph of anything, subjects and styles recurred across the archive. These themes provided points of crystallisation for my analysis.

## ALTHOUGH YOU PLOTTED MAJOR THEMES IN CONTENT, YOUR RESEARCH DID NOT PIGEONHOLE PHOTOS ON THE BASIS OF WHAT THEY DEPICTED. INSTEAD YOU FOCUSED ON PHOTOS AS OBJECTS WHICH ACCRUE DIFFERENT MEANINGS AS THEY ARE MADE, USED AND REUSED. WHY WAS THIS?

I was aware that the photographs had performed different functions at different stages of their existence. Although it was important to consider the original intentions behind the making and submission of photographs, I saw this as just one part of their potential meaning in a larger 'cultural biography' (Kopytoff 1986). It was relevant, then, to look at the journeys that the photographs have taken, and the meanings that they have acquired along the way. Insofar as this is traceable – and in many cases, the problem is that it isn't – the context, uses and expectations made of photographs proves a more illuminating means of ascertaining value than the interpretation of their formal content. It demands a substantial investment of time, but can result in the enrichment and remobilisation of what might otherwise be reduced to a mass of mute, still images.

## WHAT STRATEGY DID YOU DEVISE TO WORK WITH ALL THESE PHOTOS?

As well as the painstaking process of looking at every photograph in the archive, I worked on selected samples. I assembled four groups of photographs corresponding to each of the four stages in the ODfL project's layered filtration system, and logged these in databases. These included the entire list of published winners (350 photographs), the shortlist of finalists (c.700 photographs), and a quarter of the camera-club 'longlist' (c.1,000). As a vertical incision into the largest part of the archive – the 'rejected' photographs, which remain unsorted – I chose one archival box at random (c.1,000 photographs) by drawing numbers from a hat. Into these four databases, for the purposes of cross-comparison, I logged the name, address and gender of the photographers; a short description of the photograph;

any inscriptions on the reverse, including title and marks made in the judgement process; plus further notes on format, location, condition, publication etc. These databases provided an opportunity for fine-grained analysis. As there is scant supporting information in the archive about who took part in ODfL and how, I was able to use these systems to ascertain information about the gender demographic of participants (largely female) and to note patterns in submissions. Although these databases helped me to ascertain stylistic and subject tropes across the samples, I did not pursue a quantitative typological analysis of the ODfL photographs; what a photograph might appear to be 'of' was not an adequate measure of what it was 'about' or 'for'.

## WHAT SOURCES HELPED YOU EXPLORE SUBSEQUENT USES AND MEANINGS?

To reconstitute the various meanings accumulated through use and reuse, I researched ODfL's history. This involved consulting newspaper and television archives of the period, and contacting people involved in its original phase. I sent questionnaires to around 400 participants in the competition (and received 135 responses, of which I interviewed around 20). Additionally, I contacted ODfL organisers, judges and publishers, as well as those who had been involved in archiving, curating and classifying the photographs since their arrival at the MOA.

## ONE LAYER OF MEANING YOU EXPLORED WAS HOW THE ODfL ORGANISERS EVALUATED THE PHOTOS. HOW DID YOU TRACE THIS?

Only a minority of the photographs have been sorted and the original organising structure of the project is thus still evident in the archival order, which is made up of the 'rejected' majority; the 10% selected as a 'longlist' by camera clubs; the shortlist made by the professionals, and the final winners chosen by the publishers. Each show the commercial and aesthetic processes of stratification and thus illuminate the value judgements applied to amateur photography.

## THROUGHOUT YOUR RESEARCH YOU WERE CONCERNED 'TO LOOK BEYOND WHAT THE PHOTOGRAPHS ARE "OF" TO WHAT THEY ARE EXPECTED TO "DO"'. HOW DID YOU RESEARCH THIS FROM THE PERSPECTIVES OF THE PEOPLE THAT SUBMITTED THE PHOTOS TO ODfL?

In questionnaire and interview, participants were asked to describe their photograph, its significance, its relation to ODfL and its typicality in terms of their photographic practice. Participants were also asked to classify their photography in 1987, and to

*(Continued)*

provide details about other photography events that they participated in. The rich responses at both points in time illuminated the diverse motivations and purposes ascribed to photographs that might appear to be superficially similar in the archive. For many participants, the significance of the photograph lay beyond the frame, in the reasons for taking part, or in the personal stories attached to the photographs that are not visible on the surface of the print. Thus, photographs of apparently banal or 'typically amateur' subjects such as kittens, cottages and sunsets could carry complex and hidden subtexts, sometimes in relation to illness and death. Entered into a national photography competition in aid of cancer charities, personal photographs could make public statements, and variously contest political identities, create memorials for lost loved ones, compete aesthetically, perform 'everydayness', and make history.

Pollen's account highlights some of the practical issues that researchers encounter when using archival collections. Though I do not discuss archival research in general as other texts do this (e.g. Gidley 2004; Hill 1993), it is useful to review specific issues that confront the researcher who uses archives or who works with non-archived large photo collections. Drawing on insights from Pollen and studies discussed in Chapter 5, I suggest the following issues are particularly pertinent when doing research with photos.

## Locating photographic materials

Photo researchers need to be persistent and resourceful in locating sources; unless an archive is primarily photographic it tends not to be organised to facilitate the location of photographic evidence. It is therefore important to factor in time to find sources.

## What you can look at

Researchers often encounter constraints on how they work with photographs. Sometimes photos are available only on microfiche or online. This limits what you can see and is particularly frustrating if you adopt a material approach which requires attention to the physical characteristics of photos such as their size, presentation and signs of use (see Chapter 2). But even where photos are available for scrutiny it is not always possible to see the back as they can be pasted into albums or displayed so the rear is not visible. Some archives let users have only a few images at a time which, as Edwards (Chapter 5) laments, is problematic if you are interested in tracing patterns of practice or in doing longitudinal comparative image analysis. When planning research it is useful to check what forms photographs are available in and the implications for what you can do with them.

## Strategy

You need a clear strategy for working with large collections of photos as it is easy to be overwhelmed by visual data. Researchers utilise various strategies, often in combination, depending on their research questions and objectives.

Looking at a whole collection is not always possible or even necessary. For example, in her study of the photographic survey movement in England, Edwards (see Box 5.3) looked at 17 surveys yielding a dataset of roughly 55,000 photographs. Such a vast number of photos could easily be overwhelming, but it was not necessary to look at all the photos in detail because the answer to Edwards's research questions lay in identifying themes in photographic content, format and presentation: 'With so many images, detailed analysis of specific images can obscure as much as it reveals.' In other instances, looking at everything in a collection is both feasible and instructive.

Alongside an overview of an entire collection, researchers often want to undertake more detailed and complex analyses that necessitate working with fewer photos. This is particularly the case where the researcher is interested in photographic practices, materiality and the complexities of meaning. What to research in detail can be decided using standard sampling procedures (e.g. Pollen, Box 6.2). Another strategy is to identify examples of typical and atypical photos, this involves prior emersion in the field so as to know what is and is not usual (e.g. Newbury, Box 5.2). In a study of two Japanese-American family photo collections and the cultural practices that shaped them, Richard Chalfen and Lyne Horiuchi overviewed the collections and then adopted a case study approach, focusing on individual albums (Box 5.1).

## Keeping track of photos

Keeping track of material is essential when working with large collections. Where photos are in magazines or newspapers, the date and page numbers provide an obvious means of identification and record. Archival reference details are also valuable for keeping track of photos. Especially when working with family archives, collections might not have a ready-made identification and in these cases you need to devise your own. With all photos it is helpful to keep a record of basic details (what is salient will depend on your project) but particularly with large numbers of photos it can be helpful to also have a quick and simple reference system. You could simply number photos, but it is usually better to devise a system that corresponds to the main concerns of your research. This brings me to a related practical issue, if you are working with photos you have accumulated you can mark the photos with your identification system, but this is not usually possible when working with other people's photos. Making copies of collections, or parts of them, and marking these up is useful if you want to work closely with photo materials, it is also helpful if doing photo-elicitation with large photo collections.

## Revisiting photographic data

To work with large collections requires thought about the practical issues of how to revisit photographs for the purposes of analysis. In his research on South African photography, Newbury digitally photographed images and organised them in small albums so he 'had an easy at-hand set of visual references that I could consult as I was writing and thinking' (Box 5.2). In their study of Japanese-American photo collections, Chalfen and Horiuchi produced facsimiles of people's albums (Box 5.1).

# Digitalisation

Digital technologies and the web have transformed how researchers work with photos. In this section I reflect briefly on the contribution of digital photography to research before considering issues relating to the use of digital photographic resources.

## The contributions of digital photography

Digital photography has transformed access to images and what researchers can do with photos for the purposes of analysis and presentation. I comment briefly on each of these points.

Photographic images are now increasingly easy to search for, access and repeatedly revisit from the comfort of your own desk; this saves time, money and effort. Pre-digitalisation, many important photograph collections were too disorganised or dispersed to be easily accessible and some photographs were too fragile to be studied, even by researchers working on site (Miller 2007). While digitalisation has facilitated wider and easier access to images, it has also changed how researchers use archives and lessened the time spent in them. Instead of taking notes or making poor quality but expensive photocopies, it is often possible to make your own digital images for scrutiny at a later stage.

Digitalisation and related software has had a tremendous impact on comparative photo analysis: 'Software provides researchers with capabilities for comparison of images that were previously extremely difficult if not impossible using traditional magnification and photographic techniques' (Margolis and Rowe 2011: 342; for a graphic example, see Klett 2011). Digitalisation has also changed how you can work with individual images. Being able to enlarge and enhance images enables you to identify details and study them more closely. It can also facilitate a fresh perspective on photographs generated in a project and change how you view familiar public and personal photos. Viewing enlarged versions of personal photos or ones taken for a project also opens up new ways of seeing for interviewees. You also have innumerable opportunities to mark up images you have generated or downloaded from archives, which can facilitate analysis but also playful strategies as discussed in Chapters 1 and 3.

The use of digital technologies to present academic research is still in its infancy, but as seen in Chapter 3 only modest skills are necessary to create interesting visual representations of research. With more advanced skills and resources the presentational possibilities include the interactive (Coover 2011; Klett 2011).

# Digital photographic resources

Digital photographic resources are expanding at a phenomenal rate due to public and commercial digitalisation projects and the uploading of old and new personal photos. These photographic resources vary tremendously; there is a huge difference between an image found through Google Images or Flikr, and one found through a digitalised collection produced by a small archive or from a funded database for academic research. Convenience and the excitement of easily locating photos can lead to complacency in how we treat these images, but it is essential that researchers interrogate digital sources critically. You need to ask yourself: is this image genuine? How has it got here? Who took it, when and why? Is it typical or atypical? In the following I discuss key practices that shape digital photographic archives that have implications for how researchers use and interpret the images they find: selectivity; descriptions; search and viewing facilities; presentation. To illustrate my points I use the example of the International Mission Photography Archive (IMPA), which makes available images from Protestant and Catholic missionary collections held at several centres in Europe and North America. The IMPA is a recently created and well-designed digital resource, the result of a project jointly undertaken by the Centre for Religion and Civic Culture and the Digital Archive at the University of Southern California.[2]

## Selectivity

Most digital collections represent a selection of images from a larger collection/ archive or set of collections. You need to ask: how were these images selected? Who selected them? What criteria were used? What audiences and purposes were to the fore in informing these choices? Public databases rarely provide this information and so it is difficult, and sometimes impossible, to ascertain the authenticity and status of the photos, how they were chosen and from what pool of images. Fortunately, well-resourced research databases tend to provide clear accounts of this process. The IMPA website, for example, presents a clear account of the IMPA's practice and this can inform use of the resource. The IMPA is partial and consists of layers of selection; only certain photos from specially chosen archives are made available. The selection criteria are varied – the skills of staff, 'representative samples' (how are representative samples decided?), and a desire to 'include the "thickest" series of pictures, such as those produced by a particularly prolific and skilled photographer or identified with a particularly important place, cast of characters, or set of historical events.' Fundamentally, the selections of the IMPA, as of equivalent digital archives, are guided by a realist approach to the image with a focus on the type of information that the photo can offer about the subject depicted.

## Description

How researchers interpret a photo is shaped partly by how it is described through caption and metadata. Metadata provides information about a photo, for instance, when and where it was taken and by whom. As with all descriptions you need to consider the criteria determining these accounts. What is and is not worth noting? Is the original context acknowledged? Returning to the IMPA example, we see that it provides information about the content of the photo, its production and accompanying textual information (captions, descriptions and associated documents). But the quantity and quality is uneven and some photos have only the barest details recorded. As Toni Weller (interview; see also Weller 2012) points out, high-profile archives employ archivists and historians to produce metadata, but this practice is not universal and standards vary tremendously so it is always necessary to consider the credentials of the person or organisation providing this data. The IMPA has reached an interesting compromise between the authority of the expert and knowledge possessed by the public. It is hoped that users of the website will contribute information but the curator will decide whether or not to incorporate it into the database.

## Facilities to use, search and view

An important point is how researchers can use, search and see photographs in online digital databases. Working with digital databases you need to consider how the database is designed – the interface, search and display facilities (e.g. keywords for searching and linking, bookmarking, themed galleries and facilities to create a personal photo gallery) – because design features shape what you can find and how you can engage with photographic data. The technical side of databases (interface, search facilities etc.) are not usually designed by historians or social scientists, although well-resourced research databases are increasingly the product of collaborative work (Weller interview).

A related issue is how the search facility works. Does it pick up only index categories or does it search captions and metadata too? As always, you need to find the right search terms otherwise you may not find what you are looking for; you cannot assume a photo is not there just because you cannot find it. Searching for photos is also very different from searching for text (Weller interview). It is increasingly possible when working with text online to search for the occurrence of a word or phrase, not just in the heading or metadata, but in the body of the text. Such a facility is not possible with photos and the researcher has to rely on a textual account of the image. There is typically a wealth of visual details in a photo and it is not usually possible to describe them all. What is deemed worthy of description will depend on the knowledge and skills of the person who inputs this data and the classification criteria that are used.

Serendipity has always been an important element in research but, according to Weller (interview), this is less likely to occur when working with digital resources. When working with hard copies of source materials – family albums, magazines etc. – the eye scans a host of material as you flick through to find your photos and unexpected material can catch the eye. As digital databases have search facilities this type of scanning is not usually undertaken although, particularly in well-designed sites and where thumbnail photos are available, search keys can bring up surprising images.

Another search issue is the opportunities increasingly available to work across different collections. Discussing the United States National Archives and Records Administration and the 'American Memory' archive created by the Library of Congress 'to document the American experience',[3] Margolis notes that the independent collections that make up these two archives are losing their distinctive identities and becoming 'submerged in the digital archive. Even though each image retains its citation and whatever additional supporting data exists, the fact that one can search across collections by topic begins a process of homogenization' (1999: 10–11; see also Sassoon 2004). On a practical level, researchers need to be wary that it is easy to lose sight of the different sources of their images.

**Figure 6.3**   Tembu women with festive headdresses, Baziya, South Africa East, photographer: Wilhelm Blohm. Moravian Archives Herrnhut, LBS.9902 [IMPA –HRN-BOX-SAO-7-09902]

## Presentation

Presentation also raises interesting issues as digitalisation mediates the encounter with each photo. What does the presentation reveal but also obscure or hide from sight? What aspects of the photo are not represented when a photo is presented solely as a visual medium? The IMPA database is particularly sophisticated and has digitalised not just the images but the photographs 'as encountered visually in the archive' – the imperfections on the print, visible traces of use, writing on or around the image, and the immediate framing such as the borders of the print, their torn edges and sometimes their mounts (see Figure 6.3). Additionally, though the photos are usually black and white, the scanning is done in colour to reveal subtleties of tones and shades; a calibrating colour bar is featured along the left-hand side of each image. But even in the IMPA collection there are limits to what researchers can 'see'; for example, you cannot see what is on the back of a photo or the arrangement of several photos on a page of an album or, in most cases, the mounts used to display the photos in the original presentational forms. As Joanna Sassoon (2004: 188) argues, digitalisation results in the 'translation' of a photograph from material to digital form. This process 'emphasises the aesthetic qualities and image content of a photograph' but 'obscures' observable physical clues that researchers often use to make sense of photographs (p. 191).

Digitalisation practices limit the kinds of questions you can explore, especially if you are interested in photographic practices and photos as objects with biographies. Jon Miller (2007: 90) is overly optimistic when he claims that 'These visual collections can be used in ways that are limited only by the curiosity of the researchers who visit the website'. An inspection of the unique photographic resources at the Women's Library is a useful reminder of the benefits but also the limitations of digitalisation and the importance, where possible, of visiting archives and reflecting on the multi-dimensionality of photographic sources (see Box 6.3).

## BOX 6.3   THE WOMEN'S LIBRARY*

**Figure 6.4**   Women's Social and Political Union photographic postcard album (7JCC/0/1). © The Women's Library

The Women's Library houses the most extensive collection of women's history in the UK. The collection includes textual, visual and material resources, including photographs. To date, the archive and museum collections have identified and catalogued over 7,500 photographs, a number that continues to rise. The postcard collection is of a similar size and contains many 'photographic' cards. Like many libraries and archives it is gradually digitalising its holdings to offer easier and wider access. Digitalisation is ongoing, as is the pursuit of improved ways of presenting digital resources.

When to work online and offline, is an important question when using archival resources such as The Women's Library. Although it is sometimes tempting to rely on digital resources, these are rarely representative of the entirety of large collections, not least because libraries and museums need copyright clearance for each digitalised image made available through a publicly accessible catalogue (copyright expires 70 years after the date of the death of the artist or photographer, see Chapter 10). Moreover, the richness, and sometimes the limitations, of archival materials are often invisible, as the following three examples illustrate.

## MILLICENT FAWCETT'S COPY OF THE CONCENTRATION CAMPS COMMISSION REPORT (1902) (7MGF/G/1)

Fawcett led this commission which was instructed during the Boer War (1899–1901) 'to inquire into conditions in concentration camps in South Africa to ascertain how English charitable funds could best be spent'. Fawcett's copy of the report is in the form of a large and heavy volume that was specially made and bound in leather, probably at Fawcett's request and expense, and which includes pages from the official report interspersed with leaves of plain paper. On most of the plain sheets Fawcett affixed photos with captions, also other textual commentary and one poem. A letter from the Secretary of State, thanking Fawcett for her work, is copied out and inserted at the end of the report. This volume is a personalised record of the camps and Fawcett's experiences while serving on the Commission.

The volume is not digitalised, although some photos are digitally available but removed from their visual and material context. Although it is conceivable that the volume is digitalised in future, the materiality would be difficult to appreciate fully. The volume is evidence of photographic practices amongst affluent women at the turn of the twentieth century. Moreover the visual and material relationships between the photos, text and official report provide fascinating insights into Fawcett's experiences of, and views on, the camps, also her experiences of undertaking the enquiry in South Africa. Many of the photos are poor quality or seemingly uninteresting and not priorities for digitalisation, but looked at in the context of the page and volume, and other photos and texts, they are illuminating.

## WSPU PHOTOGRAPHIC POSTCARD ALBUM (7JCC/0/1)

The second example is an album intended to display photographic postcards of suffrage campaigners (see Figure 6.4). The front of this 8 × 12 inch green album is impressed with one of the logos of the Women's Social and Political Union (WSPU) under which, inset in silver script, is the word 'Postcards'. Originally it was owned by suffragette Grace Roe (1885–1979), before being given to feminist Jill Craigie (1911–99) and subsequently donated to The Women's Library in 2007 by her husband Michael Foot.

This album embodies both the pleasures and frustrations of archival work with photos. The WSPU had an early appreciation of the value of photography (Crawford 1999; Tickner 1988) and this now rare postcard album is testament to

*(Continued)*

this and the photographic practices of at least some of the WSPU's supporters. However, one frustration is that for preservation purposes the postcards were removed from the album and are now displayed in plastic sleeves. Fortunately, the postcards were removed in the order that they were held in the album, though some had already fallen out or were tucked in rather than fixed, and they have been carefully numbered to express this order so the Library can recreate the album if required. The empty album is also enigmatic in another way. On various pages there are headings written by Roe, indicating how she organised her postcards, but Craigie had a different agenda and she scrubbed out these headings, reordered the postcards and added her own collection. We can only surmise how the postcards were arranged originally, but the archaeology of the album is a tantalising testament to its biography and shifting place in suffrage history. This complex history eludes an online database.

**Figure 6.5**   Cartes de Visites. © The Women's Library

---

### CARTES DE VISITE (3AMS/G)

My third example is from The Women's Library's extensive collection of cartes de visite used by Josephine Butler and the Association for Moral and Social Hygiene, some of which are accessible online (see Figure 6.5). While the library's database shows the photographs on the front of the 3 × 2 inch cards, what it does not convey is their place in social life. Encountering the cartes in the archive, as presented in see-through plastic sleeves, one is struck by their size and the ease with which they would fit into the hand. Looking at the rear of the cartes reveals the often elaborate advertising and, in some cases, the scribbles that locate these objects in everyday interactions: 'acknowledge receipt of stamps'.

*From January 2013 The Women's Library is housed in the Lionel Robbins Building at the London School of Economics.

---

## Summary

Researchers need to reflect on what kinds of histories are preserved, reworked and obscured in archives and online photographic databases. In this chapter I have explained that layers of practice shape archives and digital databases. These practices have implications for how you can use archives; you need to think about what is present and absent and reflect on how archival practices – for example, of classification and presentation – confer meanings on photos. Doing archival research can be exciting but also daunting and I discuss five practical issues: locating photos; checking how photos are available – online, in plastic sleeves, loose – and the implications for what you can do with them; devising strategies to manage large quantities of photos; keeping track of the photos you look at; and working out how you can revisit photographs, particularly at the analysis stage of your research. Many photos are now available in digital form and researchers need to treat these resources critically, attending to how images are selected for inclusion in online databases, how they are described, the facilities available for searching and viewing images and modes of presentation. Where feasible, I suggest that it is useful to visit the archives where your images are deposited and engage with the materiality of your photographic sources to ascertain what you may miss by relying solely on digital images.

## Notes

1  Images can be viewed at http://americanhistoryreinvented.com/main.html
2  See http://crcc.usc.edu/initiatives/impa/. Last accessed 10 August 2012.
3  'American Memory' is composed of materials from the collections of the Library of Congress and other institutions, it documents 'historical events, people, places, and ideas that continue to shape America, serving the public as a resource for education and lifelong learning', see http://memory.loc.gov/ammem/about/index.html

# 7
# Generating Photos: Researchers

This chapter examines how researchers can generate their own photos as part of a research project. Taking photos is an established practice in studies of landscape and material culture, also ethnography where 'a camera has been an almost mandatory element in the "tool kit" for research for several generations' (Pink 2007: 65). Heightened interest in visual methods is, however, likely to create a wider interest in taking research photos. Taking photos can be integral to research in three main ways. First, researchers can take photos to generate visual data. Second, photos are taken to facilitate interviews; they are a tool for generating data (see Chapter 9). Often these two purposes are intertwined as photos are taken to produce visual materials, some or all of which is then discussed in a photo-elicitation interview. Third, photos are taken as an aide-memoire; in ethnographic research they may be incorporated into a research diary.

This chapter focuses on researchers taking photos to explore aspects of social life and material culture in the past and over time; it engages with process, change and continuity. To provide a foundation for this discussion I begin by introducing general points about researcher-generated photography, this includes: why researchers take photos; key variations in approaches to research photography; technical considerations; and what you need to think about, and do, when undertaking analysis of your photos. Following this general discussion, I look in detail at specific methods: documentation, making photos for use in interviews, and generating and sometimes collecting photos for the purposes of overtime comparisons. It is not possible to address all methods in which the researcher takes photographs, for example photo diaries (Chaplin 1994, 2004, 2011).

## Why do researchers take photos?

It is useful to start by identifying and evaluating the reasons researchers take photos and whether this is always a productive research strategy.

One advantage of taking photographs is that the researcher can easily and quickly produce a visual account of what they are researching. This is useful if the focus of the research is changing or moving, or visible for only a short time because it is fleeting or access is restricted as in archived materials. For instance, Historian Karen Harvey takes photos:

> so I have a record of sources that I cannot copy and because photos allow me to see things that I sometimes cannot see with the naked eye: this is especially true of objects and images, where with good quality images I can zoom in to small details that my eye missed when confronted with the real thing. (Personal correspondence)

Additionally, in studies of change 'visual changes can be very subtle or so complex that they are virtually impossible to document adequately without the use of a camera, which permits "freezing" a scene in extraordinary detail' (Rieger 1996: 6). I use the word 'account' because, as discussed in Chapter 1, photos, including those generated by the researcher, are constructions offering particular versions of people, things, places and practices. These visual accounts are not objective or complete, but they do offer a wealth of information that can be analysed fruitfully if the photo's construction is kept in mind. Because visual accounts are always partial, it is important to also produce a verbal or written record of the research/fieldwork experience and to note how photos were taken, points I will return to.

Photos produce a visual account of the look of people, places, things and practices. They are also generative in that, through accident or design, images can suggest new ways of seeing and thinking about a topic (see also Chapter 3). Viewing a two-dimensional representation of what is typically encountered in three dimensions, or seeing what is usually invisible to the eye or missed, can be illuminating. In this context, one of the advantages of photos is that they record in excess of what is required; there is typically more in a photo than intended by the photographer. Incidental visual information can stimulate new ideas and research questions. For instance, in a study of residential care for the elderly, the background details in photos unexpectedly pointed to 'the social nature of corridors as "inner streets" within the homes' (Rolph et al. 2009: 437).

Photos are also widely valued for capturing the 'texture' (Latham 2004: 129) and feel of places. Although photos undoubtedly convey a sense of place, it is debatable whether this can always be achieved more effectively with photographs than with words. Unless a researcher is a skilled photographer, it can be difficult to capture the researcher's experience of the atmosphere of a place; it takes considerable technical skill to produce in a photograph what can be observed or felt in the research setting. Moreover, photographs can convey a different impression of a research scene to that experienced and possibly remembered by the researcher. How many of us have been disappointed by the feel of our holiday photos because the light and colours are not as we remember them?

Another advantage of taking photos is that they enable researchers to revisit data at later stages in a project and to discover new details or follow up fresh ideas and questions. At the analysis stage of a study of gentrification, Charles Suchar (1997: 52) found that photographs facilitated a 'closer link' between what he had experienced and observed in the field and his abstract conceptualising: 'The photographs ... allow for a preciseness of recall which give the resultant conceptualizations an enhanced richness of texture and detail.'

Photography is clearly useful in studies that explore visual phenomena, such as aspects of personal style or the appearance of homes and localities, all of which relate to complex social, economic and cultural processes. It is also valued as a means to trace and explore change, indeed, visual phenomena are often studied explicitly as indicators of social and economic change. However, as Jon Rieger (1996: 5) explains, the relationship between visual change and social change is complex. For instance, following a flood, the immediate effects of change may be visible – damaged homes – but not the long-term structural consequences such as the relocation of households. Visual change can also lag behind social change, as in the effects of closing a large local business where the resulting unemployment and decline in the community may not be visible for some time. The strength of the relationship between visual change and social change also varies: 'Some visual changes seem to have little social significance, and there are social changes that may not have very obvious or prominent visual manifestations.'

So far I have considered reasons why researchers take photos, but is this always a valuable addition to a research design? Ask yourself the following questions: (1) is what you want to photograph accessible to you and your camera; (2) is it ethical to take photographs; (3) do you possess, or can you develop, the necessary technical skills to make suitable photographs for the purposes of addressing your research questions; (4) what is the point of taking photos given your research questions? This last question involves thinking about whether there are visual dimensions to what you are interested in and whether these visual aspects are significant for addressing your research questions. If you plan to take photos for use in interviews then consider why it is preferable to use photos you have taken rather than found ones or those generated by your research participants.

# Approaches to generating photos

There has been much discussion about how to classify different approaches to taking photos. I look at four aspects that are particularly important:

- How are photographs perceived by the researcher?
- Whose perspectives influence photo taking?
- Whose meanings are addressed in interpreting the photos taken?
- Do the photos stand alone or are they incorporated into a word analysis?

## How are photographs perceived by the researcher?

There are two important distinctions. First, between a naive realist and cautious realist conceptualisation of photographs: a naive realist approach assumes it is possible to produce an accurate visual record of what has been photographed, whereas a cautious realist approach acknowledges the construction of photos. As discussed in Chapter 1, a naive approach is no longer tenable though people sometimes slip into treating images in this way. The second distinction concerns the researcher's conception of their part in constructing an image and their relationship to what they are researching (see also Pink, 2007, on 'realist' versus 'reflexive' approaches). A non-reflexive researcher does *not* acknowledge that the visual data they generate is inevitably shaped by their subjectivity and photographic practices, whereas a reflexive researcher does (see Chapter 1). As Martha Macintyre and Maureen Mackenzie (1992: 163) explain, 'the experience, the motivations and the social positions of the photographers are intrinsic to the images' (cited in Pink 2007: 69). Jon Prosser and Dona Schwartz's (1998: 122–3) distinction between 'visual record' and 'visual diary' exemplifies the difference between a non-reflexive and reflexive approach; it 'reflects differing positions with regard to the capacities of photography to provide an "unbiased" record of a reality'. They prefer 'visual diary' because 'cameras don't take pictures, people do'; the notion of photographs as a visual diary acknowledges that the images generated are 'the unique result of the interaction of a certain researcher with a specific population using a particular medium at a precise moment in space and time'.

## Whose perspectives influence photo taking?

Is photography directed solely by the researcher's theories, agendas, perspectives, or is it shaped in part by the views of research participants (photos generated by research participants are discussed in Chapter 8)? The involvement of research participants in directing the researcher's photography varies. It occurs when participants are interviewed or involved in shaping decisions about what to photograph and how. It is also a defining feature of 'collaborative photography' (Banks 2001; Pink 2007) whereby ethnographers are instructed to take photographs by their informants. It also occurs when the researcher's photos are shown to participants and discussions with them lead to the refinement of subsequent photography (e.g. Caldarola 1985; Harper 1987; Woodward 2008). Incorporating the views of other people into the production of photos is possible only in overt research; covert research necessarily excludes research subjects' involvement.

## Whose meanings are addressed in interpreting the photos taken?

Are photos interpreted principally by the researcher or are other people's interpretations important? In many cases, photos are discussed in photo-interviews and, in this way, research participants' meanings are embraced, albeit to varying degrees.

## Do the photos stand alone or are they incorporated into a word analysis?

Is the visual explained through words or is the image treated as a medium of knowledge and critique in itself? Gillian Rose (2007) differentiates between 'supportive' and 'supplemental' uses of photography. Supportive research is where photos are 'worked over for what they offer in the way of evidence to answer a research question' (p. 239). Photo-elicitation and documentary photographic projects are typically supportive. In contrast, supplemental research is where photos are presented without explanation; they are given space 'to have their own, perhaps rather unpredictable [as far as the researcher is concerned], effects in the research process' (p. 246).

Rose (2007) suggests there are two supplementary things that can be done with photos. First, photos are good at capturing what is difficult to convey in words particularly the atmosphere and feel of places. Second, photos can be instances of what Howard Becker (2002: 5) calls 'specified generalisation': 'photos are specific instances of the general argument' because photos are 'always of someone or something specific, not an abstract entity or a conceptual creation'. Discussing John Berger and Jean Mohr's textual and photographic study, *A Seventh Man* (1975), in which photos are intended to be 'read on their own terms', Becker argues that the real life depicted in the photos can create a different understanding from that produced by a written account and can work to persuade the viewer/reader of the veracity of the abstract written account. Additionally, photos impel the viewer to become an active participant in making meaning because images are ambiguous and because the experience of flicking through photos generates new perspectives as a montage of (bits of) photos form in the reader/viewer's head.

For academic purposes it is debatable whether it is useful to use photos only as supplemental. Though some advocate photo essays (Banks 2001), the prevailing view is that photos need some written accompaniment though scholars differ as to the precise relationship between pictures and words. Discussing ethnography, Sarah Pink (2007: 6) argues that findings can be presented creatively using photos but that theory needs words: 'visual representations bear an important relationship to, but cannot replace, words in theoretical discussion'.

Photos can be used productively as supplements in academic studies. But while photographs can enable different understandings and experiences than words, the success of this strategy depends on the reader's engagement. Especially in academic contexts where words are typically prioritised over images, readers may skim or skip pictures with little appreciation of how they might contribute to the findings; readers may also be unwilling or unused to shifting between words and images. If you want to use photos as supplementary you need to explain clearly why you are using them and present your photos in ways that encourage readers to shift how they look at the page or screen. Because of the ambiguity of images, I agree with Rose (2007) that it is helpful to provide written guidance on how to approach the images you present; at minimum an interpretative framework.

# Technical considerations

Taking photos is something almost all of us do in everyday life, but how can you take photos for research purposes? In this section I introduce general points about taking photos.

The question of how to photograph is easily overlooked, yet technical decisions are important because they contribute to what photos look like and this has implications for how they are interpreted by the researcher, interviewees and other viewers. Researchers are sometimes professional photographers or of professional standard and they take great care with technical specifications. However, most researchers are not of this standard and technical issues can seem daunting. Though it is not necessary for researchers to become expert photographers, they do need to be aware of basic technical decisions and their implications.

While there is no right or wrong way to take photos it is worth reflecting on what you want to use the photos for and the implications of basic technical decisions. Basic considerations include: the effects of lighting on the visibility of detail and the representation of atmosphere; the type of lens used (normal, telephoto, wide angle) and the implications for what can be photographed from a particular vantage point; whether the photos will be in colour or black and white and the different impressions produced by this. Another point is whether to take and present sequences of photos or individual shots. Sequences are preferred by some researchers for capturing the dynamics of social life, including cause and effect (Becker 1974), and for presenting a more nuanced account of culturally unfamiliar practices than individual images or words can convey (Chaplin 1994; Collier and Collier 1986). Ricabeth Steiger (1995) advises researchers to present a record of technical matters to viewers so that they can take them in to consideration when looking at the photos. While basic information is useful when presenting your photos as research evidence, this is not necessary in photo-interviews because this would be a distraction and interviewees may not be interested in or informed about the implications of technical decisions.

In producing photos for a photo-elicitation study in Switzerland of professional women in the transition to motherhood, Steiger (1995: 31–2) thought carefully about the effects of her technical choices. Her study involved taking photos of women and their interactions with their children, also of the interiors and exteriors of the women's homes. The use of lighting in photographs had important implications for the detail captured and the feel of the spaces and interactions photographed:

> Social life is strongly influenced by the nature of the light which surrounds it. Inside rooms, where I made most of my photographs, there was usually natural light coming from windows. This light tends to be focused, full of contrast and rapidly decreasing throughout the room. While the eye can compensate for such differences, photographic material cannot. If I used a flash, I would record many details in the scene, but I would not record the way the light naturally appears there.

> If I photographed in the available light, I would record an impression of the ambience of the rooms, but it would be incorrect: the contrast would be so extreme that few details would appear in the shadows or highlights. In addition, given the low level of natural light, a large aperture would be necessary, making the depth of focus in the photograph very narrow.[1]

Steiger also deliberated on how to frame her photos of domestic scenes:

> Perception works in ways the still camera cannot imitate. The eye produces a picture that is about equivalent to that of a 'normal' lens, but this lens records only a small amount of what a human perceives. (p. 32)

> That is why a series of 'normal' lens photographs cannot give the same impression one has looking around in that room. A wide angle lens gives more information about the room but makes it look bigger than it really is. (p. 32)

There are further examples of researchers' technical decisions later in this chapter.

Whatever your level of expertise, it is useful to experiment with technical choices and consider the likely implications of these selections. Pilot work can be valuable, especially if you intend to use your photos in interviews: are you producing the right kinds of photos to facilitate feedback from your interviewees? There are also other reasons for getting to grips with technical matters before starting research. As Prosser and Schwartz stress (1998), visual researchers need to be familiar with their equipment, to handle it competently and with assurance. This is to ensure that the researcher engenders confidence and trust in the people around them (research participants, research facilitators, observers) and to aid the researcher in efficiently and effectively taking photos in the field. Researchers who are unfamiliar with their equipment can easily miss important photographic opportunities.

A further point to note when taking photos is the need for meticulous records. It is always sensible when doing research to keep a note of when, where and what is photographed. This includes documenting even those photos taken initially as purely personal resources because they may later become data (Pink 2007). Digital cameras usually have a function that dates each image but other details need to be recorded. Pink (2007) also suggests that ethnographers keep a reflexive diary in which they chronicle their photographic practice and the motivations and ideas that informed taking each picture.

## Analysing photos

Analysis and interpretation of images is an important aspect of research. Researchers often gloss over how they analyse the images they have generated, and because analysis is often embedded in the research process it can be difficult to see precisely what people do with their data. In the following I discuss what you need to think about, and do, when undertaking analysis.

# What to think about when doing analysis

Four general points need consideration early on in your research, the first before you get started.

First, when are you going to do the analysis? In quantitative research, analysis typically occurs at the end of data collection. In contrast, qualitative research is commonly iterative; the analysis is undertaken at different points during the research so that there is 'interplay' between interpretation and data generation such that the analysis can shape the next stage of data generation (Bryman 2008: 372). Most research discussed in this chapter is iterative, the exception is systematic rephotography. In iterative research it is essential to think about methods of analysis before you start and how the research and analysis are related (Pink 2007).

Second, how do you perceive photographic images? As discussed earlier in this chapter under 'Approaches to generating photos', a naive approach should be avoided. If you use photos as visual evidence a cautious realist approach is essential combined with reflexivity about how and why you took your photos.

Third, whose meanings are addressed? If you rely on your own interpretation, your analysis should acknowledge that this is only one way to understand your images; it is also important to think about how you have produced your interpretation. If you are interested in what your visual data mean to the people whose lives they relate to, you need to seek out their understandings of what you have photographed and analyse their accounts.

Fourth, how will you integrate the results of different types of analyses, for example the results of visual and interview analyses?

# Doing analysis

In the following I introduce four common methods of analysing your own photos, starting with quantitative content analysis, and then looking at three types of qualitative data analysis – qualitative content analysis, narrative analysis and combining interview data with photo analysis. Sometimes methods are combined.

## Quantitative content analysis

This is a systematic method for counting the frequency with which visual details appear in photos and can be useful if working with a lot of images. However, it generates a very limited account of your data unless used alongside qualitative techniques of visual analysis or photo-elicitation. This method is discussed further in Chapter 8.

## Qualitative content analysis

This is what Alan Bryman (2008: 552) describes as 'turning data into fragments' and it involves coding or indexing your data. Qualitative content analysis puts emphasis on: the role of the researcher in the construction of meaning; allowing categories to emerge out of the data; the context of visual details. There are several ways of doing this; I outline three variants starting with analyses that code the image, then a method that codes your description of each image.

1. *Identifying themes in photos using qualitative coding* – This involves labelling or coding the content of photos according to themes you have preselected and/or that emerge as the research unfolds; you then interpret the patterns that surface (see Bryman 2008; Seale 2004). For instance, if you are interested in children's attire in school you might code items of clothing and how they are worn. The patterns you identify – for example, about how children wear their ties – are then interpreted in relation to ideas about identities and resistance.

2. *Combining enumeration with thematic coding of each photo* – This method systematically maps the content of images, counting how often details appear in each photo; it is useful for detailed comparison of images. Jon Prosser and Andrew Loxley (2010: 208–10) use this technique to analyse and compare photos of primary school classrooms, identifying similarities and differences between them (see Figure 7.1). The researchers began by identifying categories of visual details (e.g. 'furniture', 'interactive materials') to describe what was in their photos. They then studied each photo, counting the number of times visual details fitted into each category and recording brief comments. The categories were identified through joint scrutiny of some of the images 'to assess content and, drawing on their theoretical and disciplinary frameworks, what this content might mean'. Though based on counting, this method differs from quantitative content analysis in that the researchers engage reflexively with what they see in their photos: the method has a 'reflexive twist to it as it is less concerned with procedural exactitude and focuses upon the way in which researchers interact with material to not only construct the categories but also determine how different segments of data are selected for allocation' (p. 208). For example, the researchers might include comments about their assessment of the different properties of the 'interactive materials' they spotted in their photos or add notes on unusual features. A table was used to record the systematic (based on counting) and thematic understanding of what was visible in their pictures. The results were then interpreted.

3. *Describing photos and coding your descriptions* – This approach starts by generating a description of each image in its entirety. The advantage of working in this way is that you engage with the interrelationship between details within each image. Unlike the previous two methods it does not fragment individual images in order to identify and trace patterns or trends across a group of photos (your description of each image may, however, be fragmented when you analyse it). One way to do this is to look at each image and describe how it addresses your research questions and record your initial thoughts and interpretations of the visual data. You can then identify themes and patterns in your written accounts using qualitative coding as described in (1) above. An example is Suchar's research, discussed later in this chapter.

## Narrative analysis, or integrating the image and its 'story'
This approach considers the content of each image in relation to the 'story' around it, in other words how the photo was made and why, and how you are engaging with

**Figure 7.1** Classroom, 2001. Courtesy of Jon Prosser and Andrew Loxley

it in the context of your research. To do this you can work through the five lines of enquiry detailed in Chapter 2. One way of conceptualising this task is in terms of what Marcus Banks (2001: 11) calls 'internal and external narratives'. An internal narrative refers to the content of an image, 'the story ... that the image communicates'. This story is not integral to the image but generated by the researcher or other viewers as they engage in the act of interpretation. The external narrative is 'the social context that produced the image, and the social relations within which the image is embedded at any moment of viewing', it embraces contexts of production, encounter and what happened to the photo over time. In combination, the internal and external narratives generate a contextualised and reflexive description of each image you have generated.

## Interview data combined with photo analysis

What participants say about photos can be analysed (see Chapter 9) and used to complement the researcher's interpretation produced using methods already mentioned. There can also be collaborative analysis of photos by researcher and participants; participants' comments are integrated into the researcher's analysis of the images shaping how they are described, an example is Harper's research discussed later in this chapter.

In this section I have introduced common methods that researchers use – sometimes in combination – to analyse their own photos; this is not an exhaustive list of methods of analysis, nor of the variations within each. These analytic techniques can be used also with research-participant photography and found photos.

In the remainder of this chapter I shift from discussing general points to examining different types of researcher-generated photography in detail, namely, photo-documentation, taking photos to use in interviews and rephotography. These methods have a broad range of applications but I focus on how they can be used to explore and attempt to explain everyday processes, the past and social change.

# Photo-documentation

Rose (2007: 243) describes 'photo-documentation' as a method in which 'photos are made systematically by the researcher in order to provide data that the researcher then analyses'. This method is well established in the social sciences. It takes various forms and is frequently followed by, or sometimes combined with, photo-elicitation interviews. In this section I look at scripted documentary photography. Typically the script is worked out at the beginning of the research although it can emerge after an initial period in the field (e.g. Becker 1974).

One way of researching change is to identify 'new' phenomena and photograph them. In this case, the researcher needs to have some knowledge of what 'new' phenomena are, which presupposes identification of the 'old' or 'unchanged' and what these look like. In Suchar's study of neighbourhood change and gentrification in Chicago in the 1990s, these changes are various additions and modifications to houses and gardens; their status as signs of change is that they are either new (e.g. exterior art work), renovations (e.g. freshly painted doors) or recently added (e.g. antique coach lamps or period decorations), which presumes that pre-gentrified houses did not have these features. Suchar had visual evidence of what pre-gentrified houses looked like, but there is a danger that pre-change is assumed. One potential pitfall of this is that a homogenised version of the past is constructed and used as a point of comparison.

Drawing on his experience of researching gentrification, Suchar (1997: 34–5) offers a helpful account of his method. He regards the documentary role of photography as the 'process of asking and answering questions – based on field observations or archival research, and engaging in a discovery process'. To guide his photography he uses a shooting script, this is a list of research topics or questions that can be examined via photographic information. The script 'provide[s] a means by which photography can be grounded in a strategic and focused exploration of answers to particular theoretically-generated questions'. Suchar argues that shooting scripts and grounded theory are compatible research tools in that both rely on the creation of categories for the collection, organisation and analysis of observational data. Suchar combines these tools to provide a means of organising and interpreting the rich visual data he generates. Shooting scripts help structure his daily fieldwork, but they also 'provide the flexibility needed for a sociological discovery process that draws

from field observations to visually grounded abstractive and conceptual development... This [method] ... permits the field worker to become more sensitive to the
recognition of patterns and therefore enhances seeing'.

Suchar identifies six main stages in using a shooting script; the analysis is interwoven with data generation:

1   Establish an initial shooting script drawing on the researcher's general
    understanding. In Suchar's research the shooting script included questions
    on the nature of renovations to property.
2   Take photos to answer or respond to questions in the initial shooting script.
3   Scrutinise each photo and write a descriptive narrative identifying how it
    addresses, or responds to, a question from the shooting script. Also note
    initial interpretations of the meaning or significance of photos.
4   Coding. The researcher adds labels (codes) to each descriptive narrative. The
    labelling process is of organisational value, it also provides a means of refin-
    ing ideas/concepts and facilitates comparison of images which can generate
    new codes, code categories (groups of codes, such as 'Victorian-style
    changes'), questions and theoretical understandings.
5   Revision of the shooting script. A shooting script is not a straightjacket:
    'The hunches, speculations, and insights that come out of this process help
    us to take new directions in our field research. Most significantly, they help
    us to ... reformulate the photographic shooting script' (Suchar 1997: 39).
    After each coding session, Suchar asked: what possible answers to these
    shooting-script questions have yet to be explored? What other questions
    do these answers raise? The shooting script is revised and more photos
    are taken.
6   The accumulated narratives, codes and photographs become the basis for
    further comparative analysis. A new round of coding takes place to make
    connections between code categories and to reveal patterns. In the process
    of comparing images and narratives across code categories, analytic and
    descriptive notes are generated which help to 'integrate the ... interpreta-
    tions of visual data into more abstract conceptual understandings and state-
    ments' (Suchar 1997: 40). These notes can prompt further photography
    with the purpose of developing the emerging theory. The emerging theory
    can be refined using photo-elicitation, these interviews allow the researcher
    to triangulate their data.

A clear guide to direct documentary photography is important, not least because it
is easy to lose direction or to overlook evidence. In his photographic study of changes
in America's Midwest, specifically the growth of the non-farm population and relative decline of the farm population, Rieger (1996: 37) found that a clear hypothesis
(or shooting script) helped counter his 'reflexive inattention' to the non-farming
aspects of the country landscape. Like Suchar, Rieger's research was based solely on
contemporary photographs, but for Rieger this represented a compromise. Although
he lacked an earlier set of photos with which to compare his contemporary set, it

remained important to Rieger to convey something of what had been before. To address this, as he explains: 'In framing the picture, I usually included enough of the surrounding landscape to give a sense of the context or physical setting of the residence, so that the reader could intuit what it was probably like before it became a non-farm residence' (p. 37).

Rieger (1996) also suggests that another way to research ongoing change is to photograph many individual instances of it, each at a different stage of the process. He suggests that by arranging the photos in appropriate sequence, researchers can construct a facsimile of the larger social change process and present this as an approximation of what longitudinal evidence would show. An issue with this cross-sectional approach is that it may not be clear what the final stage of the social change process may look like, indeed social change can be open ended.

# Taking photos to use in interviews

Taking photographs is often combined with photo-interviews (see Chapter 9). Sometimes there is a preliminary interview with research participants to help identify a schedule for the researcher's photography. The photo-elicitation interview follows after the photographic research and is a means of doing one or more of the following: checking what is depicted in the photo; exploring the meanings that photos have for participants; refining and developing an emergent theory; and generating supplementary personalised accounts. Sometimes photo-interviews intersperse and inform the direction of the photography, this is the case in Douglas Harper's ethnographic study *Working Knowledge* (1987).

Set in a poor, rural area in the United States, *Working Knowledge* is a study of the craft and workplace culture of Willie, a garage owner with mechanical and engineering skills, who repairs motors as well as 'repairing, redesigning and rebuilding' all manner of local machinery, equipment and facilities. The dialogue between Harper and Willie guides the photography and is key to the success of this study which explores both social change at the micro level and the processes of complex craft activities.

The project started as a purely photographic study of Willie's shop, but this proved unproductive as Harper (1987: 10) explains:

> I had a hard time getting down to serious photography, primarily because I didn't want to call attention to myself. At first I hung around in the background taking snapshots in an offhand manner. The photographs were uninteresting because the details of the work were missing. Furthermore, the shop was dark, and using a strobe would have drawn yet more attention. I realized after a few unsuccessful attempts to photograph this way that I would have to explain my plans – as, of course, I also needed to do for ethical reason – and to begin photographing in a forthright and even aggressive manner.

Harper discussed his project with Willie, who was keen to be involved, and then started again:

> I began photographing with a strobe and a short telephoto macro lens to concentrate the camera on the hands and materials; the small details of jobs in progress. Switching periodically to a wide angle lens made it possible to photograph the work in its context. The photographs, lighted by the strobe, showed the detail I had wanted from the beginning. As long as I took care not to flash the strobe in Willie's face while he was working it did not pose a serious problem.

Returning to the earlier discussion of technical issues, Harper's account reveals the need to work out in advance how best to take photos and the importance of involving research participants in the process (see also Collier and Collier 1986: 74).

Technical matters were not, however, the only challenge for Harper. A key question was what to photograph given that the purpose was to explain Willie's work. Harper drew inspiration from Becker (1974: 11) who explains that 'good' photographs, as far as the visual sociologist is concerned, are underpinned by understanding: the researcher needs to have 'acquired a sufficiently elaborate theory to alert them to the visual manifestations' of the 'complexity' of their subject matter. Becker continues, 'In short, the way to change and improve photographic images lies less in technological considerations than in improving your comprehension of what you are photographing'.

Harper wanted to convey Willie's perspective rather than that of 'an interested outsider'. To achieve this he used photo-elicitation interviews to both understand what he had photographed and to refine his subsequent photography: 'The photo elicitation interview points the photographer in new directions as the subject tells what is missing in the photographs and what should be included in subsequent ones' (Harper 1987: 12). Each interview of between 2–4 hours was organised around specific themes and projects. The most useful photos were sequences that showed the progress of a job; talk about these enabled Harper to 'disassemble intuition' (p. 31) and explore the workings of Willie's 'hand knowledge' (p. 121). The photos (e.g. Figure 7.2) isolate a moment in the work process and elicit a description from Willie of what he usually experiences:

> ... it looks like I'm holding the file real tender like. But you've got to shift that pressure from one hand to another – as you go across the saw the pressure shifts on your file. If you hold it hard you can't feel the pressure. You're not gripping the file, you're more or less letting it float or glide right through. (p. 120)

The photo sequences and photo-interview transcripts were subsequently 'digested' by Harper and integrated with previous interviews and notes from his research journal.

**Figure 7.2**    Willie at work. Photograph by Douglas Harper

Harper was fortunate in being able to photograph Willie at work and to use these photos to facilitate discussions with Willie about the detail of his craft. Sometimes it is not possible to take or find suitable photographs to use in photo-interviews. In these cases Rieger (2003) suggests that the researcher consider photographing reconstructions. In his study of changes in the wood industry in North Michigan since 1920, Rieger used photo-elicitation to understand recent and past practices. However, while Rieger could take or find photos of contemporary practices to use in interviews he discovered very little visual evidence of early practices. Older and extinct practices around the felling, stripping, debarking, cutting and moving of trees were, therefore, harder to investigate. When an interviewee offered to demonstrate an old technique using original tools, Rieger took the opportunity to photograph the demonstration. These photographs were subsequently used effectively in photo-interviews with other workers.

# Rephotography

This section focuses on projects where the researcher takes photos to facilitate comparison between two or more points in time; this is a particular type of photo-documentation. The aim of such projects is to explore social and cultural change over a time period that can extend from a few days to years or even decades. The process is variously called 'repeat photography', 'rephotography' or 'overtime comparison'. I use the term 'rephotography', which I define loosely as the practice of taking photographs with the purpose of facilitating overtime comparisons. I start by introducing types of rephotography – prospective and retrospective – and then two main approaches – 'systematic' and 'reflexive'. I then discuss the three stages of a rephotography project.

There are two main types of rephotography – prospective and retrospective. Prospective research explores the possibility of *change from the present* (working forwards), whereas retrospective research *compares the present with some point(s) in the past* (working backwards). In prospective research, photographs are taken by the researcher typically at two or more points (sometimes designated Time 1, Time 2 etc.). In retrospective projects the researcher uses pre-existing photos for the first set (Time 1) and compares these with photographs they have taken more recently (Time 2 etc.). Whereas in prospective research all photos are taken with the purpose of facilitating the exploration of change, this is not the case with retrospective projects.

Whether you chose retrospective or prospective methods depends on your research question. You would choose prospective research if, for example, the aim is to explore how town-centre space is used by young people before and after a planned redevelopment, the researcher can take photographs at a point in time before the development (Time 1) and then once the redevelopment is complete, perhaps in the first month (Time 2) and then 6 months later (Time 3). However, you would choose retrospective research if the aim is to consider how current primary school classrooms compare with those of the 1970s, the researcher would not be able to take the initial set of photos. In this case, s/he would need to locate a pre-existing photographic survey of primary school classrooms (Time 1) and follow this up by taking photos of classrooms today (Time 2).

There are two main approaches to rephotography in social research: 'systematic visual measurement' (Rieger 1996: 6) and 'reflexive' (Rolph et al. 2009: 431). Systematic measurement is, as its name suggests, an attempt at a scientific and objective measure of change using photographic images: change is deduced from a close inspection and comparison of the detail of images once all the visual data is collected or generated. This approach, championed by Rieger (1996), has its origins in natural science initiatives to monitor landscapes, most notably changes in glaciers. A reflexive approach, in contrast, approaches photographic data as the product of the researcher's views and practices within a particular socio-historical context. It is concerned foremost with comparability at a macro rather than micro level; researchers do not automatically rephotograph everything that featured in the first photo study or replicate the vantage points from which these photos were taken, but ensure that the content of the first and subsequent sets of photos facilitate meaningful comparisons between points in time. Change is assessed by comparing contextualised photo studies made at different points in time rather than by principally comparing the content of photos taken of the same type of subject matter. In both approaches, photos are used alongside words to present and discuss overtime comparisons.

# The three stages of rephotography

Rephotography has three main stages: stage 1 – setting up the research and generating or acquiring the Time 1 photos; stage 2 – rephotographing; and stage 3 – comparison and analysis of the photos. Stages 2 and 3 are similar for both prospective and retrospective projects and are considered together. Stage 1 differs in important ways for prospective and retrospective approaches, so I will discuss them separately.

## Stage 1 – Working forwards: prospective research

Rieger presents a model for systematic prospective research. The first stage involves working out a clear research question, followed by identification of 'visual indices of change' (Rieger 1996), deciding the time frame and frequency of rephotography, and finally taking the initial set of photos. The researcher's prior knowledge and theory informs these decisions.

Identification of visual indices of change is of particular importance in prospective rephotography: 'Does the change process ... have visual manifestations, and to what extent can visual changes be trusted as indicators of social structural change?' (Rieger 1996: 42). It is easy to assume that what *looks* different *is* different, but this is not always the case. You need a general understanding of the phenomenon in order to identify likely indices. As Rieger acknowledges, this is not a foolproof approach to the identification of indices of change and researchers need to be receptive to other indices as they undertake the first stage of photography. Deliberations about visual indices also inform decisions about the type of photos you need to take and the photographic equipment and skills required – distance, close-ups, and night-time or daytime photography.

A decision also needs to be made about an appropriate time frame; this is shaped by your research question and the time and resources available for the study. The time frame is also shaped by the likely speed of changes you are researching: will these changes be captured in the proposed time frame? You also need to decide on the frequency of rephotography and whether it is necessary to take photos at more than two points, although decisions about frequency can be adjusted in light of the results of the initial photo set. Once you know what you want to photograph, how often and over what period, you can concentrate on taking the initial set of photos.

Rieger advises keeping records of where and when each photo was taken, also the content including the identification of people and places featured in them. I suggest that you also engage reflexively with the research process by keeping an account of your fieldwork. All research is necessarily partial and this needs to be acknowledged and thought about. One aspect of this is keeping notes of why and how you take photos and the context in which you did this. Your fieldwork notes become part of the evidence generated at this first stage and they inform your subsequent analysis.

## Stage 1 – Working backwards: retrospective research

These are projects in which the researcher takes photos of aspects of the present to compare with pre-existing photos. Clearly the time frame is determined in part by available photographs, in most cases flexibility is necessary. You can start with a pre-existing photographic survey and follow this up, or start from an interest in the present and look for a pre-existing photo set. The latter can be time-consuming unless you are already familiar with a suitable archive or published study that uses photographs.

Rieger (1996: 43) is wary of using existing sets of historical photos for research on social change, mainly because his ideal is a controlled and 'systematic' study:

> Since the Time 1 documentation has, in effect, already been accomplished, the researcher is … limited to those dimensions of a particular phenomenon that the original photographer chose to document, and by whatever bias and selectivity may be contained in the photo-documentary record. To make matters more complicated, such photographs are rarely accompanied by an adequate record of the precise circumstances or context in which they were made.

Retrospective research is constrained by the focus of pre-existing photos. For example, if researching cultural life in schools it would be relatively easy to locate pre-existing photos of classrooms and possibly playgrounds, but despite their importance for school culture, school corridors are less likely to have been the focus of photography even if they sometimes feature incidentally. Rieger's reservations about the selectivity and bias of the original photographer are important, but not insurmountable. Selectivity and bias are always features of research. With pre-existing photos the researcher needs to be able to reconstruct information about the selectivity and purpose of the original photos using other visual and textual sources, this entails preliminary analysis of the stage 1 photographs. This is necessary because it is inadvisable to assume old photos depict material or social life as it was (naive realist approach) and to simply rephoto-graph with the aim of showing change or continuity. Even the 'scientific' photographic studies that Rieger prefers for retrospective rephotography need to be evaluated for their standpoint: what was the purpose of the original photography project? Why was a particular field, barn or street photographed at a particular time of day and year rather than other places and buildings at other times? Was the scene typical? Was it chosen to be illustrative of an argument?

Take a simple example. If you are interested in changes in consumption you might decide to do a retrospective rephotographic study based on Humphrey Spender's photos of a Bolton market taken in 1937-38 for Mass Observation. Before doing this you would need to ask various questions about the original photos (e.g. Figure 7.3): were they typical market stalls and typical of what region (Bolton, the north of England …?), were these all the usual stalls or just those that caught the photog-rapher's eye, did the photographer focus on the outlandish rather than the com-monplace, was he most interested in the stalls or the shoppers and why? It is hard to work with pre-existing photos when little is known about their provenance because it is difficult to evaluate their content. You need to establish what the original set of photos represents before deciding how to use them as a basis for rephotography and overtime comparisons, as demonstrated by Sheena Rolph, Julia Johnson and Randall Smith (2009).

**Figure 7.3** 'Working man's hair specialist' by Humphrey Spender. ©Bolton Council from the Bolton Library and Museum Service Collection

Evaluation of the construction of photographs (individually and as a collection) is key to a reflexive approach to rephotography as demonstrated by Rolph et al.'s (2009) retrospective study of residential care. In 2005/6 they revisited Peter Townsend's seminal study of residential care for the elderly undertaken in the 1950s. In the book based on his study, Townsend (1962) argued that workhouses should be demolished and replaced by supported housing schemes and inpatient hospital care; this argument was informed by a study of 173 residential care homes using observations, interviews and 100 photographs. Rolph et al. (2009) revisited 20 of the original care homes using similar methods of data collection to Townsend, including photography. The aim was not to replicate Townsend's study, which would have been impossible given changes in legal and ethical approaches to academic research, but to generate comparable data. To decide what kinds of photos would provide useful overtime comparisons, Rolph et al. started by evaluating critically why Townsend had taken certain photos and what the original set of photos conveyed. This evaluation involved comparison of Townsend's photos and his written text, an assessment of the collection of photos that he took and an interpretation of individual images. It also involved asking Townsend questions about his intentions in producing the photographs. The researchers' analysis provided the foundations for stage 2 (what and how to photograph) and 3 (how to compare the photos), which I discuss shortly.

## Stage 2 – Taking follow-up photos

This stage, which is common to both retrospective and prospective research, involves taking follow-up photos; how this is done depends on your topic and approach (systematic or reflexive). Whichever strategy is employed, you need to make detailed written notes of what and how you are photographing. It is sometimes useful to adopt a systematic approach but there is still a need for critical and ongoing evaluation of what you are researching and its broader context, and reflexivity about your research practices.

In a systematic study of place, Jon Rieger (1996) suggests taking repeat photos from the same position from which the first set of photos was produced, although it is not always possible to replicate this precisely. Rieger illustrates this with examples from a retrospective study he undertook in 1985 of migration away from rural communities in the western part of Michigan; this study revisited the sites of photos he had taken in a separate study in 1970:

> From the information on the back of each photo, I knew what lens to use and the approximate spot the photo was taken from. With my camera in hand and the print on a clipboard, I would relocate the original vantage point as nearly as I could by lining up key benchmarks in the scene so that they matched their configuration in the photo …
>
> Lining up the geometry of the scene sensitizes one to what has changed and what has not over the period of time since the original was taken. (Rieger 1996: 44)

Although some rephotographic projects replicate vantage point, time of year, lighting conditions and time of day, Rieger sees this as 'elegant' but unnecessary. He advises researchers to get as close to the original vantage point as necessary, but as the aim is to permit an analysis of social change an exact replica is rarely necessary. He describes how, when he came to rephotograph a particular street scene, there was a car in the way. He had fretted about whether to wait until the car went but eventually took the photo; if the vehicle had been a lorry that substantially interfered with his attempt to rephotograph the scene he would have waited until it moved. Alongside replicating the location, Rieger also recommends retaking photos at approximately the same time of year. I disagree. Many projects do not extend over years. More importantly, the degree of replication necessary between photos at different points in time should always be assessed in relation to the needs of each project.

In concentrating on pictures of pre-selected visible signs there is a danger that the completed research will miss novel and unexpected changes. To counter this problem Rieger advises photographing as much as possible and gathering other types of data: 'the conscientious researcher will document any and all aspects of the phenomenon that could contribute to an understanding of it sociologically' (p. 42). This does not seem systematic, but here I agree with Rieger. Even if a systematic approach is adopted, researchers need not be constrained by it. I suggest embedding a systematic survey within a critical and ongoing evaluation of what you are researching. It seems sensible to reflect on changes since the first set of photos was taken. Once the repeat photos have been taken it may be useful to support these with additional photos that enable you to contextualise your photographic topics or respond to changes.

Comparability between the original and subsequent photos is essential. In systematic rephotography, this needs to be at the level of individual photos, but this is not necessary in reflexive rephotography as long as there is comparability between *sets* of photos. What constitutes comparability is not standardised and must be worked out for each project, informed by a clear sense of the point of using rephotography and drawing on contextual research to anchor and explain the original photo set. For the purposes of social and historical research I argue that the reflexive approach to rephotography is useful even if you eventually decide to replicate aspects of some, or all, of the original photo set.

The reflexive approach has two important advantages over the systematic, especially in studying people, practices and institutions retrospectively. First, while prospective research can pre-decide specific visual details to trace and compare over time, in retrospective research it is not always helpful to follow up details featured in the original set of photos. This is because the original photos were not produced to address the researcher's questions and so rephotographing the original details may not provide a basis for meaningful historical comparisons. Second, as Rolph et al. (2009) explain drawing on Charlotte Davies and Nickie Charles (2002), in a re-study it is necessary to consider methodological, analytical and social changes in the period between photo sets. It may not be feasible or necessary to repeat individual photos either in terms of subject matter or vantage points.

Stage 2 of a retrospective study can be challenging, as Rolph et al. (2009) discovered when they researched continuity and change in residential care for the elderly since Townsend's study in the late 1950s. How can you make meaningful photographic comparisons 50 years after an original survey? The challenges that confronted Rolph et al. were threefold and they used a reflexive approach to tackle them. First, the researchers' photos were taken to develop a different argument from Townsend's, in part because they were researching change and continuity. Rolph et al.'s decisions about what to photograph were, therefore, shaped by Townsend's choices but not constrained by them; for instance, they also photographed details, and signs of change and continuity that caught their attention as they visited the homes. Second, there were technological issues, namely whether to copy Townsend and use a Leica camera to take black and white photos or to employ the latest technology to produce digital colour ones. This led to reflection on the different impressions created by monochrome versus colour photos. The researchers decided to use both:

> The upbeat appearance of our colour photographs is undoubted and often does not coincide with our memories or fieldnotes concerning a particular home. By comparing them with our monochrome versions of the same scenes, we can achieve a more balanced view. The colour photographs ... can warn us against adopting too gloomy an interpretation. They enable a perspective which moves from one that is in our mind's eye, habitually black and white (following Townsend), to one that is still capable of shocking, but also in many cases creates a more positive effect. (p. 433)

Third, there were ethical issues. Townsend 'was able to snap off photographs in a way that is impossible today' (p. 433), whereas contemporary research photography is circumscribed by rigorous ethical guidelines (e.g. informed consent, privacy and dignity issues) and administrative procedures (see Chapter 10). As a result, it was not possible to take the same kinds of photographs in 2005/6 as in the 1950s, and the recent photos therefore convey a very different impression of residential life than the earlier ones. For instance, Rolph et al. could not photograph how people used communal spaces because of difficulty in securing consent from everyone pictured, nor could they photograph people in circumstances that might be demeaning. Because Rolph et al. adopted a reflexive approach – indeed this was the only feasible way to produce a comparison over time – they were able to tackle this issue directly and to discuss why they could not produce comparable photos.

## Stage 3 – Comparative analysis

The third stage of rephotography involves comparing photos from different times; tracing details over time, particularly pre-selected 'indices of change', but also attending to incidental details in the photos. (In retrospective rephotography, preliminary analysis of stage 1 photos will have already been undertaken.) The third stage entails comparison of individual photos, it can also involve reflection on and comparison of the sets of photos generated at different points in time using analytic techniques discussed earlier. How do the overall visual accounts from different times compare: are there gaps in the visual records or differences in atmosphere? How do you explain these differences? At this point it is useful to draw on your field notes and your evaluation of the different photographic sets. How might the selectivity of the original photo set, as of subsequent sets, contribute to similarities and differences? Where a reflexive approach is adopted, the analysis can also take account of what is revealed by the modifications that are required to repeat a study at a later date.

Whether doing prospective or retrospective research, researchers need to be cautious in drawing conclusions from overtime photographic comparisons and wary of misinterpreting similarity or differences in photos from different points in time. Assuming linearity can lead to similarity being misinterpreted as continuity when, in fact, there has been short-lived or intermittent changes between the points considered. Similarly, visible differences between photos taken at different points in time may not be an indicator of permanent change but rather of a fleeting occurrence. Additionally, invisibility in photos should not be conflated with absence. At the comparative analysis stage it is important to draw on data gathered from other sources and by other means, including photo-interviews, to anchor and explain photographic details and impressions of change and continuity.

For rephotography to be a constructive exercise it is essential that photography provides answers to your research questions. In a discussion of how rephotography can be used to track 'the witnesses' of change, Rieger (1996: 28) considers Bill Ganzel's (1984) photograph in 1979 of the people (Florence Thompson and her daughters) who featured in Dorothea Lange's famous Depression photo from 1936. Lange's 1936 photo depicts a woman pea-picker sitting in a makeshift tent. She is clearly very poor;

she wears tattered clothes and clasps a baby close to her chest while two young children huddle close and hide their faces from the camera. The woman rests her chin
in her hand and her forehead is furrowed as she looks into the distance. Although it
is interesting to look at Ganzel's recent photo of this iconic figure from the 1930s,
the exercise provides an unconvincing example of how rephotographing people can
trace and explain change for three main reasons. First, differences between the production of the two photos are not considered, such as differences in genre (documentary versus family portraiture) and purpose. Second, Ganzel uses photo–elicitation
with Florence Thompson to reflect on the time the first photo was taken and how
things have changed for her since then. Although the recent photo is an interesting
illustration, and shows that Mrs Thompson and her daughters survived and are now
seemingly living in improved circumstances, it is the interview that is informative
about the present: even in old age Mrs Thompson was never far from poverty, a story
that is not obvious from the photo. The interview points to the ambiguity of the
second photo as evidence, indeed it reminds us that the 1930's photo does not speak
for itself. On its own the recent photograph is a poor indicator of the extent and
complexity of change; for academic purposes the interview would have sufficed. A
third reason this example is unsuccessful is that it is unclear what academic purpose
the photo serves.

The presentation of the analysis and conclusions needs to evidence clearly the
process, choices and basis of conclusions. This is important for systematic and reflexive research, but researchers who adopt a reflexive approach are particularly at risk
of the accusation of cherry picking examples that suit their argument. Whereas a
systematic approach compares the content of one or more photos of the same place,
people, practices, a reflexive approach does not necessarily have fixed points of comparison and it can be unclear how researchers have decided what to compare. It is
for this reason that the basis of the comparison must be presented clearly to readers.
Rolph et al. are very careful in doing this.

A related issue is how to present convincing overtime conclusions. In this respect
I am not entirely satisfied by Rolph et al.'s rephotography. My criticisms hark back
to a point I made in Chapter 3 about the importance of presenting clearly how
conclusions are reached. Rolph et al. are very careful in how they analyse the photographs produced by Townsend in his early study, but they do not apply the same
critical and reflexive methods consistently to their own photography and the process
of making overtime comparisons. For example, they compare a 1962 photo captioned
'Assistant matron and matron' (2009: 424) with one they have taken (not published)
as revealing 'significant changes over time: the ethnic minority background of staff'
(p. 435). Even if I could see the 2005 photo, a simple comparison with the 1962 photo
would not in itself establish this point. We know from other sources that there were
Afro-Caribbean women in care work in the 1950s and 1960s, though probably not
at assistant matron level. There may well have been Afro-Caribbean women working
in the 1960's home or in other homes surveyed by Townsend, but these do not appear
in this photograph and it is not clear if they appear in other photos; Rolph et al. do
not comment on this. Moreover, though Rolph et al.'s 2005 photo indicates ethnic

diversity amongst senior staff in one home this does not establish 'significant changes' in the ethnicity of staff per se. Rolph et al. proceed to comment on other differences between staff that they identify as signs of change: 'In Townsend's photographs the matrons often appear formally posed, uniformed and forbidding compared with the more relaxed pose of the staff in 2006 ... whose facial expressions, gestures, body language and even the variety of their uniforms indicate a degree of informality' (p. 435). It is possible to compare the photo of the 'Assistant matron and matron' with the photo taken in 2005 of four women standing close together entitled 'Manager and staff'. The recent photo does portray women in a more informal style than the earlier photo, but what, if anything, does this mean? A lack of critical and reflexive analysis of the recent set of photographs leads to a naive realist assumption about what the 2005 photo reveals about staff and how they work. Do the staff's smiles for the camera indicate that they have different working practices from their predecessors, perhaps that they are more caring? Or might these smiles and poses be a product of a different relationship to photography and the photographer in 2005 than in 1962?

## Summary

In this chapter I have explained how you can generate photos as part of a research project, this includes photos for use in interviews, photo-documentation and rephotography. I have also shown that before deciding to generate your own photographs, you need to consider whether photos would be a valuable addition to your research design, and to reflect on what approach is appropriate. Once you are committed to generating your own photos you need to reflect on the implications of technical decisions about lighting, lenses, the use of black and white or colour photography, and the value of taking single photos or sequences. How you will analyse your photos is another decision undertaken before you start taking photos.

Photos are often generated for the purpose of facilitating an interview and photo-elicitation is sometimes used to check or complement the generation of visual data. If you are interested in using photo-elicitation this chapter is best read alongside Chapter 9, which focuses on listening to what people say about photos. Chapter 8 considers asking research participants to take photos.

## Note

1  Aperture is the size of the opening inside a photographic lens; together with shutter speed it regulates the amount of light that passes into the camera. Aperture also affects the 'depth of field', which is the zone of sharpness in front of and behind the subject that is focused on. A large aperture allows in more light but results in a shallower zone of sharpness.

# 8
## Generating Photos: Research Participants

In studies of contemporary life it is increasingly common for research participants, especially young people, to be mobilised as photographers (Luttrell and Chalfen 2010; Pink 2007; Tinkler 2008). In this chapter I introduce the main types of research projects in which participants generate photographs and consider why researchers find it useful to ask participants to take pictures. I then outline how to set up a project in which respondents generate photos, including what guidance to give and technical matters. In the final section I discuss the analysis of participants' photos addressing approaches to image analysis, the importance of contextualising images and ways of incorporating participants' accounts of their photos into your investigation. Many projects involve talking to research participants about the photos they have taken so this chapter is best read alongside Chapter 9 in which I discuss photo-elicitation.

## Types of projects

There is variation in how participant-photography projects are conducted, but typically there are the following features: an initial interview or meeting with research participants; participants take photos according to guidance given, and if required, provide captions or brief descriptions; the photos are then returned to the researcher for analysis; in some instances the photos are discussed with participants individually or in groups on one or more occasions. Within this general format projects vary in two main ways.

First, they vary in terms of the photographic task. Research participants are typically asked to do one of several tasks: generate a photographic self-portrait (e.g. Ziller and Lewis 1981); produce documentation of aspects of their lives or interests (e.g. Allen 2009; Bolton et al. 2001; Croghan et al. 2008; Samuels 2007; Luttrell 2010; Richards 2011); take photos and then create a visual presentation – such as a collage – on some aspect of their experience or views (e.g. Coleman 2008).

Second, studies differ in terms of the kinds of data the researchers aim to generate. This variation is best conceptualised as a continuum. At one end studies are principally focused on generating visual data, they are 'photo-focused'. These studies typically attend to what participants think about their photos by asking them to produce captions or a brief written or verbal description (e.g. Damico 1985; Kenney 1993; Ziller and Lewis 1981; Ziller and Smith 1977). In some photo-focused studies, photos are accompanied by extensive written and sometimes verbal commentary or they are one aspect of a broader qualitative study and analysed alongside other textual, verbal and observational data relating to participants' experiences and perspectives (e.g. Bolton et al. 2001, see Box 8.2). Research at the opposite end of the continuum is concerned principally with what participants have to say about their photographs, they are 'talk-focused' (see Box 8.1). Though participants' photos may be valued principally as a means to generate interview data, in practice it is unusual to ignore the photographic image; attention to participants' photos is necessary to understand what participants speak about and why, and to identify themes for discussion. Some research is positioned in the middle of the continuum because both the photos and interviews are important sources of data; they are talk-focused *and* photo-focused (e.g. Luttrell 2010, see Box 8.3; Radley and Taylor 2003). The importance attached to photos and talk can shift in the course of a project; photos can become an important source of data in projects that are initially talk-focused and vice versa.

# Why ask research participants to generate photos?

There are several interrelated reasons why researchers ask participants to take photos. I start by commenting on enjoyment, then look at different types of data – visual and talk – before considering 'voice'.

## Enjoyment

A common reason for enlisting participants as photographers is the assumption that people enjoy taking pictures. Participants, especially young people, often embrace participatory photography with enthusiasm. For example, in a longitudinal study of working-class immigrant children in public schools in the United States, Wendy Luttrell (2010: 227) refers to participants' 'palpable excitement' at the thought of taking photos, though there was also some trepidation about having responsibility for a camera. In her research on sexual cultures in schools, Louisa Allen (2009) noted that this method was more attractive to potential research participants than interviews or surveys; the method also appealed to children from groups that were under-represented in academic research. The downside was that some children were unwilling to be interviewed about their photos.

## Visual data

In many projects, photos are important and distinctive sources of visual data about people and their lives. Sometimes researchers ask participants to take photos in order to gain a peephole into aspects of the participant's subjectivity or everyday life. For instance, some social psychologists approach photographs as evidence of the photographer's personality or self-concept. The thinking that underpins this approach is that the 'perceiver [is] perceivable through photography': 'photographs are images of the photographer's information processing and traces of his [sic] interaction with the physical and social environment' (Ziller and Smith 1977: 172–3). More often researchers adopt participant photography as a means to peer in to the everyday lives of participants, because the camera can go where the researcher cannot (e.g. Blinn and Harrist 1991; Bolton et al. 2001; Moore et al. 2008). This is what Gerry Bloustein and Sarah Baker call 'ethnography by proxy' (2003: 72).

Using photos as data is not straightforward because of issues relating to production and meaning. Limitations include research participants not using cameras in ways envisaged by the researcher, which may be the result of participants' inhibitions or resistance to revealing aspects of their lives to the researcher or simply because they have misunderstood the instructions. There are also constraints on what participants can photograph and ethical issues concerning the possible voyeurism of the researcher, particularly in research involving children and marginalised social groups (see Chapter 10). Other factors include technological limitations and the skills of participant photographers; photos sometimes fail to show details that photographers intended or that are necessary for appreciating the points they wish to convey. As discussed in Chapter 1, photos are constructed so researchers should avoid a naive realist interpretation of images, in other words photos should not be viewed uncritically as visual evidence of aspects of participants' lives and experiences. The meaning and significance of what is visible in a photograph is another issue in using photos as data. Images are polysemic and photographers' meanings cannot be ascertained simply by studying the images they have generated (see Bolton et al. 2001; Radley and Taylor 2003; Williams 2010). It is debatable whether photos can in and of themselves tell us much about either the outer or inner dimensions of participants' lives. This is not to say that participants' photos are redundant, far from it, but that their value depends greatly on understanding how they have been produced and discovering what they mean to their creators. Most photo-focused research incorporates some guide to participants' meanings, these include captions or, more usefully, detailed written and verbal commentaries (see Box 8.2).

Photography is sometimes adopted in photo-focused studies because it is regarded as a relatively easy way for research participants to convey information: 'Through photography we instantly become artists. Moreover, we are able to communicate vast amounts of information effortlessly' (Ziller 1990: 37). Although it is fairly easy to take photos, researchers need to be wary of assuming it is easy for people to convey their experiences and thoughts *through* their photographs for three reasons. First, it is not always easy for people to create the pictures they envision without a high level of photographic expertise. Second, as mentioned above, the meaning of photographs is not transparent and the research participant and researcher may see different things in the same picture. Third, participants may experience difficulties deciding what to photograph or working out how to represent their experiences (Frith and Harcourt 2007; Radley and Taylor 2003). Sarah Drew, Rony Duncan and Susan Sawyer (2010: 1682) discovered that roughly half the young people in their study about living with chronic health conditions experienced problems deciding what to photograph; the researchers subsequently spent much time on the telephone 'coaching' young people through these difficulties.

## Interview data

For many researchers, the attraction of using participant-generated photography is that it is a means to get participants talking. People are often keen to talk about the photos they have taken and this facilitates discussion about aspects of their lives and experiences that might otherwise be difficult to explore. This was why Jennifer Mason used this approach when researching children's relationships (see Box 8.1, also Tipper 2011). The process of deciding what to photograph is also valued for prompting participants to concentrate their thoughts and feelings on a subject. For example, a novice monk in Sri Lanka explained to Jeffrey Samuels (2007: 216) that the process of taking photos to address a script of questions about important aspects of his life encouraged him to reflect on his experiences before the interview. The photographs that the monk generated were reminders of the thought he had put in to decisions about taking each picture: 'If we look at a photograph taken by someone else, then we would simply see the photograph and think ... "this is a Bo tree [sacred tree]." However, these photographs have a lot of meaning ... and value for us now because we had to think about it [sic].' Taking photos similarly concentrated the thoughts of the mature women entrants to higher education interviewed by Lynn Blinn and Amanda Harrist (1991; see also Liebenberg 2009). The researchers asked the women to take ten photos about aspects of their experience of higher education, discuss them with their families and then write about them prior to interview using the following guide: 'when I look at this picture I feel ... When my family members look at this picture they think ... The title I would give the picture is ...' (Blinn and Harrist 1991: 190). Blinn and Harrist concluded that 'conducting the interviews without this prior cognitive processing would have provided data which was at a much more superficial level' (p. 189) because the participants would not have had the impetus to work out, and reflect on, what they were experiencing and how they thought and felt about it.

Deliberations about what photos to take to address the researcher's questions are sometimes an explicit focus of participant-photography projects because of the insights they afford into participants' thinking. For example, Tina Cook and Else Hess (2007) asked children to generate photos about their experiences of school. The researchers tape-recorded the children's collective discussions about what photos they would take and interviewed the children about the photos that they did take. Children's conversations proved more useful than their photos in helping the researchers understand children's perspectives on the world. Similarly, in their ethnographic research, Bloustein and Baker (2003) used videos and cameras respectively to understand how the girls 'play with these tools' and explore identities with them (p. 75), and how the girls related to the photos they had taken of themselves at different points in the project.

Generating photos is also valued as an adjunct to interviews because it can help research participants focus on particular points in time and space. Alan Latham used this method to get at the detail of people's interactions as they moved about in the course of a day: 'The problem is that a single interview does not provide respondents with a robust enough set of narrative resources that they can productively work through and recount the detailed patterns of their everyday life-worlds' (2004: 123). To counter this, Latham asked diarists to chronicle their daily movements – where they went, when, why, who they went with and who they met – and to supplement this by taking photographs; the visual details led diarists 'back to the materiality of the world being described' (p. 127).

## 'Voice'

Giving participants a 'voice' in research is a feature of all participatory research, particularly action research 'where a group of people ... are involved in every stage of the research process and directly benefit from the outcomes' (Richards 2011: 1). There is a widespread assumption that generating photos enables research participants to represent their views and to exert some control over the research agenda (Luttrell and Chalfen 2010); in other words, to have an 'authoritative voice' in the research (Bloustein and Baker 2003: 72). This is a rationalisation of both photo-focused (e.g. Ziller 1990) and talk-focused studies. In some participatory photo projects, especially those using 'photovoice',[1] transformation, self-development and activism are primary objectives and the opportunity for participants to have a voice in the research is of central importance (also a host of non-academic projects which are beyond the scope of this book). For example, Alice McIntyre (2003) gave cameras to working-class women living in Belfast and invited them to provide an account of their daily lives which was then used to produce an exhibition about the relationship between place and identity. The purpose was to encourage the women to reflect on aspects of their lives and to be empowered to engage in individual or collective action to improve their circumstances.

Several issues arise when considering claims about voice in participatory photo projects. First, the extent of control that research participants have over the agenda is variable and dependent on the level of specificity in guidance about what to photograph, also by ethical and legal junctures and other physical, social, technical and cultural constraints on who can take photographs, of what, where, when and how. Bear in mind, though, that some guidance on what to photograph can help a person focus their thoughts and sharpen their ideas. Second, as discussed in relation to photos as data, the meaning of photos is not transparent and it is debatable whether partici- pants' views can really be appreciated by looking only at their photos. How much you can learn about a person's views will depend on how the research has been conducted; projects are most successful when researchers also attend to what participants think about their pictures and this entails photo-interviews or asking participants to write detailed comments. Third, to paraphrase Wendy Luttrell and Richard Chalfen (2010: 199), it is sometimes difficult for researchers to discern whose 'voice' is represented and, in turn, whose story is being told. The production of photos is not always a solo activity and family, friends and researchers sometimes help in producing these. It can be difficult to differentiate the 'voices' of participants from those of researchers and project directors, especially as participants' voices are selected, interpreted and pro- cessed by others.

---

### BOX 8.1   CHILDREN CREATING KINSHIP: AN INTERVIEW WITH JENNIFER MASON

This ESRC project (2004–6; 'Children Creating Kinship', RES-000-230-271) was designed to explore how children aged 7–12 create their own kinship and relationships. It involved listening to what children said about their own lives and relationships that were important to them. The research team was Jennifer Mason, Becky Tipper and Jennifer Flowerdew.

#### Why did you decide to ask children to take photos?

We wanted to think creatively about how to encourage children to tell us about important relationships in their lives, in case this was difficult for them to do in words alone. We decided to use ethnographic interviews and also to ask children to take pictures that evoked or were reminiscent of their relationships. We did not imagine that the pictures themselves would represent the children's important relationships and kinship in any straightforward way, and we felt that the content of the pictures might ultimately be less important than the discussion that they could potentially stimulate.

#### How did you go about this?

In an initial meeting with the children we gave them a single-use disposable cam- era with simple instructions asking them to take pictures that made them think about important relationships. We gave them a stamped addressed envelope so they could send the cameras back to us when they had taken all the pictures, and we explained that we would get the pictures developed and give them a copy, whilst

*(Continued)*

keeping a copy for the research project. We took the children's copies along when we interviewed them, so this was the first time the children had seen their pictures. We audio recorded the interviews, and subsequently transcribed them, and this means the audio recordings and the transcripts include the moments when the children first saw their pictures, as well as the discussion that ensued.

## Was this method successful?

The method was very successful couched, as it was, in the context of an ethnographic interview. This meant we could look at the pictures with the children, and ask them about what they contained, what they were unable to take pictures of, what was important about the people, animals, things, places and times or moments that they had tried to capture in their pictures, and so on. The pictures stimulated much discussion about important relationships and how these were contextualised. They enabled the children to engage in a detailed discussion with us about the circumstances of the pictures – usually events and things that had happened in the last few days – which helped us understand relationships in context, as we had wanted to do. The children also for the most part were able to respond in a very articulate manner to our questions about who or what they had been unable to include in the photographs, which helped broaden our discussion into their kin relationships as a whole, and not just those represented in the pictures.

Looking at pictures together was good as a warm up for the rest of the interview, and meant that the children got very engaged at an early stage. They were excited to see their pictures, and to explain them to us, pointing out people, things and places with great enthusiasm. The research was conducted prior to the era of mass ownership by this age group of digital devices that can take instant pictures, so the excitement and surprise in having had pictures developed, and opening the pack to discover them, was palpable. This also meant that the children (with only one or two exceptions) were excited about the exercise from the start because it meant being given a camera for their own use, albeit a single-use one.

We learned a lot from the pictures that would have been hard to get in any other way. For example, there were many pictures of things (birthday cakes, pictures stuck on the fridge and so on) which helped us understand their role in children's relationalities. Similarly, photographs of places helped to open up discussion of the importance of particular places and spaces in the ways that children practiced their kin relationships. It would have been difficult to find out about these particular aspects simply by asking questions in an interview, and our sociological understanding was enhanced by being able to see what these things looked like rather than relying only on verbal description. It was also interesting to see how children took the pictures. For example, there were many pictures of animals, which did not in itself surprise us because we knew that animals were an important part of children's experience of kinship. But many of the photographs were taken at extremely close range so that the pictures show seemingly enormous rabbits and guinea pigs, for example, or just part of the face of a dog (see Figure 8.1). This was suggestive to us of the physical closeness and tactility of children's relationships with animals, and indeed the physicality of their orientation to the world, and this became an important part of our understanding of what kinship is like for children.

**Figure 8.1**   Dog. © Jennifer Mason and Becky Tipper

## Would you do it again?

Yes, but it would work differently with the ubiquity of digital photographic devices. A single-use disposable camera is unlikely to be something that would excite the children in the same way and they may be less motivated to use it in the first place because of this. However, if they did use it and take some pictures, there would be a novelty in the current context of having a set of printed pictures put into their hands, and the excitement of having researchers interested in you and your pictures would remain. Not being able to see, judge and delete pictures instantly, as one can do with digital devices, is actually advantageous for a project of this sort. We would have missed a great deal if the children (or their friends and relatives) had been able to edit out the pictures they thought were not good enough – for example, the accidental shot of the lawn at their grandparents' house last Sunday, or the unflattering one of their Auntie with her eyes shut.

# Setting up research

In this section I consider how to set up a project in which research participants generate their own photos, this includes deciding what guidance to give participants, considering technological matters and ethics.

## Guidance on what to photograph

Some guidance on what to photograph is essential, but how much? This is an important question with implications for the agency of research participants. It depends, in part, on the objectives of the research: do you want to research specific questions or explore aspects of the participants' experiences from their perspectives and according to their agendas?

There are several strategies:

- Leave the photographic exercise *open*. In Baker's ethnographic study of 8–11-year-old girls growing up in Australia, girls were encouraged to photograph any aspect of their lives that they wished: 'The invitation in essence was to "play" with the camera, using it to explore their worlds freely' (Bloustein and Baker 2003:67).
- A variant of the open strategy establishes a general focus for the photos so that the photography is *contained*. An example is Rosaleen Croghan et al.'s (2008) study of young consumers in which a group of young people were asked to take photos of consumer goods that were meaningful to them.
- In contrast to the open and contained approaches, many researchers opt for a *scripted* approach in which research participants are asked to take photos to address a list of pre-decided topics or questions (e.g. Samuels 2007). Usually the questions are based on knowledge of relevant research in the area or the results of pilot or preliminary interviews.
- A variant of the scripted approach involves research participants devising the script; this works well when participants are able to work collaboratively. This strategy is often a feature of action research. For example, in her study of the experiences of Irish women living in Northern Ireland, McIntyre (2003) invited the research participants to identify the script that would guide their photography (see also Cook and Hess 2007).

It is important to choose a strategy that is appropriate given your research objectives and research participants. This is not always easy to predict and pilot work can be helpful. Samuels's (2007) research provides a good example of the importance of selecting an appropriate strategy. In his study of boys' experiences of Buddhist life in a temple in Sri Lanka, Samuels undertook two photographic studies, one in 2003 and another in 2004. In both projects he asked the boys to take photos of aspects of monastic life and then interviewed them about their photos. His aim was to explore 'what constitutes an emotionally satisfying experience of Buddhism' (p. 198). The principal difference between the two studies was in the directions that Samuels gave the boys. In the 2003 study, drawing on previous research in Sri Lanka, he generated a script of eleven topics to guide the photography of his research subjects. Topics included: an ideal monk and what is difficult about being a monk. One year later he again asked young monks to take photos, but this time he decided to ask the boys to photograph ten things that they liked. This change in practice was influenced by scholars who advocate giving children agency; Samuels questioned the assumptions embedded in his scripted project and wondered whether it hampered children in being 'active arbiters of their own experience' (p. 217). Samuels discovered, however, that the scriptless photographic study was far less successful than the scripted one. Although some of the novice monks talked at length about their photos most 'were much less able to articulate their own thoughts behind why they took each photograph and what attracted their heart/mind to their photograph' (p. 218). This was because the scripted approach encouraged the boys to work out what would be the best photo to take for each topic; this decision-making encouraged reflection on their experiences and feelings.

You need to think carefully about the instructions you give participants about what to photograph. In a study of how people 'belong' to their locality, Julia Bennett (2011) asked participants to keep diaries for a week, detailing the places they visited, who they met there and what they did. Participants were also asked to photograph each place visited; these photos were to help participants talk about places in subsequent interviews. However, one participant, 'Beryl', did not respond to the task as Bennett expected. Beryl took a photo of the church she had been attending for 45 years, but she photographed it from an unusual perspective (Figure 8.2). In the photo-interview, as Bennett explains (personal correspondence): 'Beryl was initially confused by the photo and denied taking it until she recalled, "I took that because it had the statues in".' When Bennett asked Beryl to elucidate on the photo, to explain what she felt about this place, Beryl could only say 'it doesn't look familiar'. Rather than facilitating talk, in this instance the participant's photo initially inhibited it. A further point to remember when setting up projects is that it is helpful to ask participants to keep a written record of the photos they have taken, a diary entry or a description on a log sheet (for an example, see Moore et al. 2008).

## Technological matters

Camera technology has implications for what and how things are photographed. Whereas in the past researchers relied on disposable cameras, and occasionally cheap instamatic cameras and Polaroids, today's researchers utilise cheap digital cameras and disposable cameras, as well as research participants' camera phones. Many accounts of the technical details of pre-digital research now seem dated, but the issues are not always very different. Modern technologies do not guarantee problem-free research, nor do they enable researchers to bypass questions about what type of camera is most appropriate.

**Figure 8.2**    Beryl's photo. © Julia Bennett

Cost is a consideration, but there are also other factors that will be influenced by the specifics of your research design. You should ask yourself the following questions. Is it necessary for the camera to be easy to use? Does the camera need a self-timer so that the photographer is not dependent on an assistant for self-portraits? Do you need to limit the number of photographs that research participants can take? If this is the case, a disposable camera which typically has 24–36 exposures or a cheap film camera may be a better choice than a digital camera which allows a photographer to take hundreds of pictures and to edit their shots. Is the quality of the image important, perhaps because you want to study the content of the images and the details need to be clear? Are aesthetics important? This might be an issue if you want participants to use their photographs to express their points of view on a topic and produce an exhibition of their work. These were the reasons why McIntyre (2003) wanted her research participants to have control over the look of their photos. To facilitate this she gave participants a disposable colour camera and an inexpensive 35 mm camera for black and white prints. McIntyre also discussed with the women the implications of photographic choices: how black and white prints evoke different responses than colour prints and the difference between taking photos close-up and at a distance. Is it advantageous for research subjects to have almost instant access to their photos so they can reflect on, and write about, their photos while the reasons for taking them are still fresh in their minds (e.g. Blinn and Harrist 1991)? Digital cameras can provide instant access to photographs, but access to a computer is necessary if you want participants to view and comment on the detail of images. How much training should you give research participants? It is imperative that participants know how to use the cameras they are given but, as in McIntyre's (2003) study, sometimes it may also be useful to provide guidance on the implications of photographic choices. To provide the necessary guidance, you must be competent and confident in using and explaining how to use photographic technologies.

## Ethics

It is important to discuss issues around etiquette and ethics with research participants as these may determine what can be photographed and how. Often there are common courtesies to consider and agree on. Usually research must comply with the ethical specifications of your institution, funders or other agencies. These specifications can be demanding, particularly when the research involves people from vulnerable groups, such as children. You also need to explain to participants what you will do with their photographs or digital images. Ethical issues are discussed more fully in Chapter 10.

# Analysing participants' photos

Analysis of research participants' photos is central to photo-focused studies. It is also undertaken in many talk-focused studies as an adjunct to photo-elicitation; how people talk about their photos is discussed in Chapter 9. Sometimes photo analysis is not part of the researcher's initial plan, but the participants' photos seem too interesting to be treated only as a stimulus for discussion (see Box 8.1).

In Chapter 2 I introduced five lines of enquiry that are usually involved in image work; most are relevant to analysing photos generated by participants. Identification of the basic details of a photo (when taken and by whom) is always necessary; bear in mind that some participants' photos may be taken or directed by their friends or family members (see under 'Voice'). The materiality of photos is typically of little importance in analysing participant photography, though it plays a part in how participants talk about their photos. Typically the main lines of enquiry in analysing participant photography are a combination of: a close examination of the content of images; exploration of their contexts of production and engagement, in this instance the contexts in which you and your participants interpret the images; and the meanings you and your research participants ascribe to the images.

In the following I look at approaches to analysing images, the importance of context and ways to incorporate research participants' accounts of their photos in to your analysis. The division of this section is for convenience; in practice the analysis of images often involves consideration of participants' accounts of what they have photographed and, particularly in photo-focused studies, contextual research. A combination of these analytic strategies characterises the study of children's part-time work, which is discussed in Box 8.2.

### BOX 8.2   RESEARCHING CHILDREN'S LABOUR

Participant photography was one component of a project by Phil Mizen, Angela Bolton and Chris Pole examining part-time work among school-age children in England and Wales. Though the participant photography was principally photo-focused, the bigger study also involved participants in talk-alone interviews, group discussions, casual conversations and the production of written diaries. The researchers insist that participants' photos generated distinctive data.

Young people were given disposable cameras and asked 'to take photographs of their work, which showed what it was like to work and what that work meant to them' (Bolton et al. 2001: 513). Once their photos were developed, each partici-pant was asked to select six and write about these in a diary. Some wrote exten-sively about each image while others wrote a few lines: they explained why they had taken the image, what it meant to them and what they thought it communi-cated about their working lives (Mizen, personal correspondence).

Initially, the researchers thought participants' photos 'disappointing'; empty workplaces and equipment featured prominently but there were few pictures of people or the children working (Figure 8.3). 'Several of those who had spent the first half of the year talking in interviews and writing in diaries about busy working environments duly presented us with photographs of empty shops and hairdressing salons at the beginning or end of the working day' (Bolton et al. 2001: 510). This initial assessment was soon revised.

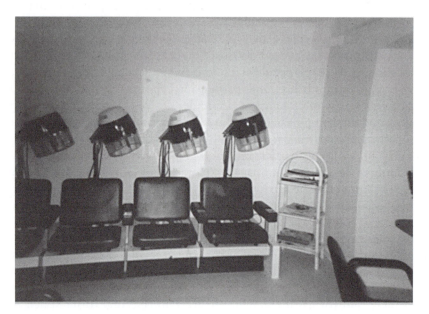

**Figure 8.3**   Hairdressing salon, Becky, 15, South Wales. © Phil Mizen

The researchers insist that participants' photos contributed something distinctive to their research, but they are equally insistent that they are of little value if considered in isolation from other sources. The distinctive contribution emerged in part from the visual record that the photos provide. To use photos in this way required a 'critical but realist or materialist approach' (Bolton et al. 2001: 505), akin to the cautious realist position on images outlined in Chapter 1. (If using photos in this way you need to be careful how you think about and refer to photos; it is easy to slip into a naive realist position that overlooks the construction of photos and describes them simply as portraits of reality.) The researchers acknowledge that images are constructions and the product of the photographer's selectivity, but argue that by taking these points into account photos provide visual evidence of aspects of young people's work and perspectives. The distinctive contribution of photos is, however, inseparable from understanding the contexts in which children worked and in which the photos were produced, this information was provided by participants' written commentaries and gleaned from other sources and methods used in the project. The value of photos also emerged from using children's written commentaries (and some conversations) to pinpoint the meaning and significance of their photos. As Mizen explains (personal correspondence):

> this was important to us because we knew that we could not take for granted our own interpretations of the images and it quickly became apparent that the meaning of the images was not always self-evident. In fact, one of the principal lessons we learned was that the images quickly confounded many of our assumptions about the children's lives.

In a nutshell, photo analysis involved:

- A methodical approach to the analysis of images, 'naming everything that is seen with the object of making the taken-for-granted rise to the surface, breaking down the privileging of the central image or object of focus' (Bolton et al. 2001: 513).
- Attention to contexts of production, namely how and why participants selected, composed and generated their photos.
- Study of photos in relation to other forms of data – including sources about participants' biographies and young people's written accounts of their photos – to identify what was present or absent in the photos.
- Exploration of how participant photographers understood the images they generated.

By triangulating methods the researchers identified three ways the photos were revealing. First, the photos provided a visual record of aspects of children's work, particularly the equipment they used and aspects of their work environment – stockrooms,

*(Continued)*

backrooms, rubbish skips, toilets – places that are often behind the scenes and invisible to researchers. Through their photos, the children 'expanded upon the context and detail of their jobs in ways that their words had never quite conveyed, or which familiarity had rendered inconsequential to interview, discussion or written diary' (Mizen 2005: 129). Second, the form of participants' photos proved revealing, particularly of children's lowly work status. Most photos were taken when workplaces were empty, because this was less disruptive of the young person's work or because the participant was concerned not to antagonise their employer. Third, the photos were evidence of the children's perspectives on their work:

> Their choice of what to include in the frame and what to leave out provides us as the researchers not merely with data as illustration, but with a form of data which has been selected and subject to a process of analysis for its significance to the culture of the research participants. (Bolton et al. 2001: 507)

Clearly, the selectivity of the photograph is an important feature of the data, but understanding the viewpoint depends on an explanation of what it means to the photographer.

For example, John, age 12, worked on his father's sheep farm, and one of the photographs (Figure 8.4) he wrote about depicted him seated on a quad bike surrounded by fields:

**Figure 8.4**   Working on family sheep farm, John, 12, South Wales. © Phil Mizen

> It could have been a photograph of any boy showing off a treasured posses-
> sion with no relation to working practice. But he [John] wrote, '*(T)his is when
> I go out on my quad to check all the sheep to see if they are all right*' ... Without
> alternative data sources we risked interpretations which missed, concealed or
> skewed the nature of John's work. (Bolton et al. 2001: 514– 5)
>
> Comparison of different data sources also highlighted omissions in the photos. For
> instance, in interview John talked about herds of sheep but these were never visible
> in his photos. However, from discussing this point with John it emerged that he did
> not regard a flock of sheep as a fitting representation of his work because the sheep
> were usually scattered across the hillsides. In the context of a triangulation of meth-
> ods, John's photo provides graphic evidence of the scale of his work.

## Approaches to analysing images

Your approach to analysing participants' photos will depend on how much emphasis
you place on photos as data; the content of images is usually of secondary importance
in studies that are only talk-focused, whereas it is central to photo-focused studies.

### Talk-focused: identifying general themes and patterns
### that can be explored further through photo-elicitation

One strategy is to look at participants' photos to identify prominent themes or patterns of content, tone and treatment, perhaps taking into account participants' captions and descriptions. Some people go no further than this before discussing their
findings in photo-interviews, while others revisit photos (taken by individual participants or a group) to count up how often themes appear before exploring these
in photo-interviews. For example, in their study of the experiences of women
returning to education, Blinn and Harrist (1991: 180) began by studying each of
their participants' photos and the accompanying comments to draw out key themes:
'The written comments ... were critical because they allowed the researchers to go
beyond the categorization of surface content and quickly begin to understand the
motives and feelings of the photographers.' Blinn and Harrist then counted up the
frequency with which each theme appeared in their participants' photos before
using photo-elicitation interviews to pursue the themes further.

### Photo-focused: doing a detailed analysis of image content

Detailed analysis of image content is necessary if your research is photo-focused;
bear in mind the guidance in Chapter 2 on scrutinising images and ascertaining
meaning. Qualitative methods of photo analysis are explained in Chapter 7, so here
I introduce quantitative content analysis and how it can be used alongside qualitative methods of data analysis.

Quantitative content analysis is a method for counting up the frequency with
which observable content is featured in a sample of texts. It can be used with found

photos (e.g. Lutz and Collins 1993) and generated ones (e.g. Luttrell 2010; Ziller 1990). This type of analysis is useful, particularly if you are working with a large number of images and you want to identify themes, compare photos produced by different groups of research participants, or trace changes over time.

Studying photos generated by participants, or a sample of these, involves the following steps:

1   Identifying, and defining precisely, categories of visual content that you will record in your analysis (e.g. location, gender of subjects), these are called 'coding categories'. Coding categories are based on your research questions, theories or other information that emerges from a preliminary survey of the photos; ensuring that categories map on to research questions is essential for the validity of your analysis (Rose 2007).

2   Each coding category is broken down into specific codes; these codes are the precise visual details that you record in your analysis of each image. For example, the coding category 'location' is broken down into the codes of 'office', 'home', 'shops', 'other'. The codes within each coding category must not overlap; they must be mutually exclusive. It is essential that codes are worked out carefully and that they are unambiguous, such that another researcher would independently replicate how you have coded a particular photo.

3   Coding, that is, recording which codes appear in each photo. For every photo, one code must be given for each of your coding categories. To inform the coding process you need to construct a coding manual or data dictionary that defines precisely what each category and code means; for an example, see Figure 8.5.

4   Counting up the frequency with which each code appears across the collection or sample of photos.

The meaning and significance of content is judged by the frequency with which it appears. More complex analysis involves noting the relationships between different coding categories; often, but not always (e.g. Lutz and Collins 1993, cited in Rose 2007), this uses quantitative techniques and software to identify associations, correlations, cross-tabulations. Advice on doing quantitative content analysis is provided in several good texts (e.g. Bell 2001; Rose 2007; Seale 2004).

For the purpose of analysing participants' photos, quantitative content analysis has four main limitations. First, important but infrequent visual features are marginalised in the findings. For example, in a project on children's experiences of urban space a police officer appears only once in the set of generated photos, but though this single appearance may be important for understanding children's use of urban space, it would probably be ignored because quantity of appearances are the criteria for assessing significance. Second, absences are not automatically considered though these may be important. For instance, the lack of photos of particular places or practices might indicate that these were out of bounds or taboo but, despite the importance of this finding for understanding use of space, it would not be flagged. Third, quantitative content analysis fragments images so that the interconnections between elements are not appreciated and the mood or tone is unacknowledged (Rose 2007). Fourth, account is not taken of what the image means to the photographer; researchers often misjudge what features of a photo are most important to the photographer (see Orellano 1999). This last limitation is sometimes rectified partly by drawing on participants' written descriptions of their photos or by interview input at the coding stage (e.g. Ziller 1990). Nevertheless, many scholars do not rely solely on quantitative content analysis because it offers a skewed assessment of the meaning of texts; it is 'a necessary but not sufficient methodology' (Bell 2001: 13). As discussed earlier, it is debatable how much can be learned from studying photos without input from participants.

Quantitative content analysis can be useful in combination with other techniques of image analysis, principally the study of the production context of an image and the meanings attributed to images by participant photographers. This is the analytic strategy adopted by Luttrell in her project, 'Children Framing Childhood', see Box 8.3.

---

## BOX 8.3  CHILDREN FRAMING CHILDHOOD

In 'Children Framing Childhood',[2] a participatory-photography project with school children, Wendy Luttrell (2010) analysed both the content of children's photos as well as the multiple meanings inscribed in these by participants as they talked about them in different contexts. 'Children Framing Childhood' is part of a larger, longitudinal study of how working-class immigrant children 'perceive and navigate linguistic, cultural, race/ethnic and economic differences, family–school relationships, and self and identity changes over time' in the context of schools in the United States (p. 224). Luttrell started from the premise that 'there are multiple layers of meaning in any single photograph and that children have intentions and make deliberate choices (albeit prescribed) to represent themselves and others'; 'It was with *an eye and an ear* for hidden transcripts of power expressed in children's photography that I crafted this project' (pp. 224–5, my italics).

Participants were equipped with disposable cameras and instructed to 'imagine you have a cousin your age that is moving to town and coming to your school. Take pictures of the school, your family and community that will help him/her know what to expect' (p. 227). Films were developed and the children invited to talk about them in four successive 'audiencings'. The first audiencing was a one-to-one interview in which the children discussed their photos with a researcher, explaining what was happening and what was important about each picture and saying why they had taken them and whether there were photos they

*(Continued)*

would have liked to take but could not. The children were also asked to select their five favourite photos; this process was video-taped. The second audiencing involved the children in peer group discussion of their favourite photos, focusing on 'what they noticed about each other's images, and ... questions they might have of the photographer' (p. 228). In the third audiencing the children were shown videos of their accounts of their favourite photos and asked if they would like to comment further or remove any photos. The fourth session involved the children curating an exhibition of their photos, which generated different discussions about their images.

These methods proved very successful, but finding a means to systematise and 'honour' the 'wealth of information and affect being communicated with and through children's photography' was 'daunting' (p. 225). Luttrell opted for a two-pronged analysis attending to the content of participants' photos and children's narratives about them (themes and patterns in what they had to say about their photos and the process of producing them); these 'two lenses of interpretation' (personal correspondence) enabled Luttrell to engage with various 'sites' (Rose 2007) of meaning making – picture taking, picture viewing and picture content – as well as the meanings made and remade as children used their photos to make claims about themselves or to express feelings etc.

The analysis started with a form of quantitative content analysis, what Luttrell (personal correspondence) calls a 'categorical approach', identifying patterns and themes across all the images to answer the question, what role, if any, does gender, race/ethnicity, immigrant status, age and cohort play in shaping what images were taken? The aims were to be 'systematic and transparent about one way of seeing/ reading the photographs and to identify patterns that might be "too subtle to be visible on a casual inspection"' (Lutz and Collins 1993: 89) (Luttrell 2010: 229). The content analysis involved the formulation of a list of categories and codes derived from theory (e.g. Goffman 1979), other content analyses (e.g. Lutz and Collins 1993), what teachers noticed about the photos and information that emerged as the children talked about each other's photos in the context of peer-group audiencing (e.g. brand names). The following codes were covered: setting (e.g. family, school, community, inside/outdoors); people (e.g. children/adults, male/female; age and gender mix); things; genre (e.g. snapshot, landscape, portrait); posture, poses and glances; activity type (e.g. work, play, socialising); activity level (i.e. high, medium, low); gaze (i.e. looking at the camera or away); and whether smiling or not. Coding was based only on what was visible in the photos. A team of assistants coded a random selection of photos; reliability was tested and discrepancies discussed. Category headings (e.g. 'setting', 'activity level') were explained further. After another round of reliability testing, all photos were coded and the data entered into a statistical analysis package. Figure 8.5 provides excerpts from the data dictionary that was devised to assist coders; Figure 8.6 is an example of how one photo was coded.

| Code | Meaning |
|---|---|
| CODEDWHO | Enter YOUR FIRST name |
| CODEDWHEN | Enter date photo was coded (mm / dd / yyyy) |
| INSIDE | Is the photograph taken inside? (0=no; 1=yes; -1=not ascertainable) |
| SETTING | What is the setting of the photo? (1=home; 2=school; 3=community; 4=other [including photos of parents' workplace]; -1=not ascertainable; -9=does not apply) |
| SITE | What type of room/location is the photo taken in? (1=bedroom; 2=living room; 3=kitchen; 4=dining room; 5=hallway/stairs; 6=classroom; 7=technology lab; 8=library; 9=lunch room; 10=gym; 11=playground/park; 12=religious center; 13=store; 14=restaurant; 15=neighborhood street; 16=government building [e.g. fire station]; 17=performance space; 18= private residence; 19= other -1=unable to ascertain from context of photo; - 9 = does not apply [e.g. in the case of a photo of a photo]) |
| GENRE | What is the overall genre of the photograph? (1="scene" [e.g. people in the act of doing something]; 2="site" [e.g. photo of a place/building/room]; 3="portrait" [e.g. posed people/pets, objects on displa]; 4='meta' (photo of a photo); -1=unable to ascertain from context of photo) |
| PEOPLEPHOTO | Are there any people in the photo? [Code only real people, so don't code people if it's a photo of a photo or people on TV as 'people'] (0=no; 1=one person; 2=two people; etc...13=thirteen OR MORE people; -1=not ascertainable) |
| BABYPHOTO | Are there any babies in the photo ? (0=no; 1=one baby; 2=two babies; etc...13=thirteen OR MORE babies; -1=not ascertainable) |
| BRANDNAME | Do any of the objects pictured feature a brand name and/or logo? [code for foregrounded objects, e.g. a shirt someone is wearing, an object someone is holding, or when the object is the focus of the photo. (0=no brand names/logos on object(s); 1=at least one brand name/logo object present [e.g. Fubu shirt, Roco jacket, Hello Kitty pen]; -1=not ascertainable) |
| DISPLAY | Do any objects (including pets) appear to be purposely displayed or organized for the photograph? (0=objects not purposely displayed/arranged; 1=one or more objects on display [e.g. trophies lined up on a table; vaccum cleaner placed in front of couch; book placed on the middle of a couch]; -1=not ascertainable) |
| DECORATION | Are indicators of decoration present in the photograph? [Curtains, pillow covers, indoor plants, mouldings, etc count as indicators of decoration] (0=no; 1=yes) |
| ANGLE | CODE ONLY OBVIOUS ANGLES: 1=PHOTO TAKEN FROM ABOVE, FROM A HIGHER STANCE THAN THE SUBJECT; 2=PHOTO TAKEN FROM BELOW, I.E. LOOKING UP TO THE SUBJECT/OBJECT; 3=PHOTO TAKEN AT EYE-LEVEL ON 'EQUAL FOOTING'; -1=NOT ASCERTAINABLE |
| "FEMCUL" | 0=NO INDICATORS OF FEMININITY; 1=YES INDICATORS (COLORS, RIBBONS, GLAMOUR PRODUCTS, CURTAINS, Kitchens, tools for household chores/ child-rearing, etc); -1=NOT ASCERTAINABLE/NOT APPLICABLE [femcul/mascul codes are not mutually exclusive; same for childcen/ adultcen) LOOK FOR EVIDENCE OF "DOMESTICATING A SPACE" |
| MASCUL | 0=NO INDICATORS OF MASCULINITY (I.E. SPORTS INSIGNIAS) 1=YES; -1=NOT ASCERTAINABLE/NOT APPLICABLE |
| CHILDCEN | 0=NO INDICATORS OF child-centeredness; 1=INDICATORS (TOYS, GAMES, STUFFED ANIMALS, CARTOONS ON THE TV); -1=NOT ASCERTAINALBE/APPLICABLE  ASK YOURSELF, "WHO WAS THIS SPACE SET UP FOR?" |
| ADULTCEN | 0=NO INDICATORS OF ADULT-CENTERDNESS; 1=INDICATORS (ALCOHOL, CARS, FURNITURE that's not meant for kid's use); -1=NOT ASCERTAINABLE/NOT APPLICABLE  ASK YOURSELF, "WHO WAS THIS SPACE SET UP FOR?" |
| DISTANCE | 1=PHOTOGRAPHER WITHIN TOUCHING DISTANCE OF THE SUBJECT/OBJECT (AT ARM'S LENGTH, SO TO SPEAK); 2=PHOTOGRAPHER AT BODY'S LENGTH AWAY FROM SUBJECT/OBJECT, LET'S SAY 3-5 PACES AWAY); 3=FAR AWAY; 4=EXREMELY UP CLOSE (LIKE A DETAIL SHOT); -1=NOT ASCERTAINABLE |

**Figure 8.5**   Extracts from Data Dictionary. © Wendy Luttrell

| PhotoNumber | INSIDE | SETTING | SITE | GENRE | PEOPLEPHOTO | BABYPHOTO |
|---|---|---|---|---|---|---|
| 10120507 | 1 | 1 | -1 | 3 | 0 | 0 |

| BRANDNAME | DISPLAY | DECORATION | ANGLE | "FEMCUL" | MASCUL |
|---|---|---|---|---|---|
| 1 | 1 | 1 | 1 | 1 | 0 |

| CHILDREN | ADULTCEN | DISTANCE |
|---|---|---|
| 1 | 0 | 1 |

**Figure 8.6**   Child's photo - 10120507 (stuffed animals) – with extract from coding sheet. © Wendy Luttrell

*(Continued)*

Following the content analysis, Luttrell then did 'a case-based, narrative analysis to flesh out the meanings that the children attached to their images and their intentions when taking the photo, which among others things, brought to the surface assumptions that the coders were making about what was going on in a photograph' (personal correspondence). Alongside this, Luttrell compared what the children had to say in one-to-one interviews with what they said amongst their peers.

## Contextualising photos

Where images are regarded as an important aspect of a project, whether treated as texts or evidence of the material and social dimensions of participants' lives, it is important to contextualise images by examining their production. What is featured in a photo is influenced by a host of factors that have implications for your interpretation of the images and also, in photo-elicitation studies, what participants talk about. This is not to deny that research participants have choices when they take photos, but to acknowledge the factors that shape their photography (material, cultural, social, physical) and to recognise that their images are shaped by what they have been asked to do. In the following I consider pre-existing photographic practices and factors specific to the research context. I also examine claims that the processes involved in participant photography are worthy of analysis in their own right.

Understanding pre-existing photographic practices is important, in part because these influence how research participants interpret and respond to the photographic assignment. Where the use of a camera is novel (see Mason, Box 8.1), participants may be excited and empowered by the prospect of taking photos and approach the task differently from those who are used to producing their own pictures. Prior experience of taking photos might also influence the skill with which people generate research photos. Cook and Hess (2007) realised that the children in their study did not share their experiences and understandings of cameras and they wished they had looked at this more closely before starting the project. This resonates with Jon Prosser and Catherine Burke's advice that 'children should not necessarily be viewed as apprentice adult photographers since they exhibit their own distinctive intentions and products' (2006: 14; see also Sharples et al. 2003). Participants' understandings of photographic genre conventions can also shape how they respond to the research task. As Croghan et al. (2008: 348) explain of their study of youth consumption: 'In giving young people disposable cameras, we invited them to participate in a genre of personal snapshot photography that has a particular history and set of expectations associated with it'. Alongside genre conventions (conventions of style and subject matter typically associated with different types of photographs such as passport photos or family snaps) there are also prevailing and sometimes rapidly shifting conventions around the depiction of particular types of people and experience. For instance, since adolescence is constructed as a time of fun and freedom from responsibility, Croghan et al.'s respondents produced lively and affirming images. Talking with participants about their photos can reveal how genre and other conventions shape their pictures. To review research participants' prior relationships to photography, a brief interview can be undertaken with each at the beginning of a project, perhaps looking at the cameras they use and the kinds of pictures they usually take.

What people photograph is also shaped by the research task and context including how participants perceive their audiences (the researcher, possibly other research participants and readers/viewers of the research). Some studies invite participants to imagine specific audiences when producing photos. For example, Keith Kenney (1993: 252) invited Chinese and American students to each make photographic self-portraits and to 'select one image to enlarge ... to give a true impression of yourself ... this picture will be sent through the mail, along with your classmates' pictures, to a group of (Chinese or American) college students.' Clearly, the photos will be shaped partly by how participants conceptualise their audience, but Kenney's comparative research takes no account of the different ways in which American and Chinese students perceive one another and the implications of this for their self-portraits.

Interpersonal relations, and the power dynamics between research participants and their 'assistants' or photographic subjects, will also influence what is photographed. Participants often take 'obligatory' photos of family or friends (e.g. Blinn and Harrist 1991: 189). Sometimes participants ask 'assistants', typically family members or friends, to take photos (Drew et al. 2010; Luttrell 2010). In some studies it is assumed that participants will seek help; for instance in Cindy Clark's (1999) study of children with chronic illness it was expected that child photographers would be assisted by parents or peers. Interestingly, many studies do not comment on the collaboration involved in generating pictures, but interpersonal relations between the photographer and her or his 'assistant' are likely to shape the content of photos and have implications for photo-elicitation; to return to the earlier discussion of 'voice', collaborative photography raises the question of whose story is being told.

How research participants respond to the researcher's task will also be shaped by photographic opportunities, such as how and where the photographer can move and what they can access. Age-related restrictions and freedoms are particularly pertinent when working with children. Physical capabilities are also a factor to consider. Young children are usually restricted in the height at which they can take photos and will, for example, photograph through fences and railings rather than over them. The duration of the study will also have consequences for the kinds of photos participants have the opportunity to generate (Moore et al. 2008); loss of cameras and photographs is also more likely to occur in long-term than short-term projects.

So far I have discussed ways that participants' images are shaped by contexts of production, but the process of participant photography can be an important source of data in its own right (Cook and Hess 2007; Frith and Harcourt 2007; Radley and Taylor 2003). In an ethnographic study of the experiences of hospital patients, Alan Radley and Diane Taylor (2003) asked participants to photograph up to twelve things that they thought significant about their hospital stay; photo-interviews were undertaken in hospital and when the participants returned home. Because of restrictions imposed by the hospital, a researcher stayed with each participant while they were selecting and taking their pictures, this proved advantageous for the researchers: 'We gained knowledge of the context in which the pictures were taken and became aware of the kinds of questions that arose when patients decided what (or what not) to photograph' (p. 82). Radley and Taylor noted that the act of taking photos shifted participants' perspectives on their environment and experiences, encouraging them to objectify what they had been living – to 'turn on' their environment (p. 82); it also prompted participants to account for things they could not easily explain or that they did not wish to explore. Witnessing (and recording in their field notes) the processes and deliberations involved in producing these shots, researchers gained unexpected insights into participants' experiences. Their analysis subsequently included 'both what the patients did to make the pictures and what they said to make them meaningful' (p. 83). Radley and Taylor were determined that their analysis should not privilege any one aspect of the material they collected: '[We] listened to the tapes of the interviews with the photographs in front of us, making detailed notes of what was said about the images and relating this to the notes we had made at the time of photography and after the home interview' (pp. 89–90). The researchers' field notes about each participant's 'act of photography' helped make sense of the photos and talk and facilitated their integration. Radley and Taylor argue that much is gained by the researcher being present when participants take photos; though this is not always feasible or desirable, photo-interviews can be used to unpack participants' experiences of deciding what and how to generate photos.

## Incorporating participants' accounts of their photos

If your research is concerned with the content of generated photos, the issue is whether to address the interviewee's account of what they have photographed and why. Captions can help researchers see the photographer's intended meaning and avoid gross misinterpretation of an image, but not everyone can provide a caption, moreover even clear captions are not usually enough to explain a picture. Written descriptions are more helpful. Typically, research participants are not asked to write extensive accounts of their photos: indeed, this could be counterproductive given that this method is supposed to be fun and accessible and is sometimes used to avoid an over-reliance on words. Moreover, some of the questions that researchers may want to ask about the photos may be difficult for participants to think and write about without some prior training and reflexivity which would position participants differently in the research. Whilst written descriptions can assist in categorising photos at a general level, they are usually unable to address all the factors necessary to contextualise an image. To understand participants' photos, Bolton et al. drew on earlier talk-alone interviews with their participants and other sources of information as well as ad hoc photo-elicitation (see Box 8.2).

Talk is usually the best way to explore what a photo means to the photographer because what is seen by one person is not always visible to another. Researchers always need to be wary of presumptions about meaning, but this is particularly the case when working with research participants whose everyday culture is different from that of the researcher. In her work with children and urban space, Orellano (1999: 78) reports that, 'In many cases, what kids focused on in their talk about the photos was not what seemed most salient to me.' Her research points clearly to the limitations of relying only on what is in a photo:

> These conversations with the children about their photographs revealed that the children and I literally did not see the same things in the same physical space. Not only did we notice different physical details, but the children saw what I could not – a web of complex and engaging social relationships that both filled and gave meaning to the physical landscape of buildings, streets and cars. (p. 84)

There are also prosaic reasons for talking to research participants. As Orellano discovered, her respondents did not always photograph what they had intended to, which, she stresses, is a good reason to listen to photographers talk about their work and 'a good reminder not to over psychologize our interpretations of photographs' (p. 86).

## Summary

Research participants are asked to generate photos so the researcher can learn about participants' lives, subjectivities and views. There are various types of projects but the key difference between these is whether the researcher is interested in the generation of visual data (photo-focused) or interview data (talk-focused). In this chapter I have evaluated common reasons why researchers ask participants to take photos. I have argued that to learn about the lives and views of participants, photo-focused research must engage with how images have been produced and why, and what they mean to the participant photographer; this can be achieved using photo-elicitation, extended written narratives, or a triangulation of sources.

Participant-photography projects need to be set up carefully; this involves deciding how much guidance to give participants about what to photograph, selecting an appropriate camera and reflecting on how much preparation participants need to take photos. Ethical frameworks are also important; this topic is pursued more fully in Chapter 10. Analysis of participants' photos depends on the types of data the researchers aim to generate. In studies that are only talk-focused, analysis usually involves identification of general themes and patterns for discussion in photo-interviews; photo-elicitation is pursued further in Chapter 9. Photo-focused research typically employs detailed analysis of images including qualitative techniques and quantitative content analysis, sometimes in combination.

## Notes

1  Photovoice (Wang and Burris 1997) is a method that involves participants taking photos of their daily lives from their own perspectives and then discussing and working with these photos in various ways; the aim is to facilitate personal and community change.
2  The 'Children Framing Childhood' website is at http://wendyluttrell.org/framing-childhoods/. The site also includes a description of the follow-up study, 'Looking Back'.

# 9

# Photo-interviews: Listening to Talk about Photos

Listening to what people have to say about photos is an increasingly popular method in social and historical research, known widely as 'photo-interviewing' or 'photo-elicitation'. But what is the purpose of using photos in interviews, what do they contribute? And how can researchers make sense of what people say about photos; how do photo-interviews work? These fundamental questions are the focus of this chapter. Though I tackle them separately, these two questions are interwoven; understanding how photo-elicitation works is pivotal to deciding whether and how to use photos in interviews.

To address these two questions the chapter is organised in two parts. In part one I focus on the purpose of using photos in interviews, starting with an overview of how researchers have used them. I then evaluate the two main benefits that are claimed for using photos in interviews: that they encourage dialogue and generate useful data. The first part concludes with an overview of practical questions that researchers need to consider before doing a photo-interview. In the second part of this chapter I concentrate on how photo-interviews work and the implications of this for what people do and don't say as they look at photos. Understanding this process can help researchers make decisions about methods and inform the analysis and interpretation of photo-interview data. This discussion engages with how interviewees conceptualise photos, the temporalities of the visual–verbal relationship, and the relationship between photos, memories and stories. I conclude by drawing out key strategies for incorporating photos into interview analysis.

## Part One: Key purposes of using photos in interviews

Before evaluating photo-elicitation it is useful to reflect on the main ways that researchers use photos in interviews. Increasingly, photo materials are a tool for social and historical research and deliberately 'inserted' into interviews to prompt discussion, reflection and recollection (Harper 2002: 13), sometimes alongside other visual and textual materials (e.g. Bagnoli 2004). Some interviews use found photos, including interviewees' personal pictures (Chapter 4), but often the talk focuses on photos the researcher (Chapter 7) or research participants have generated for the research (Chapter 8), the latter is sometimes called 'autodriving' (Heisley and Levy 1991). Often, especially in historical research, photos are not deliberately inserted into an interview for a specific purpose, rather personal photo collections are studied in their own right, sometimes alongside other documents and objects, and interviews are used to make sense of these collections and what they might reveal about the past and the people that created and used them (e.g. Langford 2001, 2007; McLelland 1997; Thomson 2011a; Tinkler 2010, 2011; see also Chapter 5). Photos are also drawn into interviews on an ad hoc basis as and when they are volunteered by interviewees (see Pink 2007).

Researchers seem increasingly keen to discuss photos in interviews, but what are the attractions of doing this? Advocates of the practice identify two main reasons it is helpful to use photos in interviews: photos facilitate dialogue between the interviewer and interviewee, and they generate useful data. I now consider each of these benefits. Though people often relate differently to impersonal found photos, personal ones and those generated by the researcher or themselves (Pink 2007), as the following discussion demonstrates, there is no simple relationship between the type of photo and what happens in an interview.

## Photos facilitate dialogue

Photos are widely praised for facilitating interview dialogue. An important aspect of this is that they encourage people to talk and can serve as an icebreaker. Sighted people are generally used to talking about photos, especially family ones, although people may approach this differently in non-Westernised cultures (Collier and Collier 1986). Photos can also foster a relaxed atmosphere because they lessen the pressure on an interviewee. One way they do this is by acting as a 'third party' in interviews (Collier and Collier 1986: 105) so that an interviewee no longer feels they are the centre of attention. As Dona Schwartz (1989) discovered, people often respond directly to the photographs and pay less heed to the interview context and the interviewer. In photo-interviews there is also less need for eye contact and the 'potential tension generated by face-to-face contact is lessened by mutual gazing at a photograph' (Prosser and Burke 2006: 9).

According to proponents of photo-elicitation, photos facilitate interviews by 'building bridges' between the interviewer and interviewee, this can occur with all types of photos (e.g. Collier and Collier 1986; Harper 2002; Pink 2007). As the interviewer and interviewee pore over photos together and discuss what they see and what this means, communication is encouraged and rapport and trust are built. While photos decentre the interviewee in terms of the interaction, they simultaneously create space for the interviewee's meanings and perspectives: when 'people discuss the meaning of photographs they try to figure out something together' (Harper 2002: 23), leading sometimes to a 'negotiated understanding' (Heisley and Levy 1991). This is important because people often see things differently. For example, in conversations with children about the photos they had generated, Marjorie Orellana (1999) found that the children and researcher literally did not see the same things in the same physical spaces. Where the researcher generates the photos, photo-elicitation can help the photographer see their pictures from different perspectives: 'the photographer, who knows his or her photograph as its maker ... suddenly confronts the realization that she or he knows little or nothing about the cultural information contained in the image' (Harper 1998: 35). These features are reasons why photo-interviews are sometimes seen to shift the balance of power in interviews, empowering research participants and giving them more 'authority' (e.g. Clark 1999).

All these features make photo-interviews particularly useful when working with people who are not used to interviews or who may feel intimidated by them. This is why some scholars (e.g. Clark 1999; Clark-Ibáñez 2007; Prosser and Burke 2006) embrace photo-elicitation as a child-centred method: 'words are the domain of adult researchers and therefore can be disempowering to the young. Images and their mode of production on the other hand are central to children's culture from a very early age and therefore are empowering' (Prosser and Burke 2006: 408).

### Photos don't always facilitate the talk researchers want

Researchers often find that photo-interviews elicit longer and more comprehensive responses than talk-alone interviews and are less taxing for respondents (e.g. Collier and Collier 1986). But this can have downsides as Katherine Davies and Jennifer Mason discovered (see Box 9.1). Photos can elicit an outpouring, and contrary to John Collier's experience (Collier and Collier 1986) they do not always encourage focus and engagement. In interviews based on personal photos, interviewees may end up pursuing their own agendas rather than engaging with the interviewer's questions.

---

**BOX 9.1   THE CHALLENGES OF PHOTO-ELICITATION: AN INTERVIEW WITH KATHERINE DAVIES**

Interviewee's photographs were a valued resource in the project on family resemblances undertaken by Jennifer Mason and Katherine Davies. In combination with other methods, photo-elicitation was revealing, though not always in ways that were anticipated; it also posed challenges (Davies 2011; Mason and Davies 2009).

The social pressure to say the right thing was felt particularly keenly by Davies as she conducted the photo-elicitation. Interviewees often looked to her as an 'expert' on family likenesses and she felt considerable pressure to identify these correctly as she looked at interviewees' photos. Visible likenesses often mattered

*(Continued)*

---

greatly to the interviewees, especially when these were perceived as evidence of a special relationship or a link with someone who had died. It also seemed rude not to 'see' what someone was pointing out in a picture and this linked to the practical consideration of helping the interview flow smoothly.

Photos could, however, be a distraction, especially when the interviewee had a clear image in their mind's eye of a likeness and went rummaging through stacks of pictures searching for a concrete instance of it. The sifting through loose photos that often accompanied these searches made it difficult, sometimes impossible, to keep track of the relationship between verbal comments and specific photos. But 'seeing their struggle to find a photo that sums up, often intangible, likenesses, was revealing about the nature of family resemblances' and the inadequacy of a two-dimensional image to convey what people conjure up in their minds. The 'inadequacies' of photographs were almost as revealing as the likenesses they seemingly depicted, but the experience of remaining engaged throughout this process and of trying to redirect the interviewee's attention was sometimes exhausting.

In the first interviews in which interviewees often volunteered their photos as a starting point, the photos had a tendency to dominate and to redefine the interview agenda. For these reasons, and because Mason and Davies were keen to avoid an over reliance on photos in case this led to a conflation of 'likeness' with the visual, they shifted to a talk-alone interview followed by an examination of photos.

## Not all photos get people talking

While too much talk is sometimes an issue, the reverse can also occur. Photo-interviews do not always encourage relaxed and full responses from interviewees. Silence can be a productive part of an interview (though sometimes disconcerting for the interviewer) during which the interviewee reflects on photos before offering comment, and this space for reflection should be preserved. But sometimes interviewees seem to have little to say. This can be because they perceive that photos require no explanation, in which case it may be necessary to ask for elaboration (Harper 1987; van de Does et al. 1992). Sometimes the problem is more complex. There are two main issues: first, the relationships that interviewees have to the photos discussed in the interview, this is particularly pertinent when working with interviewees' personal photos; second, whether interviewees engage with the content of photos.

First, the photos that seem most likely to get people talking are those that are relevant to them or otherwise meaningful, including personal photos, but this is not always the case. It can be difficult to anticipate correctly how interviewees will relate to photos, even family ones, as Alexander Freund and Angela Thiessen (2011) describe. In an interdisciplinary project 'Local Culture and Diversity on the Canadian Prairies', historians and folklorists interviewed 600 men and women aged over 70 years who had lived in the prairie provinces before 1940. Three methods were used: a survey questionnaire, a life story interview and a photo-interview. For the photo-interview interviewees were asked to select around ten photos from their personal collections and describe them to the interviewers. The researchers assumed that photos would encourage rapport, sharpen recall and elicit detailed and expansive responses:

> [W]e assumed that people would be more used to telling stories about photos than to narrating their life story or responding to oral historians' questions. This hypothesis was reinforced by assumptions that interviewees' selection of photos gave them control over the structuring of the interview, and that chronology was less constraining than in a life story interview. (p. 29)

The researchers were disappointed. A typical interviewee response was a 'hesitant, cursory description of a few words or a sentence or two. Follow-up questions were successful only with some photographs' (p. 30).

There were three reasons why the photo-interviews about life on the Canadian Prairies did not flow smoothly, all of which concern the relationships that interviewees had to their photos. First, it was not usual for interviewees to talk about family photos with people who had no personal connection to them:

> We began to understand that ... photographs' meanings were not fixed, but changed with the context. ... A photo-interview could not imitate the intimate sharing of memories among friends and family. This was a new context, and interviewees learned only during the interview which meanings the interviewers were interested in, and which meanings were safe and useful to inscribe in the photos in this particular context. (p. 30)

This should not be interpreted simply as interviewees telling researchers what they want to hear; rather, it is an acknowledgement that we all adjust what we say depending on the perceptions of our audience and the occasion of talking. The second point is that though several interviewees had inherited their photos they had only a weak connection to them, or they had not looked at them in such a long time that the photos were unfamiliar. Whereas the researchers assumed the interviewees would be familiar with their photographs and have stories to tell, the interviewees approached their pictures as outsiders would and tried to figure them out by, for example, using clothes and buildings to date them. Third, photos sometimes offered versions of the past that contradicted the interviewee's memories and hindered their storytelling. As other oral historians have also noted, photos can have a muting or silencing effect by generating difficult feelings or memories. I return to these points later.

The second reason why photo-interviews are not always successful is that some photos are better than others at promoting the interviewee's engagement. In a study of change in a farming community, Douglas Harper (2001) had mixed results with photo-interviews. Harper used archival photos of agricultural work produced in the 1940s with success: 'the historical photographs operated simultaneously on the empirical dimension (the farmers saw in the photographs details of work they had not specifically imagined for decades) and subjective dimension as the research subjects saw themselves implicitly in images from earlier decades of their lives' (2002: 18). However, photos of the farmers that Harper had taken were less productive because they were too familiar and did not encourage the farmers to reflect on what was in the pictures. A similar problem was encountered initially in Harper's study of a car mechanic (2002: 21):

> At first I ... was reproducing the perspective through which any person in the environment would gaze, and these photographs did not lead to any deep commentary from Willie, the shop owner. When I photographed from unusual angles, or from very close, it led Willie to see his activities from a new and interesting perspective.

For similar reasons, John Berger argues that black-and-white photos are better than colour in eliciting responses (1972, cited in Harper 2002). In these research contexts, I think the crux of the difference between photos that do and don't get people talking is the interviewee's assessment of how much work is required to explain a photo. When the interviewee thinks the photo is obvious, they are perhaps less likely to engage – to really look at the picture. In contrast, incomplete or unusual pictures are likely to be perceived as requiring interpretation; this explanation seems consistent with Harper's productive use of archival photos. Unusual photos are also likely to be more interesting to interviewees. Thinking back to Mason's account of research on children's understandings of kinship, it seems that the children's excitement at the pictures they had taken was a spur to looking and talking (Chapter 8). Seeing personal photos enlarged on a laptop offered a fresh perspective on the familiar for Alistair Thomson's (2011b, discussed later) interviewees in that this revealed previously unnoticed details and facilitated collaborative viewing. An unusual perspective can, however, also close down dialogue if the subject of the photo is unrecognisable (see 'Setting up projects' in Chapter 8).

This discussion of photos that do and don't get people talking has implications for designing research. Researchers need to consider what kinds of photos will be most useful at eliciting feedback and, if generated by the researcher or research participant, what guidelines should be followed in making pictures (see Chapters 7 and 8).

## Generating useful data

Scholars agree that photos can have powerful effects in interviews, although they are less sure why, a point I shall return to. Where photos do foster discussion, and this is not guaranteed, photo-interviews can generate rich and complex data: photos stimulate people to talk about their thoughts, feelings, memories and experiences, to work things out and, sometimes, to discuss subjects that are difficult to broach in talk-alone interviews. Talk is also key to understanding people's photo collections.

Photos often stimulate people to talk about what they know, think, experience, feel and remember. Aside from factual information, photo-interviews bring out the personal significance and meaning of what is depicted in photos and, if the photos are personal, sometimes the meanings attached to photo-objects. Photos can also prompt people to talk about their feelings, disrupting complacent viewing and inspiring emotionally charged responses (e.g. Emmison and Smith 2000; Mannik 2011). Memories are often stimulated by looking at photos (personal, generated, commercial etc.); this can include recollections about the events of the previous night as well as memories of years or even decades past. Discussing the mnemonic power of photographs, Annette Kuhn describes how 'the everydayness of photography... combined with the capacity of the still photographic image to "freeze" a moment in time, lends extraordinary impact to an apparently ordinary medium' (2007: 285). In my historical research, I found that personal photos provided specific, concrete and personally relevant prompts that often worked better than spoken generalities to stimulate recollection of detail, accounts and feelings. Photos portray particulars that the researcher would not otherwise know to ask about; they offer information that interviewees may have forgotten or would not think to mention.

The use of photos can also enable participants to introduce their priorities and perspectives into interviews. This is particularly likely where personal photos, or those the interviewee has generated, are discussed. Participant-generated photographs are widely valued for enabling participants to set the interview agenda and this is an attractive feature for those who research the experiences and perspectives of marginalised or disempowered people. Cindy Clark (1999: 44), for example, discovered that photo-interviews provide 'a viewfinder for the child's perspective' of chronic illness. However, as discussed in Chapter 8, you need to bear in mind that participants are not always the sole or principal creators of their photos. Personal and especially participant-generated photos can also be used by interviewees to broach topics that are difficult to mention. Rosaleen Croghan, Christine Griffin, Janine Hunter and Ann Phoenix (2008: 345) noted that their teenage participants used their photos 'to show rather than "tell" aspects of their identity that might have otherwise remained hidden', this included topics which sat uneasily with dominant notions of adolescence such as religion, or complex issues around race and culture.

Looking at photos and thinking with them can also enable people to process and articulate experiences that they may not have worked through before. This can be seen in Harper's (1987; also Chapter 7) study of the craft of Willie the motor mechanic. Reflecting on Harper's photos of his work, Willie is able to deconstruct, identify and explain the fine detail of highly skilled practices that he typically does almost without thinking. But Harper understands the limitations of this method: 'It is pushing words to expect that experience can be literally described, for the reality Willie experiences is taken for granted, a many-sided gestalt of theoretical, tactile, and auditory input. It is difficult to put into words a complicated but utterly ordinary reality' (p. 118). Photo-elicitation, using archival and researcher-generated photos, has also been used to expose and explore people's feelings and thoughts about change, as in David Byrne and Aidan Doyle's (2004) study of a County Durham community in the 1990s following the closure and destruction of local mines in the 1970s and 1980s. In order to bring to the surface people's feelings about change, the researchers used focus groups in which photos of the area taken before and after the closure of the mines were viewed and discussed.

Generating photographs and then talking about them can be particularly effective at enabling participants to work through their ideas and feelings about a topic (see also Chapter 8). The photo-interview also enables the researcher to explore how participants approached the task of photography: 'the planning, deliberating, and problems … [were] often as enlightening as the actual images' (Frith and Harcourt 2007: 1346; see also Radley and Taylor 2003). The ability of photos to help people formulate views and responses was noted by the Sri Lankan novice monks interviewed by Jeffrey Samuels (2007). In this instance, research participants were given cameras and a list of eleven topics to photograph including 'an important temple activity' and 'what makes you happy as a monk'. As one monk explained:

> The photographs are like a mirror for us. We can learn a lot of things by discussing the photographs. It is easier to speak while holding the pictures in our hand and while looking at the pictures. We can explain more when the pictures are close at hand. (pp. 216–17)

Samuels notes that:

> knowing and thinking are not merely mental processes; feeling (holding the pictures) and seeing (looking at the pictures) are intimately connected to remembering, learning, and expressing. Indeed, taking photographs and later discussing them with me enabled many novices to recall, in greater depth, their own ideas; it also provided many novices with the occasion to construct meaning in a manner that was much more personally significant. (p. 217)

This is a good example of what Gillian Rose (2004) calls the 'materiality of seeing', in other words, that touching photos is often integral to the process of seeing what is in a photo and that looking produces embodied responses. Interestingly, the photo-interviews were less productive several years earlier when Samuels asked novices to photograph 'things that they like'.

Photos may also help generate data about concepts and topics that are difficult to explore in talk-only interviews. Gillian Bendelow (1993) used found photos and other images in a study of pain and how experiences of it are gendered. She noted that images provide concrete examples for interviewees to respond to and a means of talking about personal experiences in public. In a study in which children with chronic illness were invited to generate photos about their experiences of ill health, Clark (1999) similarly found that photos facilitated discussion of experiences that were otherwise difficult for the children to talk about. The success of photo-elicitation was partly because the children could use photos of themselves – for example, injecting insulin – to describe their experiences in the third person. But whereas Clark's participants discuss photos of their lives that they have taken or orchestrated, so the veracity of the images is not questionable, when using found photos it is possible that interviewees may engage less with the content of the images and more with their production (does the image convey genuine emotion or a performance for the camera?).

It is widely acknowledged that interviews are usually helpful to understand and explain the content of personal photos and what they mean to their owners (e.g. Chalfen 1987). On the basis of studying 40 family albums, Andrew Walker and Rosalind Moulton (1989: 165) argue that different types of album – family, travel etc. – have a common structure that facilitates a general interpretation of the meaning of an album, but it is difficult to pinpoint the meaning and significance for an album's owner of individual photos by looking only at an image, captions can give clues but you usually need to talk to people. Another reason why interviews are useful is because talk often accompanies the viewing of family photos. The role of photos in storytelling is well established, but recently Martha Langford has argued that a photo album's fundamental structure is not literary but oral, 'images selected and ordered *in anticipation* of storytelling preserved visual memory in a framework of oral consciousness' (2007: 227). Elizabeth Edwards (2006b) extends the analysis of the relationship between photos and orality to embrace the sounds, gestures and physical interactions that accompany the 'performance' of family photos.

Talking to people about their photo practices is not straightforward. There is a tendency to assume that people can explain what they do with photographs and why, but the details of photographic practices are often forgotten because they were not memorable at the time or since (Musello 1979). Photo practices can also be difficult to verbalise because people are typically unused to noting and talking about them (keen photographers are a possible exception). There are ways to help interviewees recall details about their photographic practices. In contemporary studies, practices can be explored by examining photos that have been taken recently and using these as a prompt for talk. In contemporary as well as historical research it is useful to work with photos in their original presentational formats; in contemporary research this can be images on a camera phone, in historical research this is more likely to be an album or framed photo. Handling cameras can also be helpful in historical research. This memory work involves looking, also touching and holding, because memories are elicited by doing as well as by seeing and thinking. Another reason talking about photo practices is not straightforward is people are usually interviewed days, weeks or even years after they have taken or done things with their photos and they therefore rely on memory to answer questions about their practices. As I discuss later, a range of factors consciously and unconsciously shape what people remember and say. For instance, when interviewing older women about their girlhood photo collections (Tinkler 2010, 2011; see also Freund with Thiessen 2011, discussed earlier) I found they often did not recall how they took or acquired their girlhood photos, instead they worked this out in the interview using fragments of memory, what they already knew about their youth, and the evidence of their collections; the women's adult interests and priorities, as well as the interview context, influenced this process. If you use interviews to explore photo practices you need to keep in mind the complexity of the accounts provided and, where possible, use other sources to confirm recollections.

So far I have reflected on the reasons why researchers use photos in interviews, now I consider the practice of doing photo-interviews.

# Doing a photo-interview: practicalities

There are several practical questions that researchers need to consider before doing a photo-interview. These questions apply principally where photos are used as tools in interviews, although some points are relevant to other types of photo-interviews.

## How many photo-interviews and when?

Do you have one or two interviews with each research participant or are a number of photo-interviews undertaken over the course of the research, perhaps as an ongoing check on your findings? Are photos featured in all interviews or are some talk-alone, and what is the relationship between these different interviews? At what point is it useful to discuss photos and what implications might this have for the rest of the interview (see later discussion of temporalities)?

## What kinds of photos will be discussed?

This depends on your topic, the kinds of data you want to generate and feasibility. Bear in mind that some photos are better than others at stimulating talk and a pilot may be the only way to work this out.

## Do you want interviewees to think about their photos in advance of the interview?

Particularly in projects involving photos generated by research participants, it can be useful to ask participants to provide captions or write about their photos in advance of the interview.

## Which photos will be included in the interview?

Will the interview be organised around all the photos taken or collected, or focused on a selection of them? If a selection of photos is used, who decides what should be included? If the interviewee selects, do you need to know what has been excluded and the criteria for the selection? How many photos can reasonably be discussed?

## Who decides how the photos should be looked at?

Will you or the interviewee decide which photos are looked at, in which order and when? Is there value in noting how research participants navigate selections and collections? In what media will you view the photos (hard copies, digitalised images) and with what implications for what interviewees see and how they, and you, can engage with the pictures (zooming in, holding etc.)?

## Will you need strategies to stimulate or focus talk?

Photos are widely recognised as a useful stimulus to talk, but prompts may be needed when working with some social groups or when addressing particular topics. A pilot can help you decide this and what strategies are likely to be effective. For instance, when working with young children Clark (1999: 44) placed 'thought balloons' over an image of a child in a photo as a means to ask the child what s/he was thinking. Clark also suggests asking children to sort photos into categories in a game-like activity: 'tangible props in referring to situations or feelings'.

What types of data do you need to generate during
the interview and how will you achieve this?

How will you keep track of the relationship between talk and photos during the
interview? Do you need to examine the images discussed? Do you need copies
of these photos and, if so, how will you get these? Are you interested in how
people relate to photos as material objects during the interview (e.g. do they
hold and touch them in particular ways)? How will you record this (notes,
video)?

# Part Two: How do photo-interviews work?

The distinctiveness of photo-interviews is that interviewees are encouraged to
engage with photos. Though I have shown that photos are often good at generating
data, the relationship between photos and talk needs further attention. As Croghan
et al. (2008: 346) discovered, there 'is frequently an assumption that the visual will act
as a trigger to an oral response or that the visual and verbal will somehow strengthen
one another, without examining the ways in which they differ as modes of representation'. What people say as they peruse photos is often more complex than assumed.
Understanding this can help researchers make decisions about methods, and inform
the analysis and interpretation of interview data. What is the relationship between
verbal and visual representations? How do people see and use photos to talk about
themselves and their communities in the present and past? Do photos simply elicit
descriptions and explanations and trigger memories? In the following I consider
three factors that shape photo-interviews: how people conceptualise photos; the
temporalities of the visual–verbal relationship in photo-interviews; and the relationship between photos, memories and the stories people tell. This is followed by a
discussion of how to incorporate photos into interview analysis.

## How people conceptualise photos

People see different things in photos, and how interviewees conceptualise images is
an important aspect of this. According to Schwartz (1989), addressing this conceptualisation is essential to the interpretation of photo-interview data. Schwartz conducted interviews with three generations living in a rural community using photos
she had taken of the town and everyday life in it. Schwartz discovered that rather
than commenting on what she was trying to convey through the photos or evaluating the aesthetics of the images, interviewees approached the photos as capturing
what was going on in their community and it was the detail of community life that
they subsequently talked about. These findings are consistent with studies of how
Euro-American families view domestic photos (e.g. Banks 2001) and probably
explain why photos that are personally relevant, whether produced by amateur or
professional photographers, tend to stimulate talk about the social reality of the
interviewee rather than discussion about the construction of the images. But while
interviewees often view personally relevant images in a realist manner, not all photos

are viewed in this way. For example, as Marcus Banks (2001: 95) explains, commercial photos typically prompt a different type of viewing and a detached response that can shift the focus of talk from 'the personal' to 'broader sociological topics'. Presumably the viewer looks at an advertising image as something that has been staged for the camera according to a set of objectives, it is these objectives that become the subject of talk. For example, an advertisement featuring a wedding may generate talk about societal conventions around weddings and wedding photography, whereas a personal photo of a friend's wedding would be more likely to prompt talk about what happened on the wedding day or the suitability of the groom as a spouse.

## Temporalities in photo-interviews

The temporalities of photo-interviews are central to understanding the complexity of the verbal–visual relationship. Photos represent a split second, and to say anything about the content involves talking either side of this moment. Relatedly, the meaning of this moment is not transparent and so an account is required to create both context and meaning. Sometimes this context/meaning is suggested by captions or other sources such as letters, but usually much is left to the narrator's interpretation.

There is often a temporal disjuncture between taking a photo and occasions of viewing which provides an opportunity to explain and confer meaning on the occasion pictured, a point I shall return to. This temporal disjuncture is as significant in research on the 'present' as on the 'past'. Croghan et al. (2008: 351–2) used photo-elicitation interviews to explore consumption and young people's identities. Research participants were given cameras and asked to take photos of things that mattered to them with a view to talking about these pictures in an interview with a researcher. Drawing on Roland Barthes, the authors point to a 'discontinuity between the moment recorded and the moment of looking', and argue that 'photo-elicitation invites the viewer ... to bridge that moment of discontinuity in order to invent a story that explains the photograph'. Because of the illusion that a photograph captures 'authentic' identities, this bridging provided an opportunity for their respondents to engage in 'identity work'. The young people used photos to 'underline and verify verbal claims in ways that are not available through verbal means alone' and, through 'verbal editing', to 'clarify and repair any problems in the presentation of the self in the photographs'. I would argue that in some instances a bridging account collapses time and is present-focused in that the interviewee engages with the photo (of yesterday, last week or years ago) as a representation *of* the present ('what they/we *are* doing', 'how I *am*') as if the image represents a window on to the world, or a mirror. Sometimes, especially with distinctly old photos, the interviewee acknowledges that the photo depicts the past.

Another way that temporality shapes the verbal–visual relationship is the positioning of photo-elicitation in an interview, whether the interview revolves around the photo(s) or the photos come after or before a talk-alone interview. In their study of change in a Pennsylvania steel town, Judith Modell and Charlee Brodsky (1994) employed a two-stage interview to explore the relationship between photos, memories and narratives. First, they encouraged people to talk about their community in the past and present. Second, they asked interviewees to comment on photos of the places and people in their community; these included archival photos of the town, photos taken by Modell for the purposes of the project and interviewees' personal photos. The two-stage process was explained to interviewees at the outset. Modell and Brodsky discovered that after narrating an account, people used photos to confirm and expand on what they had just said: 'people chose those aspects of a scene, a portrait, or a pictured event that affirmed an articulated memory' (p. 150). Although verbal narratives do not necessarily constrain engagement with photos as rigidly as in Modell and Brodsky's study, it is likely that people look at photos differently if following a verbal narrative compared to when the photo is a starting point for talk. Many researchers prefer to do talk-alone interviews before looking at photos to avoid an overemphasis on the photographic story or on visual phenomena (see Box 9.1). However, where photographic practices are the focus of research it makes sense to wrap the interview, or the early stages of it, around the photos. Sherna Gluck (1977: 9) suggests recording interviewees' reflections on their photos and then returning to them later within the context of the interview agenda because these moments of storytelling are different: 'the second version of the story might be quite different from that first rendition – which could become a lost gem were we not to record it when the memory spontaneously surfaced'.

Viewing photos also takes place in time – at different historical and biographical moments – and this temporally specific context shapes how viewers relate to photos. People engage with photos from the vantage point of their current personal needs, interests and perspectives, including as Modell and Brodsky demonstrate, to confirm verbal accounts they have just offered. For example, a holiday snap of the interviewee with a friend, taken on board a cruise ship several years ago, might elicit a slightly different account following news of a cruise ship sinking than before (historical event) and prompt different stories depending on whether the interviewee has recently fallen out with her old friend (biographical event). Even as an interview unfolds, the shifting juxtaposition of photos, talk and memories generates different contexts within which images become meaningful: 'photographs' meanings shift not only over historical time; multiple meanings are … attached to photographs during the interview process' (Freund and Thomson 2011: 12).

Memory is another temporal dimension which I now examine more closely in the context of the relationship between photos and the stories people tell about them.

## Photos, memories, stories

Modell and Brodsky's study raises important questions about how photos contribute to memory: are they only ever used to confirm recollections and narratives? How does memory work in a photo-interview? Is memory only relevant in historical research? In the following I begin with a brief introduction to memory before focusing on remembering with photos and the difference between using selections and collections of photos.

## Memory

Even in contemporary research, memory is often drawn on to explain the content of a photo and detail the circumstances of its production. But in contemporary research the recourse to memory is often taken for granted and not discussed. In many instances researchers are interested in probing what was going on around the time the photo was taken; here, as with research that explicitly addresses 'the past', it is necessary to reflect on how people remember with photos.

There are two main approaches to memory. One treats memory as a sort of filing cabinet in which recollections are stored ready for retrieval. The language used in these types of account can be revealing. Photo-interviews are described as 'retrieving', 'releasing', 'unlocking' and 'jolting' the interviewee's mind and memory, in other words bringing out what is already formed. In contrast, cultural theorists and historians, treat memory as a construction and as dynamic (for overviews see Abrams 2011; Misztal 2003). These scholars argue that oral histories do not tell us simply about the past, memories are reworked over time in light of subsequent experiences and the meanings attached to these. These accounts are also shaped by the cultural context in which the interview takes place. The concept of 'composure' is often used to explain the process (for account see Summerfield 2004). It refers to how people try to construct an account of their memories that contributes to a version of themselves with which they feel comfortable. How do photos contribute to this process?

## Remembering with photos

Scholars agree that photographs can be a powerful stimulus to memory, but even old photos do not always prompt an active engagement with the past. Barthes (2000: 91) suggests that photos can actually 'block' personal memory because photos provide easily-recalled visual versions of the past that substitute for memories of what happened; often it is photos that come to mind rather than experiences. Moreover, interviewees may describe photos rather than try to remember with them. In some instances, photos are cues to well-rehearsed stories; photos are noted and recognised, but they do not prompt an active engagement with memories of past experiences, views and feelings. But encouraged by the interviewer's questions, it is possible for interviewees to engage in a more dynamic process of remembering.

Drawing on my own research (Tinkler 2011), I suggest that when people remember with photos there are two aspects to the photographic encounter that are, in practice, interwoven: the memory response and the processing of recalled matter. The first aspect, the *memory response,* can take two forms – reaction and searching; some photographs elicit both. In some instances the memory experience is initially one of reaction to the photograph. This flash or welling up of often vivid recollections of sounds, sights, smells and touch, is often entangled with an emotional response; the experience is akin to Barthes' (2000: 27) 'punctum' (the part of an image that is 'poignant', that 'pricks' the viewer). More commonly, the memory response emerges gradually as the viewer studies the photo and searches for – winkles out – what they can remember about people, places, events and experiences. This type of memory response has parallels with Barthes' 'studium' (an interested reading).

Stage two of the photographic encounter usually involves the *processing* of recalled matter (as discussed below, this is sometimes resisted); memory fragments, facts and meanings are interpreted, classified, synthesised and arranged into a coherent account which is articulated to self and others. This process is shaped, but not determined, by contemporary cultural resources, including language, dominant discourses and collective memories (shared popular accounts). It is also influenced by the perspectives and interests of the interviewee and the recall context, which includes the dynamics of the interview and the interviewee's perceptions of their audiences. The objectives, conscious or otherwise, of this process are to produce memories that make sense to self and others, and which present and position the self in ways that one can live with.

Photos sometimes bolster the process of memory composure in that their content seems consistent with the interviewee's recollections and can be used as visual evidence of them, or they support a particular version of the past that the interviewee is comfortable with. Sometimes photos that bear little obvious relation to the interviewee's account can also facilitate narrative. For instance, the photos that Mary Brockmeyer selected to talk about in the study of life on the Canadian Prairies were often of the men in her family and their work 'hunting, slaughtering and harvesting' (Figure 9.1), but these images 'carved a space for her' to tell stories of 'women's hard labor and men's abuse of their domestic power' (Freund with Thiessen 2011: 36). But the process of composing memories is not always successful and can result in 'discomposure' (Summerfield 2004). Memory responses that contradict the photo evidence can make it difficult or impossible for an interviewee to recount a story, as where photos of smiling people generate memories of hardship

**Figure 9.1** 'They had easy hunting'. Source: Brockmeyer collection

(Freund with Thiessen 2011; Mannik 2011; Thomson 2011b). Discomposure can also occur when a photo elicits a memory reaction, as the often intense emotional/sensory recollections can be difficult to interpret and organise into a coherent and comfortable account. The interviewee may also resist this processing. Discomposed by the photographic encounter, the interviewee may be rendered speechless or left struggling to find the right words to convey his or her recollections. As well as hindering storytelling, discomposure can also result in physical disengagement from photos, a refusal to look (Mannik 2011) or touch (Tinkler 2011).

## Using selections and collections of photos

People remember with, and talk about, photos in complex ways, but talking about a photo collection is a different experience for an interviewee than reflecting on a few photos they have selected to speak about (Tinkler 2011). A selection is a choice dictated by concerns at the time of the interview rather than when the pictures were acquired; it represents a present-day agenda. Additionally, absences as well as presences are typically revealed by looking at and talking about photo collections, but absences are difficult to detect when working with only a selection of photos. A further difference is that talking about a collection involves the interviewee composing accounts about individual photos and about the collection as a whole:

> Talk about a collection is more than a stringing together of discreet accounts about photos and is not reducible to these ... Interviewees introduce, explain and frame their collections by what they say and do. Albums also require navigation. Through what is talked about at length, merely commented on, or ignored, the subject navigates a visible path through their collection ... Preferred pathways are ... narrative threads that are not reducible to, or necessarily obvious from, the photo collection in and of itself. (p. 51)

The following example demonstrates how I traced the threads that are woven through an account of a photo collection. I interviewed Carol about the girlhood album she compiled over 40 years earlier when she was in her teens. The album is a magpie collection dominated by photos from when Carol was 16 and 17. In our interview I was able to trace Carol's girlhood agenda as she honed in on certain photos and spoke animatedly about friends (Figure 9.2), being a first-time aunt and gaining increased independence at home and at school – 'Life started for me at 16'. But two other narratives could also be discerned that related to what happened to Carol's life after the album was compiled. One of these, a narrative of loss relating to the father–daughter relationship as Carol left home and then married a controlling husband, emerged in part from how Carol framed my viewing of her album. Although there are no photographs of Carol's father affixed in her album, as Carol passed the album to me she extracted from the front cover a small, loose, black–and–white photograph of her parents that was sent to her when she left home for university. Although both parents are featured, Carol points out her father and recounts how much he had missed Carol when she left home. Having introduced her father so poignantly, the father–daughter relationship is then woven through the narration of the collection. Carol tells stories about her father and their relationship that are not visible in the photos, including stories about photos that were taken but which never made it into her girlhood album.

Understanding the relationship between photos, memories and stories can help us make sense of what people say as they reflect on the past, but various strategies are needed to discern the processes at work.

**Figure 9.2**   Carol's friends (private collection)

## Incorporating photos into interview analysis

Much has been written about analysing talk-alone interviews, but how do you take account of what happens when people talk about photos? Drawing insights from the discussion of how photo-interviews work, I suggest several strategies for analysing photo-interviews that can be used in addition to the usual techniques of interview analysis (on the latter see, for example, Mason 2002; Tonkiss 2004). Before I list these strategies I will first address analysing common features of photo stories that have only been touched on so far, namely multiple meanings, discontinuities and discrepancies.

Talking about photos creates the conditions for multiple meanings to emerge. I have already noted that there can be 'layers' of memories and meanings as people talk about old personal photos. The meanings of personal photos can also shift in the course of a single interview (Freund and Thomson 2011) or between separate interviews as in Wendy Luttrell's participant-photography project which involved children talking about their photos in four 'audiencings' (see Box 8.3). Whenever interviewees are involved in the production of photos – personal (e.g. Thomson 2011; Tinkler 2010) or ones generated for the research (e.g. Radley and Taylor 2003) – the interview also creates space for exploring the meanings made both at the point of production and in the context of the photo-interview. Discussing participant-generated photos, Sarah Pink (2007: 91) advises that interviews should 'seek to understand how the images have meanings on both of these two levels'.

Researchers can also explore the 'fissures and gaps' that emerge in interviewee's accounts (Freund and Thomson 2011: 12). Sometimes disjunctures occur between the verbal and visual as people are speaking about photos (e.g. Freund with Thiessen 2011; Mannik 2011; Thomson 2011a, 2011b; Tinkler 2011). Discrepancies and discontinuities can also emerge between a photo-interview and a separate talk-alone interview as when Maris Thompson (2011; see also Winddance Twine 2006) interviewed German-Americans about settling in the United States pre-1940. The settlers' photo albums adhered strictly to American conventions and spoke of upward mobility and cultural assimilation, themes the photo-interviews dwelt on. In contrast, the talk-alone interviews about Americanisation produced very different stories of language loss, identity issues and hostility from locals. Read together, however, the two types of account are revealing.

Juxtaposing photos and stories, also accounts of photos produced at different times, can be a fruitful analytic strategy as seen in Thomson's study of migrant women (see Box 9.2).

---

### BOX 9.2   MOVING STORIES

Productive juxtapositions are at the heart of Alistair Thomson's (2011a) book, *Moving Stories*. In this study of four British women who migrated to Australia in the 1950s and 1960s, Thomson explores the creation and interpretation of the

**Figure 9.3**   Dorothy Wright with her baby. Reproduced courtesy of Dorothy Wright

stories that the women made about their lives. Thomson is a social and cultural historian; he is interested in understanding lives in the past, but also the cultural phenomena of story-telling and remembering, 'the dynamic relationships between self, story and society' (p. 15).

Although photo-interviews often focus on a set of pictures selected or made for the occasion, Thomson's research engages with a mixture of accounts that four women constructed, at the time and since, to show and record their experiences of migration – letters, audio-letters, photos, life writing and oral history accounts. Photos are considered in relation to their captions and other commentary on them in letters of the time: 'Photo stories combined image and text, and the text conjured the meaning for an image' (p. 246). The photo stories are also examined alongside autobiographical writing and the oral history interview transcripts.

The juxtaposition of sources is treated as a productive space, and Thomson hones in on discrepancies *within* photo stories between pictures and captions or commentaries, and *between* photo stories and what the women now say about them. He asks, 'what stories do the photo collections tell, what stories do they conceal, and what stories are lurking beneath the photographic surface to be prompted into life through new remembering?' (p. 14).

Thomson uses interviews to maximise what can be learnt from photos. Photos are mined for evidence of material culture, particularly of domestic acquisition

*(Continued)*

and consumption – the new car, the roomy and well-stocked refrigerator, evidence that letters and oral histories flesh out. Interviews are also used to explore how these pictorial accounts were made – the implications of available camera technologies and conventions about where and when to use cameras, cultural expectations about how photos should look, also details about the events and interpersonal relations surrounding the construction of pictorial accounts of life in Australia. These details are scrutinised for what they reveal about past subjectivities and aspirations:

> From the ways in which photos are taken and used to create stories and make sense, and from the choices about which photos should be sent to family in England, we can explore how migrants felt about their life in Australia and explain the meanings of the new house and car or the latest domestic acquisition. (pp. 274–5)

Complex and changing narratives emerge around the photos in the course of the research.

Although in three of the four cases men were the main photographers in the women's home lives, Thomson stresses that the production of a photo involved other contributors, notably the 'stage managers', usually the women, and the 'actors': 'there were many contributors to the photographic image, and this unruly and even contested authorship makes for complex representations and meanings' (p. 256). Subsequent renditions, including the oral history interview, generate different interpretations of the photos: 'like all life stories, these accounts are ... constantly evolving and moving, they are living histories' (p. 15). For example, Thomson explores several photos that Dorothy Wright sent home shortly after her second child was born. One photo of Dorothy with her children, captioned 'End of a perfect birthday', suggests that all is well; an interpretation supported by upbeat commentary in Dorothy's letters. But in another photo of Dorothy holding her new baby, Dorothy averts her eyes from the camera, a pose that is repeated in other pictures of the young mother with her new-born baby (Figure 9.3). It is only in letters written to her mother several months later that Dorothy admitted that she was at 'screaming point' in the months after her baby's birth, but it was not until the 1980s, when Dorothy's now adult daughter was pregnant, that Dorothy realised that she had probably been suffering from postnatal depression. Dorothy brings this insight to her oral account of the 1960s' photo, but she also articulates newer interpretations relating to her sense that as a young mother she was stifled and frustrated by domesticity and thwarted ambition.

Thomson's analysis of the women's stories involved careful scrutiny of different sources about, and renditions of, the past; it also emerged from allowing interviewees time to reflect on and (re)assess their memories as they talked about their lives. Thomson conducted the first interview without photos because they 'tend to focus the discussion around what was photographed rather than what was recalled' (personal correspondence). Following this, Thomson borrowed photo albums, perused and scanned them, and then returned to talk about them with his interviewees; in some cases the women sent him selected photos on their own volition or in response to a request from him. Trust and understanding between Thomson and the four research participants were key to the success of this study. Thomson was 'guided by the aim of "sharing authority" in both the interview and its interpretation' and this, as he stresses, cannot be hurried (2011a: 324).

Condensing insights from photo-elicitations and oral histories, I suggest that researchers use the following strategies to analyse what people say about photos: look, contextualise, listen, watch, juxtapose and trace the threads. These strategies complement established techniques of interview analysis.

- Look at the photographic images your interviewees are engaging with: what do they see? What do they talk about or ignore in the photo?
- Contextualise photos to understand their place in interviewees' lives because these relationships may shape interviewees' accounts; they might also provide opportunities to explore different moments of meaning making. Try to view personal photos in their original contexts with the captions or descriptions that accompanied them. Attend to other contemporary sources, such as personal letters or diaries, that help establish the meanings of the photos at the time they were produced or first engaged with by your interviewees. In participant-photography projects, this process includes noting entries in research diaries or logbooks that record how and why photos were taken (see Chapter 8).
- Listen to accounts and, utilising established interview techniques, attend to: what is said; the silences and hesitations that may result from what is forgotten or from topics too difficult to talk about; and how stories are delivered, including fluency, detail, velocity, rhythm and tone (Portelli 1998), which provide clues as to whether tales are well-rehearsed or composed in the interview and whether they result from an experience that made an impression. Listen for evidence of the 'layering of memories' (Tinkler 2010: 268). For example, in my interview with Carol about her girlhood collection compiled in the 1950s (discussed earlier), Carol discussed a photo of her best friend. This photo generated memories about the joys of teenage friendships, but also of Carol's later experiences in an oppressive marriage during which her husband vandalised her girlhood album destroying some of her photos.
- Juxtapose accounts. When working with interviewees' personal photos, set the original photo narratives alongside other contemporary accounts produced by interviewees, and with subsequent accounts of the photos, included those produced in the photo-interviews. If using participant-generated photos, attend to

the initial descriptions of photos presented in diaries, logbooks or captions and reflect on these alongside oral account(s) produced in subsequent discussions.

- Watch how interviewees physically engage with photos and collections as visual and material things, and how they react when touching, viewing and talking about them.
- Finally, when working with collections, trace the narrative threads that are woven through an account of a collection and that are not reducible to the sum of comments on individual photos.

As with all qualitative interviews, it is important in photo-interviews to reflect on inter-subjectivity – the interaction between the two subjectivities of interviewer and interviewee (see Abrams 2011: 58–63) – because this contributes to the account generated; this includes assumptions you and your interviewee make of each other and how you interact. Two interconnected aspects of photo-interviews are worth noting. First, the production of a photo's meanings is often a collaborative affair as you and the interviewee reflect together on the image. Second, in photo-interviews it is not only the interviewee who is compelled to engage with each picture, but also the researcher. In interviews with women about their personal photos, Judith Okely (1994: 50, cited in Pink 2007: 87) emphasises the need for researchers to reflect on how they experience their interviewees' photos as this will shape the interview dynamics; she describes 'watching, listening and resonating with the emotions and energy' of an interviewee 'living through the photographs'.

## Summary

In this chapter I have argued that deciding whether and how to use photos in interviews involves reflecting on what photos can contribute and how photo-elicitation works. Researchers are increasingly keen to use photos in interviews because they are perceived to encourage dialogue and the generation of useful data. However, though photo-interviews are often very good at doing both, this is not guaranteed. Thinking about why photos do and don't get people talking has implications for designing research. Reflecting on how photos work is also a crucial consideration when designing research because what people say in interviews is often more complex than assumed. I suggest that it is helpful to reflect on three factors that shape photo-interviews: how interviewees conceptualise photos, the temporalities of the visual–verbal relationship, and the relationship between photos, memories and stories. By looking closely at what happens in photo-interviews, I draw out five strategies for analysing what happens when people talk about photos that can be used in addition to the usual techniques of interview analysis.

In the next chapter I consider the ethics and legalities of using photos in historical and social research, this includes issues relating to photo-elicitation and the presentation of interviewees' photos.

# 10

# Ethical Issues and Legalities

Ethical obligations shape how we use photographs in historical and social research. Ethics are widely agreed moral principles about what is right and wrong;[1] on the basis of these, frameworks of ethical research practice are devised by ethics committees, funders and the institutions within which we work and conduct research (on ethical regulation see Wiles et al. 2012). However, for the most part, 'compliance with regulation ... is often the minimum requirement and ethical behaviour demands more careful consideration of the issues involved' (Wiles et al. 2008: 2.1). Photographic projects pose different ethical issues depending on their aims and objectives, the people involved, the type and age of the photos that are used, the methods employed, modes of presentation and what happens to the visual data generated in the longer term. Given the range of variables, it is inadvisable to rely solely on generic ethical guidelines, though these can provide a useful starting point. Decisions about how to use photos ethically – visual ethics – need to be worked out for each research project. There are also legal restrictions on how to do research. The most common legal issues relate to people's rights to privacy and the ownership or copyright of photographs. It is also a criminal activity to make or possess pornographic photographic images of children and guidelines issued by the Visual Sociology Study Group of the British Sociological Association (2006) state that images depicting criminal activity should be given to the police.

In this chapter I consider ethical issues involved in using photos in research and legal issues relating to privacy and copyright. I focus on three aspects of research with photos: taking photos; photo-elicitation; and the presentation of photos. There is an extensive literature on research ethics (e.g. de Laine 2000; Israel and Hay 2006; Mertens and Ginsberg 2009), so this chapter addresses only those issues pertinent to working with photographs. The Visual Sociology Study Group of the British Sociological Association (BSAVSSG) and the International Visual Sociology Association (IVSA) both have useful websites that provide information on visual ethics.[2]

# Taking photos

It is increasingly common for researchers and research participants to generate photos in the course of research. Researchers need to ensure their own photography complies with the law and that it is ethical. Researchers who ask participants to generate photos are also responsible for ensuring that participants use cameras in an appropriate manner.

## Researchers generating photos

Several issues confront researchers who generate photos, these include the rights of people to privacy, whether covert photography is ethical and the acquisition of consent before taking someone's photograph. People's dignity is another important issue but I discuss this later in relation to the presentation of research. I conclude this discussion by reflecting on how legal and ethical issues shape the generation of visual data.

### The rights of people to privacy

In recent years there has been a dramatic shift in perceptions of the rights of individuals to privacy. Fifty years ago when Townsend undertook his study of residential care for the elderly, he encountered no restrictions on who and what could be photographed (Rolph et al. 2009) and his photos were taken with little regard for the self-respect or wishes of the elderly people he depicted. This was not unusual at the time; documentary forms of photography, including academic studies, have a history characterised by a lack of regard for the people that are photographed (for discussion see, for example, Price 2000; Sontag 1971, 2003). Today the situation is different because the rights of individuals are afforded more importance in legal and ethical frameworks. It is no longer acceptable for researchers to take photos where, when and of what they like, but the legal situation is ambiguous. Legally, a distinction is drawn between public and private but this is not straightforward: 'UK law enables individuals to film or take photos of places or individuals from or in a public place, including taking photos of private property', but under the European Convention of Human Rights photographing someone in a place where they have a reasonable expectation of privacy (in public loos for instance) might be considered to be an invasion of privacy (Wiles et al. 2008: 2.5). Concern not to infringe people's rights, and be sued for this, has added to the rigour with which academic institutions and funding bodies scrutinise research and its ethics.

There is a long tradition of covert documentary and social science photography but this is now considered unethical in research except in specific circumstances (BSA Visual Sociology Study Group 2006). Particularly in ethnography, covert photography is undesirable because it is perceived to militate against building trust and rapport with the people who are the focus of a study; some argue that the researcher and participants should collaborate in the production of images (Banks 2001; Pink 2007). There are also other academic justifications against covert practice, discussed in Chapter 7. Wiles et al. (2008:3.1) point out that in ethnographic research, 'Once detailed consent is obtained researchers may still choose, with participants' agreement to this practice, to take photographs or film without study participants' awareness of the specific images being taken in the interests of obtaining "natural" images.'

Researchers are usually required by law or ethics committee to seek permission from people before taking their photograph. Where a photo would feature a few individuals this is feasible, though a single refusal means a photo cannot be taken. As with all research, there is also the issue of informed consent and who can give it. Informed consent means ensuring participants understand why and how photos will be taken and used, and the implications of being photographed. Particularly with children and other 'vulnerable' groups, it is legally permissible to gain consent if a person can understand the implications of being involved in the research, but it is also advisable to seek the approval of parents or guardians. If the photos are for your use only then verbal consent can often be sufficient, although in some instances (such as photographs of children or where the subject matter is intimate) it is better to have a written or audio record. Some researchers use a single consent form to cover taking photos and using them, but it is best to have separate forms because presentation raises different issues, a point I will return to. Some researchers advocate securing ongoing consent from participants because this is responsive to the changing needs of participants and changes in the course of the research (Renold et al. 2008).

Dignity is another important ethical issue and researchers are advised to avoid producing photos that depict people in undignified ways (see under 'Presentation'). The British Sociological Association Visual Sociology Study Group (2006) also stipulates that ethical researchers should not construct images which discriminate against specific groups, for instance disabled people. It is erroneous to think that issues of dignity and discrimination are irrelevant if photos are not for publication. Because photos are commonly perceived to bear a special relationship to the people they depict, a relationship that is different to a written description or a drawing of them, people should have a say over whether you produce photos that depict them in demeaning or discriminatory ways.

So far I have outlined ethical and legal reasons why you cannot photograph whatever you like. The photographic data generated in a project is, therefore, shaped by ethical and legal constraints, also by other factors such as choices about specific methods and the skills of the researcher. It is imperative that researchers' photographic practices are supplemented by written or audio notes that contextualise the photos they take and comment on what cannot be photographed and why. The visual data you generate will shape how you remember and think about the people and circumstances you photograph and it will inform your analysis and conclusions. Rolph, Johnson and Smith's (2009; see Chapter 7) re-study of Townsend's research on elderly people in residential care provides a clear demonstration of how decisions about ethics shaped the conduct of their research and the kinds of photographic data that are generated. Using digital cameras, Rolph et al. took photos in residential homes and showed these to the residents and staff. They deleted photos that participants were unhappy with; some residents censored photos because they were uncomfortable with images of themselves as frail or old. As it was not possible in photos of public spaces to gain everyone's consent, the researchers concentrated instead on photographing small groups and individuals, though informed consent was still problematic as many residents were physically or mentally frail or suffering from dementia.

Consent was not the only issue. Rolph et al. were also concerned about the effects of photos on the privacy of residents and so they avoided taking intrusive photos. They also avoided photos that degraded residents, even if these photos provided evidence of poor conditions, and instead produced written reports on these incidents; they were unable to show 'the pathos of some of the scenes' they witnessed (p. 434). However, to gain consent the researchers had to engage with the people they photographed, and this resulted in personal and upbeat images. As a letter from one of the residents attests, the experience of being photographed could be empowering:

> I wish to give you a very big 'thank you' for the magnificent picture of myself you sent me, following our interview ... It has so much detail to it, showing ... pictures of my wife and our wedding, and other interesting details of importance to me. (p. 435)

As a result of legal and ethical frameworks, Rolph et al. generated very different photographic data from Townsend 50 years earlier.

## Summary of the discussion of researcher-generated photography

1  If you are photographing people in a place where they 'have a reasonable expectation of privacy' it is ethically, and probably legally, necessary to ask for their consent before taking a photograph.
2  When you need permission to photograph someone you must explain clearly how you are going to use the photo; consent must always be informed.
3  Decide whether consent should be formally recorded or whether verbal permission is sufficient.
4  Consider how ethical decisions and legal requirements contribute to the type of visual data you generate and the impression it might convey to you when you return to analyse it. Keep records contextualising your photographic practices.

# Research participants generating photos

Increasingly, researchers give cameras to their research participants (see Chapter 8), but this does not circumvent the issues discussed in relation to the researcher generating photos. Researchers are responsible for preparing participants to work within ethical frameworks and legal stipulations. In this section I consider how researchers can prepare participants to take photos, the possible voyeurism of researchers who use this method and the effects on participants of being involved in a photographic project.

Research participants are no different from researchers in that they can invade the rights of other people and they are required by law, ethics committees and etiquette to use their cameras in appropriate ways. It is the researcher's responsibility to ensure their research participants are well prepared for their task and that they are aware of who and what they can photograph, and where and when they can do this. In Alice McIntyre's (2003: 52) study of the experiences of a group of working-class women in Belfast, she discussed ethical issues with the participants who then arrived at 'shared understandings of when picture-taking is appropriate, respecting people's choices about their inclusion in a photograph, and clarifying the reasons for taking particular photographs'. Claudia Mitchell (2011) also stresses the importance of fostering reflexivity on the part of research participants and, with reference to her photographic research with young people in South Africa, she illustrates how this contributes to the participants and researcher acquiring a better understanding of the community in which the research is being undertaken.

Constraints on what research participants can photograph may sometimes seem inhibiting and counter to the aim of giving a participant a camera and a voice in the research. This was how Louisa Allen (2009) felt initially when she attempted to research sexual cultures in New Zealand schools. Allen asked a sample of pupils to take photos of how they learnt about sexuality in school with a view to talking with her about a selection of their pictures. Although Allen had hoped to empower her research participants by giving them some control over the research process, schools were suspicious of pupils taking photos (in part because of high-profile cases in which students had taken photos to harass their peers). The ethics application process was lengthy and the schools imposed strict ethical regulations within which the students had to work: the research participants could photograph only students aged 16 and over, with their consent and within spaces to which 'normal access is granted'; and cameras had to be returned with 'exposed film intact' (p. 555). The effects of these constraints were, however, minimised using creative solutions. For example, Allen asked students about the experience of taking their pictures and the pictures they would have liked to take. She notes also that the pupils displayed considerable inventiveness and a 'sociological imagination' (p. 557) in responding to the research task, for example by taking photos of an empty changing room or of a school fashion show. Mitchell (2011: 21) makes a similar point about creative alternatives to photographs that identify people. In her participatory research projects Mitchell teaches participants how to take photographs that are symbolic and which do not feature faces: 'a set of hands, a from-the-knees-down photo of a group of school girls, a crowd scene at a distance, a group ... with their back to the photographer'.

Asking research participants to take photos has expanded ways of doing participant research, but researchers need to question this aspect of their practice: are they using the camera to explore areas of life that are otherwise closed to them, and what issues does this raise? This question is particularly important when working with young or disadvantaged people because the voyeurism and intrusion potentially achieved by the camera are exacerbated by inequalities of power. In some research, participants are able to edit their photos. Often, however, this would be counter-productive as participants may chose to remove photos that are useful to the research because they do not think the photos are good enough or they do not like how they look in them. Sometimes, as in school-based research, it is not permissible for child participants to edit photos before they are seen by the researcher because institutions require a des-ignated adult to ensure photos comply with ethical stipulations before they are returned to the child photographers (e.g. Allen 2009). Researchers need to think carefully about the rights of their participants and the subject matter, and to draw a clear line between the photos taken and what may subsequently be reproduced in presentations. Another point to think about is whether and how participants benefit from being involved in your research. At minimum it is courteous to give participants a copy of the photos they have generated for your research.

A further consideration is the implications of giving cameras to participants. Often researchers aim to empower participants, but there can be a downside. For instance, when Bloustein (2001) gave a group of girls video cameras to explore and present aspects of their experiences of girlhood and growing up, she discovered that the girls became more preoccupied with their appearance. Though Bloustein's research involved video cameras, the point is relevant to research using cameras. It is important that researchers reflect on the implications for people of being involved in research (Tinkler 2008).

### Summary of the discussion of research participants generating photos

1  Do your research participants understand legal and ethical issues relating to taking photos?
2  Where photos might infringe people's privacy, are participants aware of ways of generating photos that do not reveal identities?
3  Are you using participants' photos for voyeuristic purposes or intruding into areas of their lives?
4  What are the implications for participants of being involved in your research? Are there any benefits?

# Interviewing

There are general ethical issues relating to the use of interviews, as Mason (2002: 79–83) explains, these concern: who you interview and the power relations between interviewer and interviewee; what you ask and how; what you 'let' interviewees tell you, and whether and how you guarantee the confidentiality and anonymity of interviewees; and informed consent. There are also ethical issues that are spe-cific to each project and in the following I consider one that can arise when you use photo–elicitation.

People often like to talk about photos, especially personal ones, but sometimes they are unprepared for what they remember and feel when they do this. In my own research on girls growing up in the 1950s and 1960s (Tinkler 2011), I interviewed women in their sixties and seventies about their girlhood and I asked them to show me, and talk about, the photo collections they compiled when they were young. Interviewees eagerly talked about their girlhood photo collections but this experience was sometimes unexpectedly discomforting. For one participant, Irene, this was because one of her girlhood photos confronted her with aspects of her teenage life, identity and aspirations that were inconsistent with how she remembered herself and how she thought of herself now. In the case of another participant, Carol, her photo album proved deeply unsettling, not because of the girlhood story she created in her mid-teens, but because pages in her album provided physical evidence of what happened later in her life when she married. Vandalised pages and missing photos stimulated powerful memories of her jealous and controlling husband.

The distinctiveness of the photo-interview compared to a talk-alone one, especially when using personal photos, is that interviewees often feel they have to account for photos and this leads them to think about and explain what they might otherwise prefer to forget or gloss over. Even when interviewees refuse to engage with a photo because it is unsettling, the photo has already had an effect (Mannik 2011). The intensity of reactions sometimes provoked in photo-interviews does not mean that researchers should avoid using photos; they can be a pleasure for interviewees to work with and researchers learn a lot from what is talked about. However, researchers do need to be attentive to signs of distress and discomfort in their interviewees. In some cases it can be best to skip a photo, sometimes take a break, and if the topic seems important, to return to it later (not necessarily with the photo).

# Presentation

There is an important distinction between the photos you collect and analyse in your research and those you wish to use in presentations and publications. In this section I address legal issues concerning the reproduction of photos, this is principally a matter of ownership. I then outline ethical issues relating to the reproduction of photos, starting with the rights of people to privacy, anonymity and dignity and concluding with a discussion of informed consent. Reproducing photos from personal websites raises particular issues that I address separately. The section concludes with a discussion of how researchers should use photos in presenting their research.

## Legal issues and ownership

To use found photos you typically require permission from the copyright holder, and for use in publications this can often mean paying a fee. It is important to include the appropriate credit as public institutions and archives are usually particular about this. Locating the copyright holder and negotiating use of a photo can be time-consuming. Permission is also required if you want to reproduce photos from private collections. If you have undertaken research that involves looking at, and reproducing, a number of photos in private possession you may not know initially which you will want to reproduce. Although you can go back to the owner when you know, it is best to seek permission around the time you copy the photos. While you can ask the owner for permission to use any of their photos in publications and presentations this does not best serve the interests of the owner as they cannot always recall the images you have looked at and they can end up agreeing to photos being used that, on reflection, they would have preferred to keep private. The best way round this is to produce thumbnail reproductions of all the photos you have copied and to number these. You can then ask the owner to specify if there are images they do not want you to use publicly. Although the owner of personal photos is typically deemed to be the person who keeps them, as Davies (2008) explains, in legal terms ownership lies with the photographer or their employing institution; in personal photography this can be difficult or impossible to work out because cameras are passed around and several people may be involved in taking a picture (Thomson 2011a). Where research participants have generated photos you may want to use, you need to request that they sign copyright over to you (Wiles et al. 2008).

## The rights of participants

I have already touched on people's rights in relation to generating photographic data, here I extend this discussion. Whether the photo is one you or a research participant has taken, or a family snap belonging to an interviewee, the question is whether it is legal or ethical to use this photo without the express permission of all the people in the photo. There is no consensus on this, and practice varies depending on the particulars of the research and the obligations within which researchers work out their ethical framework. There are three main issues – privacy, anonymity, dignity/harm.

First, there are privacy issues, specifically the right of an individual to decide whether or not to appear in a photo that will be used in public presentations and publications. Given that people's photos are constantly being taken, circulated and used, not least because most of us feature in the background of other people's photos – holiday snaps, public celebrations etc. – it is unrealistic to expect that individuals can have exclusive rights over their public image. But as mentioned, the public/private distinction is a grey area and it is difficult to define precisely what may be an infringement of privacy, and in relation to children what may be considered suspect.

Second, there is an individual's right to anonymity; this concerns whether the individual is identifiable within the context of the research. Although researchers can try to distinguish between photos where individuals are clearly identifiable and those where they are peripheral or too small to be seen clearly, with digital imagery it is possible to enlarge image details, and it is therefore important to think carefully about who needs to give consent. It is also debatable whether consent is necessary when using old photos where a person no longer bears a resemblance to their photographic image.

One solution to issues about identification is to blur faces or otherwise alter an image so people are unrecognisable; similar strategies are used to anonymise place with varying degrees of success. As Wiles et al. (2008) explain, this has provoked interesting debate about the point of using photos and what is lost when faces are indistinct; not only is visual data sometimes obscured but people are objectified. Though this strategy is increasingly essential when reproducing photos of children, it is debatable whether this is the best way of representing research. How far can we go in adjusting images before it is not worth including them? Often debates about presenting photos are concerned with not infringing the privacy rights of the people depicted, but sometimes people demand the right to visibility or do not regard identification as problematic (Renold et al. 2008; Wiles et al. 2008). Whether participants' wishes should be paramount needs careful consideration, especially if they are under 16 years of age.

The third issue is the dignity and well being of the person in a photo. You need to consider whether the photo portrays the individual in ways that degrade, embarrass or in other ways cause them harm. This is not always straightforward as harm is often difficult to assess. Sometimes it may seem obvious not to reproduce a photo, for instance, if someone is visibly distressed. It is difficult, however, for researchers to know what may be harmful. For example, researchers cannot determine if they may cause harm by publishing a photo that shows someone being in a place that they are not supposed to be, such as on a protest march.

## Photos in the public domain

Reproducing publicly available photos also raises ethical issues, particularly where photos depict people in demeaning ways. These issues are pertinent to the reproduction of recent photographs of suffering, they also apply to old photos where the people depicted are dead or no longer recognisable because of ageing. This is often an issue for researchers considering whether to reproduce colonial images that humiliate indigenous peoples (Lydon 2010), Holocaust photos (see Farmer 2010), photos taken of public rituals of humiliation (Moore 2006) or demeaning photographs of people with physical or mental disabilities.

One issue is whether it is right to contribute to the original violence of representation by re-presenting photos, even if these images are in public circulation and accessible. The point is that in reproducing photos the researcher becomes complicit in the original violence and disregard of a person's rights. Sometimes the issue is couched in terms of informed consent. For instance, discussing institutional photos of children with disabilities, Grosvenor (Devlieger et al. 2008) asks whether it is ethical to look at images that have been taken without the children's informed consent. A related issue is that looking at, and reproducing, demeaning photos can cause further harm to the people in the photographs if they are still living and cause distress to their relatives and ancestors. Lydon (2010) points out that, reproducing degrading colonial photos of indigenous Australians can also have implications for how indigenous communities construct their public identities in the present.

## Informed Consent

Where the researcher needs consent to reproduce photos this must be informed consent, which means that participants need to be clear about the implications of being identifiable in a photo used in public presentations and publications. Under the Data Protection Act researchers are obligated to store data securely and ensure against breach of agreed confidentiality, but once images are published, especially on the web, it is difficult to control their circulation and how they are used. The issue of control over images, especially future uses, is also raised by the possibility of archiving photos. Mason and Davies (Davies 2008) decided against archiving photos from the 'Family Resemblances' project because it was not possible to determine the contexts in which they would be used in future. Though blanket consent can be attained, some researchers advocate detailing the different forums in which the images may be used. However, Davies describes how it proved unfeasible in the 'Family Resemblances' project to devise a consent form whereby research participants could approve or not each of the possible outputs. Davies offers useful advice on informed consent: 'Ask yourself which levels of consent you need to seek, when you need to seek them and how formally you need to do this. Don't forget that you may not be aware of all the ways you will use the images in the future so be as inclusive as possible.' For a sample consent form see Davies (2008); Mitchell (2011) includes examples of visual as well as textual consent forms.

## Photos on personal websites

There is very little information specifically on the ethics of reproducing photos from publicly accessible blogs, personal web pages and social networking sites (SNS) such as MySpace and YouTube, but it is worth noting some general issues relating to copyright, consent, privacy and anonymity.

Under copyright law in the UK, USA and Australia, as Nicholas Hookway (2008: 105–6) explains, internet content is copyrighted as soon as it is uploaded, so bloggers and the authors of personal websites have 'exclusive rights over the reproduction of their work'. There are, however, 'provisions built into the copyright act(s) which allow for "fair dealing" of copyrighted material for the purposes of study or research'.

An issue that does affect researchers is whether they need consent from bloggers or the owners of SNS and other personal websites to reproduce photos. If a website is password protected it is technically private and permission should be sought from the owners/creators before reproducing content (Snee, interview). There is, however, no consensus on how to treat personal websites that are not password protected. The debate revolves around whether these websites should be treated as public or private sources. There are several reasons why accessible personal online sources can be treated as public: they are located in the public domain, they are publicly accessible and they are usually defined by users as public (privacy settings can be used for websites that are not for public consumption) (Hookway 2008; Wilkinson and Thelwall 2011). Accessible websites are, as Hookway puts it, personal rather than private. Nevertheless, some scholars emphasise that authors may think their websites are private and that this perception should be respected (Hookway 2008), while others stress that private and public spheres of the internet are ambiguous (Pauwels 2008). Pauwels advises that it is 'basic ethical practice' for researchers to seek informed consent from website users before reproducing their websites as screenshots, though he admits that this can be difficult as websites are often short lived. Before leaving this point it is important to stress that how you decide to treat photos you find on personal websites should take into account specific features of these websites that relate to ethics (Ess and AoIR 2002), such as whether the venue (homepage, blog etc.) stipulates ethical expectations of users.

Anonymity is particularly difficult for researchers who want to reproduce online personal photographs. Researchers who reproduce photographs from personal websites need to address the same issues as researchers working with visual data that is not online.

## How photos are re-presented

So far I have concentrated on the issues at stake in reproducing photos, now I want to address the ethics of *how* researchers interpret and present photos to their audiences.

The issues are similar whether photos are generated or found, but it is helpful to discuss each separately starting with generated photos.

### Generated photos

Photos are complex constructions and it is the researcher's responsibility to engage reflexively with how they have generated photographic data (Pink 2007; Prosser and Schwartz 1998) and consider the implications of their photographic practices for their findings and conclusions. Researchers also have obligations to be clear about the point that is made by presenting the photos they have produced. You need to ask yourself: what claims do I make for my photos explicitly or implicitly, and are these claims fair and transparent? There have been numerous controversies over the authenticity of documentary photography, and the typicality or causality they sometimes imply. For example, in 1936 Arthur Rothstein presented a photo of a steer's skull on barren ground as indicative of the devastating agricultural conditions in the United States. There was outrage when it emerged that the skull had initially been found on some nearby grass and relocated by Rothstein for the purposes of his photograph (Price 2000). Although Rothstein saw his photograph as symbolic of the conditions facing agricultural communities at the time, many viewers saw the photo as misleading because it was inauthentic and implied causality – environmental conditions (and possibly a lack of government intervention) causing the death of livestock – that was not evident from the environment in which the corpse was actually found.

In research where photos are generated, another issue is whether it is productive to present photos without explanation (Chapter 7) and whether researchers have a responsibility to provide a basic interpretative framework to ensure that their photos are not misconstrued in ways that might degrade or disadvantage the people depicted (see Newton 2009).

### Found photos

Researchers have a responsibility to their audiences to give clear and transparent analyses of the images that inform their thinking. How researchers present found photos raises ethical issues. When working with photos that depict suffering or degradation, you need to consider why you are reproducing these photos. Many scholars think it unethical to reproduce such photos merely to interest readers rather than aid understanding or develop an argument; some scholars argue that in photographs documenting people's distress, viewers have an obligation to pay attention (Azoulay 2008). The sensibilities of your audience also need consideration; is the photo necessary for your argument?

The meaning of photos is shaped by how they are framed and used, so it is crucial that researchers do not reproduce found photos and their captions without critical evaluation. Some historians who work with photos of violence and degradation insist that critical evaluation is the only ethical and scholarly way to reproduce such images in presentations and publications (e.g. Keilbach 2009; Shneer 2010). Accuracy is crucial in describing the original contexts in which images were made because photographs are perceived differently depending on how we reproduce and caption them. For instance, one photograph of a Nazi war camp is used frequently as a symbol of the Holocaust and of how the Nazis murdered on an 'industrial' scale (see Keilbach 2009 for a review of literature on this and other examples). The photo depicts a bulldozer pushing a heap of tangled dead bodies; the pile of bodies extends towards the viewer and off to the left of the photo suggesting that there are more bodies. The contexts in which this photo has been reproduced suggest to viewers that the photograph documents how Nazis treated the bodies of the people they murdered. However, this is an inaccurate interpretation of this particular photograph. While the Nazis were responsible for the deaths of the people depicted, the photo was taken by a British photographer after the camp was liberated and it documents how, because of concern to prevent an epidemic and to quickly inter the dead, Allied troops used tractors to move and bury the dead. The point of this example is that photographs can be used in inappropriate ways if they are not put into appropriate historical context. One of the concerns about repeated reuse of specific photos is that they often get used out of context and thereby contribute to simplified and historically inaccurate versions of the past (e.g. Keilbach 2009; Lydon 2010). This occurs particularly when photos shift from being used to represent particular people, places and events to being used as symbols of abstract concepts such as suffering or grief. Researchers need to investigate what photos depict, and be wary of reusing images simply because they seem to fit an argument.

The importance of accurate historical context in re-presenting photos is amplified when researchers take into account that the photographs they reproduce have implications for how contemporary and historical topics are perceived (see Belizer 1998; Moore 2006; Sontag 2003). For example, where photos were originally made and used to serve particular political or ideological purposes, uncritical reproduction can serve to perpetuate these ends. This point is conveyed by Alison Moore's (2006) analysis of photos taken of the French Tondues; these were public rituals of humiliation in which women accused of collaborating with occupation forces during the Second World War had their heads forcibly shaved (a form of sexual humiliation at the time) and were subjected to other acts of abuse. According to Moore, the production and circulation of Tondue photos at the time of the French Liberation served to sexualise female collaboration, though it is estimated that only 42% of women punished in the Tondues were *accused* of sexual collaboration (some were accused of feeding Germans or being married to men who collaborated) and not all women who had sexual relations with Germans were treated in this way. Moore argues that the repeated use of particular Tondue photographs that portray women being subjected to sexualised forms of public humiliation perpetuates the erroneous idea that women's collaboration was always sexual and it is this myth that shapes popular perceptions of this period in French history: 'the stereotype of the Tondues as sexual collaborators is at best a half truth; the shearings represented not a punishment for sexual collaboration, but rather a sexualisation of female collaboration during the Liberation and in post-war memory' (p. 149).

Another dimension to debates about the ethics of reproducing found photos concerns the politics of who is visible in history. In her study of the yearbooks produced by the National Children's Home 1920–60, Janet Fink found 'brutal' photographs of children with disability and these raised difficult issues for her (interview). On the one hand, out of respect for the children depicted, it seemed unethical to reproduce the photos. On the other hand, decisions by Fink and other scholars to protect the dignity of children with disabilities, contributes to the marginalisation of these children in the historical record, and in this particular instance it obscures the diversity of children in care homes at this time. In some instances, the concern is that invisibility actually serves a public desire to forget (e.g. Lydon 2010).

## Summary of the discussion of presenting photos

1  You must have the copyright holder's permission to reproduce photos in public contexts.

2  If photos are likely to invade someone's privacy or reveal their identity, seek their consent before using photos in presentations and publications.

3  Identify the range of ways you might use photos and what you need to ask participants to consent to.

4  Decide if it is feasible or necessary to disguise the identities of people in photographs and what might be lost in doing this.

5  If photos feature people in ways that degrade or cause them harm, ask yourself why it is necessary to reproduce them.

6  In presenting generated photos, check that your claims are fair and transparent; ideally provide an interpretive framework so your photos are not misconstrued.

7  When presenting found photos, outline their production and present a critical evaluation of them. Think about who is made visible and invisible by the photos you present.

# Summary

What is ethical research? There are no easy answers and where there are no legal or institutional regulations governing your practice, you need to find your own way through this. It is best to be upfront about the decisions you make, not least because it shows that you are a responsible researcher who has taken the time to consider the issues.

# Notes

1   There are different approaches to ethics that, as Wiles et al. (2008) explain, are based on: weighing up the consequences or costs for participants against the benefits of research (utilitarian or consequentialist); establishing key principles (principalist); and a commitment to benefit the people who are the focus of the research (ethics of care).

2   British Sociological Association Visual Studies Group (BSAVSA) http://www.visualsociology.org.uk

International Visual Sociology Association (IVSA) http://www.visualsociology.org/home.html

# References

Abrams, L. (2011) *Oral History Theory*. London: Routledge.

Adam, B. (1995) *Timewatch*. London: Polity.

Allen, L. (2009) '"Snapped": researching the sexual cultures of schools using visual methods', *International Journal of Qualitative Studies in Education*, 22: 549–61.

Appadurai, A. (ed.) (1986) *The Social Life of Things: Commodities in Cultural Perspective*. Cambridge: Cambridge University Press.

Azoulay, A. (2008) *The Civil Contract of Photography*. New York: Zone Books.

Bagnoli, A. (2004) 'Researching identities with multi-method autobiographies', *Sociological Research Online*, 9, 2. Available at http://www.socresonline.org.uk/9/2/bagnoli.html

Baker, S. (1989) *Street Photographs: Manchester and Salford*. Newcastle-upon-Tyne: Bloodaxe.

Baker, S. (2000) *Streets and Spaces: Urban Photography*. Salford: Lowry Press.

Banks, M. (2001) *Visual Methods in Social Research*. London: Sage.

Barthes, R. (1973) *Mythologies*. London: Paladin.

Barthes, R. (1977) *Image-Music-Text*, trans. S. Heath. New York: Hill and Wang.

Barthes, R. (2000) *Camera Lucida: Reflections on Photography*. London: Vintage.

Batchen, G. (1997) *Photography's Objects*. Albuquerque, NM: University of New Mexico Art Museum.

Batchen, G. (2004) 'Ere the substance fade: photograph and hair jewellery', in E. Edwards and J. Hart (eds), *Photographs, Objects, Histories: On the Materiality of Images*. London: Routledge, pp. 32–46.

Bateson, G. and Mead, M. (1942) *Balinese Character: A Photographic Analysis*. New York: New York Academy of Sciences.

Baylis, G. (2006) 'Visual cruising in South Wales in the 1860s: Tredegar patch girls', *Visual Culture in Britain*, 7: 1–24.

Becker, H. (1974) 'Photography and Sociology', *Studies in the Anthropology of Visual Communication*, 1: 3–26.

Becker, H. (1979) 'Do photographs tell the truth?', in T. Cook and C. Reichardt (eds), *Qualitative and Quantitative Methods in Evaluation Research*. London: Sage, pp. 99–117.

Becker, H. (1998) 'Visual sociology, documentary photography and photojournalism: it's (almost) all a matter of context', in J. Prosser (ed.), *Image-based Research: A Sourcebook for Qualitative Researchers*. London: Falmer, pp. 84–96.

Becker, H. (2002) 'Visual evidence: a *Seventh Man*, the specified generalization, and the work of the reader', *Visual Studies*, 17: 3–11.

Belizer, B. (1998) *Remembering to Forget: Holocaust Memory Through the Camera's Eye*. London: University of Chicago Press.

Bell, P. (2001) 'Content analysis of visual images', in T. Leeuwen and C. Jewitt (eds), *Handbook of Visual Analysis*. London: Sage, pp. 10–34.

Bendelow, G. (1993) 'Using visual imagery to explore gendered notions of pain', in C.M. Renzetti and R.M. Lee (eds), *Researching Sensitive Topics*. London: Sage, pp. 212–27.

Benjamin, W. (1931/1980) 'A short history of photography', in A. Trachtenberg (ed.), *Classic Essays in Photography*. New Haven, CT: Leete's Island Books, pp. 199–216.

Bennett, J. (2011) 'Looks funny when you take its photo: family and place in stories of local belonging', *Sociology Working Paper* No. 1, University of Manchester. Available at http://www.socialsciences.manchester.ac.uk/disciplines/sociology/postgraduate/workingpapers/documents/sociology%20working%20paper%20-%201%20Julia%20Bennett.pdf [accessed 6 June 2012].

Berger, J. (1972) *Ways of Seeing*. Harmondsworth: Penguin.

Berger, J. and Mohr, J. (1975) *A Seventh Man*. Harmondsworth: Penguin.

Bhroiméil, U. and O'Donoghue, D. (2009) 'Doing gender history visually', in M. Valiulis (ed.), *Gender and Power in Irish History*. Dublin: Irish Academic Press, pp. 159–82.

Blaikie, A. (2006) 'Photography, childhood and urban poverty: remembering "The Forgotten Gorbals"', *Visual Culture in Britain*, 7: 47–68.

Blinn, L. and Harrist, A. (1991) 'Combining native instant photography and photo-elicitation', *Visual Anthropology*, 4: 175–92.

Bloustein, G. (2001) 'Far from sugar and spice: teenage girls, embodiment and representation', in B. Baron and H. Kotthoff (eds), *Gender in Interaction: Perspectives on Femininity and Masculinity in Ethnography and Discourse*. Amsterdam/Philadelphia, PA: John Benjamins Publishing Group, pp. 99–136.

Bloustein, G. and Baker, S. (2003) 'On not talking to strangers: researching the micro worlds of girls through visual auto-ethnographic practices', *Social Analysis*, 47: 64–79.

Bolton, A., Pole, C. and Mizen, P. (2001) 'Picture this: researching child workers', *Sociology*, 35: 501–18.

Bourdieu, P. (1990) *Photography: A Middle-Brow Art*. Cambridge: Polity Press.

Brooke, S. (2006) 'War and the nude: the photography of Bill Brandt in the 1940s', *Journal of British Studies*, 45: 118–38.

British Sociological Association Visual Sociology Study Group (2006) Statement of Ethical Practice for The British Sociological Association – Visual Sociology Group. Available at http://www.visualsociology.org.uk/BSA_VS_ethical_statement.pdf [accessed 21 February 2010].

Bryman, A. (2008) *Social Research Methods*. Oxford: Oxford University Press.

Bull, S. (2010) *Photography*. Oxford: Routledge.

Burke, P. (2001) *Eyewitnessing: The Uses of Images as Historical Evidence*. London: Reaktion.

Burke, P. (2010) 'Interrogating the eyewitness', *Cultural & Social History*, 7: 435–44.

Burke, C. and de Castro, H. (2007) 'The school photograph: portraiture and the art of assembling the body of the schoolchild', *History of Education*, 36: 213–26.

Burke, C. and Grosvenor, I. (2007) 'The progressive image in the history of education: stories of two schools', *Visual Studies*, 22: 155–68.

Byrne, D. and Doyle, A. (2004) 'Visual and the verbal: the interaction of images and discussion in exploring cultural change', in C. Knowles and P. Sweetman (eds), *Picturing the Social Landscape*. London: Routledge, pp. 166–77.

Caldarola, V. (1985) 'Visual contexts: a photographic research method in anthropology', *Studies in Visual Communication*, 11: 33–53.

Chalfen, R. (1987) *Snapshot Versions of Life*. Bowling Green, OH: Bowling Green State University Popular Press.

Chalfen, R. (1991) *Turning Leaves: The Photograph Collections of Two Japanese American Families*. Albuquerque, NM: University of New Mexico Press.

Chalfen, R. (1998) 'Interpreting family photography as pictorial communication', in J. Prosser (ed.), *Image-based Research: A Sourcebook for Qualitative Researchers*. London: Falmer, pp. 214–34.

Chalfen, R. and Murui, M. (2004) 'Print club photography in Japan: framing social relationships', in E. Edwards and J. Hart (eds), *Photographs, Objects, Histories: On the Materiality of Images*. London: Routledge, pp. 166–85.

Chaplin, E. (1994) *Sociology and Visual Representation*. London: Routledge.

Chaplin, E. (2004) 'My visual diary', in C. Knowles and P. Sweetman (eds), *Picturing the Social Landscape*. London: Routledge, pp. 147–65.

Chaplin, E. (2011) 'The photo diary as an autoethnographic method', in E. Margolis and L. Pauwels (eds), *The Sage Handbook of Visual Research Methods*. London: Sage, pp. 241–62.

Chaplin, E. (1994) *Sociology and Visual Representation*. London: Routledge.

Clark, C.D. (1999) 'The autodriven interview: a photographic viewfinder into children's experience', *Visual Sociology*, 14: 39–50.

Clark-Ibáñez, M. (2007) 'Inner-city children in sharper focus: sociology of childhood and photo elicitation interviews', in G. Stanczak (ed.), *Visual Research Methods. Image, Society, and Representation*. London: Sage, pp. 167–96.

Clarke, G. (1997) *The Photograph*. Oxford: Oxford University Press.

Coleman, R. (2008) 'The becoming of bodies', *Feminist Media Studies*, 8: 163–79.

Collier, J. and Collier, M. (1986) *Visual Anthropology: Photography as a Research Method*. Albuquerque, NM: University of New Mexico Press.

Cook, T. and Hess, E. (2007) 'What the camera sees and from whose perspective. Fun methodologies for engaging children in enlightening adults', *Childhood*, 14: 29–45.

Coover, R. (2011) 'Interactive media representation', in Margolis, E. and Pauwels, L. (eds), *The Sage Handbook of Visual Research Methods*. London: Sage, pp. 617–37.

Crary, J. (1992) *Techniques of the Observer: Vision and Modernity in the Nineteenth Century*. London: MIT Press.

Crawford, E. (1999) *The Women's Suffrage Movement: A Reference Guide, 1866–1928*. London: UCL Press.

Croghan, R., Griffin, C., Hunter, J. and Phoenix, A. (2008) 'Young people's constructions of self: notes on the use and analysis of the photo-elicitation methods', *International Journal of Social Research Methodology*, 11: 345–56.

Cronin, Ó. (1998) 'Psychology and photographic theory', in J. Prosser (ed.), *Image-based Research: A Sourcebook for Qualitative Researchers*. London: Falmer, pp. 69–83.

Damico, S. (1985) 'The two worlds of school: differences in the photographs of black and white adolescents', *The Urban Review*, 17: 210–22.

Davies, C. and Charles, N. (2002) 'The piano in the parlour: methodological issues in the conduct of a restudy', *Sociological Research Online*, 7(2). Available at http://www.socresonline.org.uk/7/2/davies.html

Davies, K. (2008) *Informed Consent in Visual Research. Seeking Consent for the Use of Images Obtained in Photo Elicitation: Reflections from the Living Resemblances Project. ESRC Real Life Methods*. Realties Toolkit 1. Available at http://www.socialsciences.manchester.ac.uk/morgancentre/realities/toolkits/consent-visual-data/2008-07-toolkit-visual-consent.pdf [accessed 2 August 2012].

Davies, K. (2011) 'Making sense of family resemblance: the politics of visual perception', in L. Jamieson, R. Simpson and R. Lewis (eds), *Researching Families and Relationships: Reflections on Process*. London: Palgrave Macmillan, pp. 146–9.

Day, L. (1989) 'Photo racism in the visual archive', in W. Neidich and L. Day, *American History Reinvented*. New York: Aperture, pp. 26–46.

De Laine, M. (2000) *Fieldwork, Participation and Practice: Ethics and Dilemmas in Qualitative Research*. London: Sage.

De Ville, N. and Haden-Guest, A. (1981) *The Art of Society Photography 1924–1977*. London: Allen Lane.

Devlieger, P., Grosvenor, I., Simon, F., van Hove, G. and Vanobbergen, B. (2008) 'Visualising disability in the past', *Paedagogica Historica*, 44: 747–60.

Di Bello, P. (2007) *Women's Albums and Photography in Victorian England. Ladies, Mothers and Flirts*. Aldershot: Ashgate.

Dijck, J. van (2005) 'From shoebox to performative agent: the computer as personal memory machine', *New Media & Society*, 7: 331–2.

Doan, L. (2001) *Fashioning Sapphism: The Origins of a Modern English Lesbian Culture*. New York: Columbia University Press.

Dowdall, G. and Golden, J. (1989) 'Photographs as data: an analysis of images from a mental hospital', *Qualitative Sociology*, 12: 183–213.

Drew, S., Duncan, R., Sawyer, S. (2010) 'Visual storytelling: a beneficial but challenging method for health research with young people', *Qualitative Health Research*, 20: 1677–88.

Dyer, G. (2005) *The Ongoing Moment*. New York: Vintage.

Edwards, E. (ed.) (1992) *Anthropology and Photography 1860–1920*. New Haven, CT: Yale University Press.

Edwards, E. (2001) *Raw Histories. Photographs, Anthropology and Museums*. Oxford: Berg.

Edwards, E. (2002) 'Material beings: objecthood and ethnographic photographs', *Visual Studies*, 17: 68–75.

Edwards, E. (2006a) 'Photography and the performance of history', in P. Hamilton (ed.), *Visual Research Methods*, Vol. 2. London: Sage, pp. 239–58.

Edwards, E. (2006b) 'Photographs and the sound of history', *Visual Anthropology*, 21: 27–46.

Edwards, E. (2009) 'Photography and the material performance of the past', *History and Theory*, 48: 130–50.

Edwards, E. (2012) *The Camera as Historian: Amateur Photographers and Historical Imagination, 1895–1918*. London: Duke University Press.

Edwards, E. and Hart, J. (eds) (2004a) *Photographs, Objects, Histories: On the Materiality of Images*. London: Routledge.

Edwards, E. and Hart, J. (2004b) 'Mixed box: the cultural biography of a box of "ethnographic" postcards', in E. Edwards and J. Hart (eds), *Photographs, Objects, Histories: On the Materiality of Images*. London: Routledge, pp. 47–61.

Emmison, M. and Smith, P. (2000) *Researching the Visual. Images, Objects, Contexts and Interactions in Social and Cultural Inquiry*. London: Sage.

Ess, C. and Association of Internet Researchers (AoIR) (2002) *Ethical Decision-making and Internet Research*. Available at http://aoir.org/reports/ethics.pdf [accessed 21 February 2012].

Farmer, S. (2010) 'Going visual: Holocaust representation and historical method', *The American Historical Review*, 115: 115–22.

Fink, J. (2008) 'Inside a hall of mirrors: residential care and the shifting constructions of childhood in mid-twentieth-century Britain', *Paedagogica Historica*, 44: 287–307.

Frankenberger, L. (1991) 'Going out of business in Highland Park', *Visual Studies*, 6: 24–32.

Freund, A. and Thomson, A. (eds) (2011) *Oral History and Photography*. London: Palgrave Macmillan.

Freund, A. with Thiessen, A. (2011) 'Mary Brockmeyer's wedding picture: exploring the intersection of photographs and oral history interviews', in A. Freund and A. Thomson (eds), *Oral History and Photography*. London: Palgrave Macmillan, pp. 27–44.

Frith, H. and Harcourt, D. (2007) 'Using photographs to capture women's experiences of chemotherapy: reflecting on the method', *Qualitative Health Research*, 17: 1340–50.

Frosh, P. (2003) *The Image Factory*. Oxford: Berg.

Ganzel, B. (1984) *Dust Bowl Descent*. Lincoln, NE: University of Nebraska Press.

Gidley, B. (2004) 'Doing historical and archival research', in C. Seale (ed.), *Researching Society and Culture*. London: Sage, pp. 249–64.

Gittens, D. (1998) *The Child in Question*. London: Macmillan.

Gluck, S. (1977) 'What's so special about women? Women's oral history', *Frontiers: A Journal of Women's Studies*, 2: 3–13.

Goffman, E. (1979) *Gender Advertisements*. London: Macmillan.

Goldstein, B. (2007) 'All photos lie: images as data', in G. Stanczak (ed.), *Visual Research Methods. Image, Society, and Representation*, London: Sage, pp. 61–82.

Grosvenor, I., Lawn, M. and Rousmaniere, K. (eds) (1999) *Silences and Images: The Social History of the Classroom*. New York: Peter Lang.

Grosvenor, I., Lawn, M. and Rousmaniere, K. (2000) 'Imaging past schooling: the necessity for montage', *The Review of Education/Pedagogy/Cultural Studies*, 22: 71–85.

Hagiopan, P. (2006) 'Vietnam War photography as a locus of memory', in A. Kuhn and K.E. McAllister (eds), *Locating Memory: Photographic Acts*. Oxford: Bergahn Books, pp. 201–22.

Hall, S. (1980) 'Encoding/decoding', in S. Hall, D. Hobson, A. Lowe and P. Willis (eds), *Culture, Media, Language: Working Papers in Cultural Studies 1972–79*. London: Hutchison, pp. 128–38.

Halle, D. (1996) *Inside Culture: Art and Class in the American Home*. London: Chicago University Press.

Hamlett, J. (2006) '"Nicely feminine, yet learned": student rooms at Royal Holloway and the Oxbridge Colleges in late nineteenth-century Britain', *Women's History Review*, 15: 137–61.

Harper, D. (1987) *Working Knowledge: Skill and Community in a Small Shop*. Chicago, IL: University of Chicago Press.

Harper, D. (1998) 'An argument for visual sociology', in J. Prosser (ed.), *Image-based Research: A Sourcebook for Qualitative Researchers*. London: Falmer, pp. 24–41.

Harper, D. (2001) *Changing Works: Visions of a Lost Agriculture*. Chicago, IL: University of Chicago Press.

Harper, D. (2002) 'Talking about pictures: a case for photo elicitation', *Visual Studies*, 17: 13–26.

Harper, D. (2012) *Visual Sociology*. London: Routledge.

Haug, F. et al. (1999) *Female Sexualization: A Collective Work of Memory*. London: Verso.

Hayes, P. (2006) 'Introduction: visual genders', in P. Hayes (ed.), *Visual Genders, Visual Histories*. Oxford: Blackwell Publishing, pp. 1–19.

Hayes, P. (2010) 'Introduction: photographs and ghosts in the war for Namibia', in J. Liebenberg and P. Hayes, *Bush of Ghosts: Life and War in Namibia 1986–90*. Cape Town: UMUZI, pp. 9–25.

Heisley, D. and Levy, S. (1991) 'Autodriving: a photoelicitation technique', *Journal of Consumer Research*, 18: 257–72.

Hill, M. (1993) *Archival Strategies and Techniques*. London: Sage.

Hirsch, J. (1981) *Family Photographs: Content, Meaning, and Effect*. Oxford: Oxford University Press.

Hirsch, M. (1997) *Family Frames: Photography, Narrative and Memory*. Cambridge, MA and London: Harvard University Press.

Hirsch, M. (ed.) (1999) *The Familial Gaze*. London: University Press of New England.

Holland, P. (1991) 'Introduction: history, memory and the family album', in J. Spence and P. Holland (eds), *Family Snaps: The Meanings of Domestic Photography*. London: Virago, pp. 1–14.

Holland, P. (2000) '"Sweet it is to scan …": personal photographs and popular photography', in L. Wells (ed.), *Photography: A Critical Introduction*. London: Routledge, pp. 117–64.

Homberger, E. (1992) 'J.P. Morgan's nose: photographer and subject in American portrait photography', in G. Clark (ed.), *The Portrait in Photography*. London: Reaktion, pp.115–31.

Hookway, N. (2008) '"Entering the blogosphere": some strategies for using blogs in social research', *Qualitative Research*, 8: 91–113.

Ibson, J. (2006) *Picturing Men: A Century of Male Relationships in Everyday American Photography*. Washington: Smithsonian Institution Press.

Israel, M. and Hay, I. (2006) *Research Ethics for Social Scientists*. London: Sage.

Jenks, C. (1995) 'The centrality of the eye in Western culture: an introduction', in C. Jenks (ed.), *Visual Culture*. London: Routledge, pp. 1–25.

Keilbach, J. (2009) 'Photographs, symbolic images, and the Holocaust: on the (im)possibility of depicting historical truth', *History and Theory*, 47: 54–76.

Kenney, K. (1993) 'Using self-portrait photographs to understand the self-concepts of Chinese and American university students', *Visual Anthropology*, 5, 245–69.

Klett, M. (2011) 'Rephotography in Landscape Research', in E. Margolis and L. Pauwels (eds), *The Sage Handbook of Visual Research Methods*. London: Sage, pp. 114–31.

Knowles, C. and Sweetman, P. (eds) (2004) *Picturing the Social Landscape*. London: Routledge.

Kopytoff, I. (1986) 'The cultural biography of things: commoditization as process', in A. Appadurai (ed.), *The Social Life of Things: Commodities in Cultural Perspective*. Cambridge: Cambridge University Press, pp. 64–91.

Kuhn, A. (1991) 'Remembrance', in J. Spence and P. Holland (eds), *Family Snaps. The Meanings of Domestic Photography*. London: Virago, pp. 17–25.

Kuhn, A. (1995/2002) *Family Secrets: Acts of Memory and Imagination*. London: Verso.

Kuhn, A. (2000) 'A journey through memory', in S. Radstone (ed.) *Memory and Methodology*. Oxford: Berg, pp. 179–96.

Kuhn, A. (2007) 'Photography and cultural memory: a methodological exploration', *Visual Studies*, 22: 283–92.

Kuhn, A. and McAllister, K.E. (eds) (2006) *Locating Memory: Photographic Acts*. Oxford: Berghan.

Langford, M. (2001) *Suspended Conversations: The Afterlife of Memory in Photographic Albums*. London: McGill-Queen's University Press.

Langford, M. (2006) 'Speaking the Album: an application of the oral-photographic framework', in A. Kuhn and K.E. McAllister (eds), *Locating Memory: Photographic Acts*. Oxford: Berghan, pp. 223–46.

Latham, A. (2003) 'Research, performance, and doing human geography: some reflections on the diary–photograph, diary–interview method', *Environment and Planning*, 35: 1993–2017.

Latham, A. (2004) 'Researching and writing everyday accounts of the city: an introduction to the diary–photo diary–interview method', in C. Knowles and P. Sweetman (eds), *Picturing the Social Landscape: Visual Methods and the Sociological Imagination.* London: Routledge, pp. 117–31.

Lehmuskallio, A. and Sarvas, R. (2010) 'The agency of ICT in shaping non-professional photo use' during the NNVS workshop on 'From Family Album to Social Media – Traditions and Change', 20–22 September 2010, Stockholm.

Liebenberg, L. (2009) 'The visual image as discussion point: increasing validity in boundary crossing research', *Qualitative Research*, 9: 441–67.

Linkman, A. (1993) *The Victorians: Photographic Portraits.* London: I.B. Tauris.

Lister, M. (2000) 'Photography in the age of electronic imaging', in L. Wells (ed.), *Photography: A Critical Introduction.* London: Routledge.

Luttrell, W. (2010) '"A camera is a big responsibility": a lens for analysing children's visual voices', *Visual Studies*, 25: 224–37.

Luttrell, W. and Chalfen, R. (2010) 'Lifting up voices of participatory visual research', *Visual Studies*, 25: 197–200.

Lutz, C. and Collins, J. (1993) *Reading National Geographic.* Chicago, IL: University of Chicago Press.

Lydon, J. (2010) '"Behold the tears": photography as colonial witness', *History of Photography*, 34: 234–50.

McAllister, K.E. (2006) 'A story of escape: family photographs from Japanese Canadian internment camps', in A. Kuhn and K.E. McAllister (eds), *Locating Memory: Photographic Acts.* Oxford: Berghan Books, pp. 81–110.

MacIntyre, M. and Mackenzie, M. (1992) 'Focal length as an analogue of cultural distance', in E. Edwards (ed.), *Anthropology and Photography.* London: Yale University Press, pp. 158–64.

McIntyre, A. (2003) 'Through the eyes of women: photovoice and participatory research as tools for reimagining place', *Gender, Place and Culture*, 10: 47–66.

McLellan, J. (2009) 'Visual danger and delights: nude photography in East Germany', *Past and Present*, 205: 143–74.

McLellan, M. (1997) *Six Generations Here: A Farm Family Remembers.* Madison, WI: State Historical Society of Wisconsin.

Mannik, L. (2011) 'Remembering, forgetting, and feeling with photographs', in A. Freund and A. Thomson (eds), *Oral History and Photography.* London: Palgrave Macmillan, pp. 77–96.

Margolis, E. (1998) 'Picturing labor: a visual ethnography of the coal mine labor process', *Visual Sociology*, 13: 5–35.

Margolis, E. (1999) 'Class pictures: representations of race, gender and ability in a century of school photography', *Visual Sociology*, 14: 7–38.

Margolis, E. and Rowe, J. (2011) 'Methodological approaches to disclosing historic photographs', in E. Margolis and L. Pauwels (eds), *The Sage Handbook of Visual Research Methods.* London: Sage, pp. 337–58.

Mason, J. (2002) *Qualitative Researching.* London: Sage.

Mason, J. (2006) 'Six strategies for mixing methods and linking data in social science research.' NCRM Working Paper Series 4/06. ESRC National Centre for Research Methods. Available at http://eprints.ncrm.ac.uk/482/1/0406_six%2520strategies%2520for%2520mixing%2520methods.pdf [last accessed 6 June 2012].

Mason, J. and Davies, K. (2009) 'Coming to our senses: a critical approach to sensory methodology', *Qualitative Research*, 9: 587–603.

Mavor, C. (1996) *Pleasures Taken: Performances of Sexuality and Loss in Victorian Photographs*. London: I.B. Tauris.

Mertens, D. and Ginsberg, P. (eds) (2009) *The Handbook of Social Research Ethics*. London: Sage.

Mifflin, J. (2007) 'Visual archives in perspective: enlarging on historical medical photographs', *The American Archivist*, 70: 32–69.

Miller, J. (2007) 'Capturing the visual traces of historical change: the Internet Mission Photography Archive', in G. Stanczak (ed.), *Visual Research Methods: Image, Society, and Representation*. London: Sage, pp. 83–120.

Mirzoeff, N. (1998) *An Introduction to Visual Culture*. London: Routledge.

Misztal, B. (2003) *Theories of Remembering*. Maidenhead: Open University Press.

Mitchell, C. and Weber, S. (1999) *Reinventing Ourselves as Teachers: Beyond nostalgia*. London: Falmer Press.

Mitchell, C. (2011) *Doing Visual Research*. London: Sage.

Mizen, P. (2005) 'A little "light work"? Children's images of their labour', *Visual Studies*, 20: 124–39.

Modell, J.A. and Brodsky, C. (1994) 'Envisioning homestead: using photographs in interviewing', in E.M. McHahon and K.L. Rogers (eds), *Interactive Oral History Interviewing*. Hillsdale, NJ: Erlbaum, pp. 101–8.

Moore, A. (2006) 'History, memory and trauma in photography of the *Tondues*: visuality of the Vichy past through the silent image of women', in P. Hayes (ed.), *Visual Genders, Visual Histories*. Oxford: Blackwell, pp. 139–63.

Moore, G., Croxford, B., Adams, M., Refaee, M., Cox, T. and Sharples, S. (2008) 'The photo-survey research method: capturing life in the city', *Visual Studies*, 23: 50–62.

Musello, C. (1979) 'Family photography', in J. Wagner (ed.), *Images of Information*. London: Sage, pp. 101–18.

Neidich, W. and Day, L. (1989) *American History Reinvented*. New York: Aperture.

Newbury, D. (2006) 'Telling stories about photography: the language and imagery of class in the work of Humphrey Spender and Paul Reas', in P. Hamilton (ed.), *Visual Research Methods*, Vol. 2. London: Sage, pp. 295–320.

Newbury, D. (2009) *Defiant Images. Photography and Apartheid South Africa*. Pretoria: Unisa Press.

Newton, J. (2009) 'Visual representation of people and information: translating lives into numbers, words and images', in D. Mertens and P. Ginsberg (eds), *The Handbook of Social Research Ethics*. London: Sage, pp. 353–72.

Novak, L. (1999) 'Collected visions', in M. Hirsch (ed.), *The Familial Gaze*. London: University Press of New England, pp. 14–31.

O'Donoghue, D. (2010) 'Classrooms as installations: a conceptual framework for analysing classroom photographs from the past', *History of Education*, 39, 401–15.

Ohrn, K.B. (1980) *Dorothea Lange and the Documentary Tradition*. Baton Rouge: Louisiana State University Press.

Okely, J. (1994) 'Vicarious and sensory knowledge of chronology and change: ageing in rural France', in K. Hastrup and P. Hervik (eds), *Social Experience and Anthropological Knowledge*. London: Routledge, pp. 34–48.

Orellano, M.F. (1999) 'Space and place in an urban landscape: learning from children's views of their social worlds', *Visual Sociology*, 14: 73–89.

Panofsky, E. (1955/1982) *Meaning in the Visual Arts*. Chicago, IL: University of Chicago Press.

Pauwels, L. (2005) 'Websites as visual and multimodal cultural expressions: opportunities and issues of online hybrid media research', *Media, Culture & Society*, 27: 604–13.

Pauwels, L. (2008) 'A private visual practice going public? Social functions and sociological research opportunities of Web-based family photography', *Visual Studies*, 23: 34–49.

Pinney, C. (1997) *Camera Indica: The Social Life of Indian Photographs*. Chicago, IL: University of Chicago Press.

Pinney, C. and Peterson, N. (2003) *Photography's Other Histories*. London: Duke University Press.

Pink, S. (2007) *Doing Visual Ethnography*. London: Sage.

Poole, D. (1997) *Vision, Race, and Modernity: A Visual Economy of the Andean Image World*. Princeton, NJ: Princeton University Press.

Portelli, A. (1998) 'What makes oral history different', in R. Perks and A. Thomson (eds), *The Oral History Reader*. London: Routledge, pp. 32–42.

Price, D. (2000) 'Surveyors and surveyed: photography out and about', in L. Wells (ed.), *Photography: A Critical Introduction*. London: Routledge, pp. 65–116.

Prosser, J. and Burke, C. (2006) 'Childlike perspectives through image-based educational research', in J.G. Knowles and A.L. Cole (eds), *Handbook of the Arts in Qualitative Research: Perspectives, Methodologies, Examples and Issues*. London: Sage, pp. 407–20.

Prosser, J. and Loxley, A. (2010) 'The application of visual methodology in the exploration of the visual culture of schools', in D. Hartas (ed.), *Educational Research and Inquiry: Qualitative and quantitative approaches*. London: Continuum International, pp. 199–222.

Prosser, J. and Schwartz, D. (1998) 'Photographs within the sociological research process', in J. Prosser (ed.), *Image-based Research: A Sourcebook for Qualitative Researchers*. London: Falmer, pp. 115–30.

Radley, A. and Taylor, D. (2003) 'Images of recovery: a photo-elicitation study on the hospital ward', *Qualitative Health Research*, 2003: 77–99.

Raiford, L. (2009) 'Photography and the practices of critical black memory', *History and Theory*, 48: 112–29.

Ramamurthy, A. (2000) 'Constructions of illusion: photography and commodity culture', in L. Wells (ed.), (2000) *Photography: A Critical Introduction*. London: Routledge, pp. 165–216.

Renold, E., Holland, S., Ross, N. and Hillman, A. (2008) '"Becoming participant": problematizing "informed consent" in participatory research with young people in care', *Qualitative Social Work*, 7: 427–47.

Richards, N. (2011) *Using Participatory Visual Methods*. Realities Toolkit #17. Available at http://www.socialsciences.manchester.ac.uk/morgancentre/realities/toolkits/participatory-visual/17-toolkit-participatory-visual-methods.pdf [last accessed 6 June 2012].

Rieger, J. (1996) 'Photographing social change', *Visual Sociology*, 11: 5–49.

Rieger, J. (2003) 'A retrospective study of social change: the pulp-logging industry in an Upper Peninsula Michigan county', *Visual Studies*, 18: 157–78.

Roberts, J. (1998) *The Art of Interruption: Realism, Photography and the Everyday*. Manchester: Manchester University Press.

Robins, K. (1995) 'Will image move us still?', in M. Lister (ed.), *The Photographic Image in Digital Culture*. London: Routledge, pp. 29–50.

Rolph, S., Johnson, J. and Smith, R. (2009) 'Using photography to understand change and continuity in the history of residential care for older people', *International Journal of Social Research Methodology*, 12: 421–39.

Rose, G. (2004) '"Everyone's cuddled up and it just looks really nice": an emotional geography of some mums and their family photos', *Social & Cultural Geography*, 5: 549–64.

Rose, G. (2007) *Visual Methodologies: An Introduction to the Interpretation of Visual Materials*, 2nd edn. London: Sage.

Rose, G. (2010) *Doing Family Photography: The Domestic, The Public and The Politics of Sentiment*. London: Ashgate.

Rossler, M. (1991) 'Image simulations, computer manipulations, some considerations', *Ten-8: Digital Dialogues*, 2: 52–63.

Rousmaniere, K. (2001) 'Questioning the visual in the history of education', *History of Education*, 30: 109–16.

Rubinstein, D. and Sluis, K. (2008) 'A life more photographic: mapping the networked image', *Photographies*, 1: 9–28.

Ryan, J. (1997) *Picturing Empire: Photography and the Visualization of the British Empire*. London: Reaktion books.

Samuel, R. (1994) *Theatres of Memory*. London: Verso.

Samuels, J. (2007) 'When words are not enough: eliciting children's experiences of Buddhist monastic life through photographs', in G. Stanczak (ed.), *Visual Research Methods: Image, Society, and Representation*. London: Sage, pp. 197–224.

Sassoon, J. (2004) 'Photographic materiality in the age of digital reproduction', in E. Edwards and J. Hart (eds), *Photographs, Objects, Histories: On the Materiality of Images*. London: Routledge, pp. 186–202.

Sayer, D. (2008) 'The photograph: the still image', in S. Barber and C. Peniston-Bird (eds), *History Beyond the Text: A Student's Guide to Approaching Alternative Sources*. London: Routledge, pp. 49–70.

Schwartz, D. (1989) 'Visual ethnography: using photography in qualitative research', *Qualitative Sociology*, 12: 119–54.

Schwartz, J. (2004) 'Un beau souvenir du Canada: object, image, symbolic space', in E. Edwards and J. Hart (eds), *Photographs, Objects, Histories: On the Materiality of Images*. London: Routledge, pp. 16–31.

Schwarz, B. (2011) '"Our unadmitted sorrow": the rhetorics of Civil Rights photography', *History Workshop Journal*, 72: 138–55.

Scott, J. (1990) *A Matter of Record: Documentary Sources in Social Research*. London: Polity.

Seabrook, J. (1991) 'My life is in that box', in J. Spence and P. Holland (eds), *Family Snaps: The Meanings of Domestic Photography*. London: Virago, pp. 171–85.

Seale, C. (2004) 'Coding and analysing data', C. Seale (ed.), *Researching Society and Culture*. London: Sage, pp. 305–23.

Search 88 (1987) *One Day for Life: Photographs by the People of Britain, Taken on a Single Day*. London: Bantam Press.

Sekula, A. (1986a) 'Reading an archive: photography between labour and capital', in P. Holland, J. Spence and S. Watney (eds), *Photography/Politics: Two*. London: Comedia Publishing, pp. 153–9.

Sekula, A. (1986b) 'The body and the archive', in R. Bolton (ed.), *The Contest of Meaning: Critical Histories of Photography*. Cambridge, MA: MIT Press, pp. 343–88.

Sharples, M., Davison, L., Thomas, G.V. and Rudman, P.D. (2003) 'Children as photographers: an analysis of children's photographic behaviour and intentions at three age levels', *Visual Communication*, 2: 303–30.

Shneer, D. (2010) 'Soviet Holocaust photography at the intersection of history and memory', *The American Historical Review*, 115: 28–52.

Sluis, K. (2010) 'Algorithmic memory? Machinic vision and database culture', in A. Mousoutzanis and D. Riha (eds), *New Media and the Politics of Online Communities*. Oxford: Inter-Disciplinary Press, pp. 227–35.

Snee, H. (2011) 'Youth research in web 2.0: a case study in blog analysis', in S. Heath and C. Walker (eds), *Innovations in Youth Research*. Basingstoke: Palgrave Macmillan, pp. 178–94.

Solomon-Godeau, A. (1991) *Photography at the Dock: Essays on Photographic History, Institutions, and Practices*. Minneapolis, MN: University of Minnesota Press.

Sontag, S. (1971) *On Photography*. Harmondsworth: Penguin.

Sontag, S. (2003) *Regarding the Pain of Others*. London: Penguin.

Spence, J. (1986) *Putting Myself in the Picture*. London: Camden Press.

Spence, J. (1995) *Cultural Sniping: The Art of Transgression*. London: Routledge.

Spence, J. and Holland, P. (eds) (1991) *Family Snaps: The Meanings of Domestic Photography*. London: Virago.

Stasz, C. (1979) 'The early history of visual sociology', in J. Wagner (ed.), *Images of Information: Still Photography in the Social Sciences*. London: Sage, pp. 119–36.

Steiger, R. (1995) 'First children and family dynamics', *Visual Sociology*, 10: 28–49.

Suchar, C. (1997) 'Grounding visual sociology research in shooting scripts', *Qualitative Sociology*, 20: 33–55.

Summerfield, P. (2004) 'Culture and composure: creating narratives of the gendered self in oral history interviews', *Cultural and Social History*, 1: 65–93.

Tagg, J. (1988) *Burden of Representation: Essays on Photographies and Histories*. Basingstoke: Macmillan.

Teddlie, C. and Tashakkori, A. (2009) *Foundations of Mixed Methods Research: Integrating Quantitative and Qualitative Approaches in the Social and Behavioral Sciences*. London: Sage.

Thomas, A. (1998) *The Expanding Eye: Photography and the Nineteenth-Century Mind*. London: Croom Helm.

Thomson, R. (2010) 'Creating family case histories: subjects, selves and family dynamics', in R. Thomson (ed.), *Intensity and Insight: Qualitative Longitudinal Methods as a Route to the Pyscho-Social*. Timescapes Working Paper Series, 3.

Thomson, A. (2011a) *Moving Stories: An Intimate History of Four Women Across Two Countries*. Manchester: Manchester University Press.

Thomson, A. (2011b) 'Family photographs and migrant memories: representing women's lives', in A. Freund and A. Thomson (eds), *Oral History and Photography*. London: Palgrave Macmillan, pp. 169–86.

Thompson, M. (2011) 'Family photographs as traces of Americanization', in A. Freund and A. Thomson (eds), *Oral History and Photography*. London: Palgrave Macmillan, pp. 149–68.

Tickner, L. (1988) *The Spectacle of Women: Images of the Suffrage Campaign, 1907–14*. Chicago: University of Chicago Press.

Tinkler, P. (2006) *Smoke Signals: Women, Smoking and Visual Culture*. Oxford: Berg.

Tinkler, P. (2008) 'A fragmented picture: reflections on the photographic practices of young people', *Visual Studies*, 23: 255–66.

Tinkler, P. (2010) '"Picture me as a young woman": researching girls' photo collections from the 1950s and 1960s', *Photography & Culture*, 3: 261–82.

Tinkler, P. (2011) '"When I was a girl …": women talking about their girlhood photo collections', in A. Freund and A. Thomson (eds), *Oral History and Photography*. London: Palgrave Macmillan, pp. 45–60.

Tipper, B. (2011) '"A dog who I knew quite well": everyday relationships between children and animals', *Children's Geographies*, 9: 145–65.

Tonkiss, F. (2004) 'Analysing text and speech: content and discourse analysis', in C. Seale (ed.), *Researching Society and Culture*. London: Sage, pp. 367–82.

Townsend, P. (1962) *The Last Refuge*. London: Routledge and Kegan Paul.

Trachtenberg, A. (1990) *Reading American Photographs: Images as History*. New York: Hill and Wang.

Tucker, J. (2009) 'Entwined practices: engagements with photography in historical inquiry', *History and Theory*, Theme Issue, 48: 1–8.

van der Does, P., Edelaar, S., Gooskens, I., Liefting, M. and Mierlo, M. (1992) 'Reading images: a study of a Dutch neighbourhood', *Visual Sociology*, 7: 4–67.

van Leeuwen, T. (2001) 'Semiotics and iconography', in T. van Leeuwen and C. Jewitt (eds), *Handbook of Visual Analysis*. London: Sage, pp. 92–118.

van Leeuwen, T. and Jewitt, T. (eds) (2001) *Handbook of Visual Analysis*. London: Sage.

Wagner, J. (ed.) (1979) *Images of Information: Still Photography in the Social Sciences*. London: Sage.

Wagner, J. (2011) 'Visual studies and empirical social inquiry', in E. Margolis and L. Pauwels (eds), *The Sage Handbook of Visual Research Methods*. London: Sage, pp. 49–71.

Walker, A.L. and Moulton, R.K. (1989) 'Photo albums: images of time and reflections of self', *Qualitative Sociology*, 12: 156–82.

Walkerdine, V. (1985) 'Dreams from an ordinary childhood', in L. Heron (ed.), *Truth, Dare or Promise: Girls Growing Up in the Fifties*. London: Virago, pp. 63–77.

Walkerdine, V. (1991) 'Behind the painted smile', in J. Spence and P. Holland (eds), *Family Snaps: The Meanings of Domestic Photography*. London: Virago, pp. 35–44.

Wang, C. and Burris, M. (1997) 'Photovoice: concept, methodology and use for participatory needs assessment', *Health and Behaviour*, 24: 369–87.

Watney, S. (1991) 'Ordinary boys', in J. Spence and P. Holland (eds), *Family Snaps: The Meanings of Domestic Photography*. London: Virago, pp. 26–34.

Weller, T. (ed.) (2012) *History in the Digital Age*. London: Routledge.

Wells, L. (ed.) (2000a) *Photography: A Critical Introduction*. London: Routledge.

Wells, L. (2000b) 'On and beyond the white walls: photography as art', in L. Wells (ed.), *Photography: A Critical Introduction*. London: Routledge, pp. 253–302.

Wiles, R., Prosser, J., Bagnoli, A., Clark, A., Davies, K., Holland, S. and Renold, E. (eds) (2008) 'Visual ethics: ethical issues in visual research', ESRC National Centre for Research Methods Review Paper NCRM/011. Available at http://eprints.ncrm. ac.uk/421/ [accessed 6 June 2012].

Wiles, R., Coffey, A., Robison, J. and Prosser, J. (2012) 'Ethical regulation and visual methods: making visual research impossible or developing good practice?', *Sociological Research Online*, 17 (1): 8.

Wilkinson, D. and Thelwall, M. (2011) 'Researching personal information on the public web: methods and ethics', *Social Science Computer Review*, 29: 387–401.

Williams, R. (2010) 'Space for God: lived religion at work, home, and play', *Sociology of Religion*, 71: 257–79.

Williams, V. (1986) *Women Photographers: The Other Observers 1900 to Present*. London: Virago.

Williamson, J. (1978) *Decoding Advertisements: Ideology and Meaning in Advertising.* London: Marion Boyars.

Willis, D. (ed.) (1994) *Picturing Us: African American Identity in Photography.* New York: The New Press.

Winddance Twine, F. (2006) 'Visual ethnography and racial theory: family photographs as archives of interracial intimacies', *Ethnic and Racial Studies*, 29: 487–511.

Winston, B. (1998) '"The camera never lies": the partiality of photographic evidence', in J. Prosser (ed.), *Image-based Research: A Sourcebook for Qualitative Researchers.* London: Falmer, pp. 60–8.

Woodward, S. (2008) 'Digital photography and research relationships: capturing the fashion moment', *Sociology*, 42: 857–72.

Wright, T. (2004) *The Photography Handbook.* London. Routledge.

Yevonde, M. (1940) *In Camera.* London: John Gifford.

Ziller, R.C. (1990) *Photographing the Self: Methods for Observing Personal Orientations.* London: Sage.

Ziller, R.C. and Lewis, D. (1981) 'Orientations: self, social and environmental precepts through auto-photography', *Personality and Social Psychology Bulletin*, 7: 338–43.

Ziller, R.C. and Smith, D.E. (1977) 'A phenomenological utilization of photographs', *Phenomenological Psychology*, 7: 172–82.

# Index